Communications
in Computer and Information Science 1509

More information about this series at http://www.springer.com/series/7899

Li Cui · Xiaolan Xie (Eds.)

Wireless Sensor Networks

15th China Conference, CWSN 2021
Guilin, China, October 22–25, 2021
Revised Selected Papers

 Springer

Editors
Li Cui
Institute of Computing Technology
Beijing, China

Xiaolan Xie
Guilin University of Technology
Guilin, China

ISSN 1865-0929   ISSN 1865-0937 (electronic)
Communications in Computer and Information Science
ISBN 978-981-16-8173-8   ISBN 978-981-16-8174-5 (eBook)
https://doi.org/10.1007/978-981-16-8174-5

This Springer imprint is published by the registered company Springer Nature Singapore Pte Ltd.
The registered company address is: 152 Beach Road, #21-01/04 Gateway East, Singapore 189721, Singapore

Preface

The China Conference on Wireless Sensor Networks (CWSN) is the annual conference on the Internet of Things (IoT) which is sponsored by the China Computer Federation (CCF). The 15th CWSN took place in Guilin, China, in October 2021. As a leading conference in the field of IoT, CWSN is the premier forum for IoT researchers and practitioners from academia, industry, and government in China to share their ideas, research results, and experiences, which highly promotes research and technical innovation in these fields domestically and internationally.

The conference provided an academic exchange of research and a development forum for IoT researchers, developers, enterprises, and users. Exchanging results and experience of research and applications in IoT, and discussing the key challenges and research hotspots, is the main goal of the forum. As a high-level forum for the design, implementation, and application of IoT, the conference promoted the exchange and application of theories and technologies of IoT-related topics.

This year, CWSN received 160 submissions, including 60 English papers and 100 Chinese papers. After a careful double-blind review process, 19 revised and completed papers were selected. The high-quality program would not have been possible without the authors who chose CWSN 2021 as a venue for their publications. We are also very grateful to the members of the Program Committee and Organizing Committee, who put a tremendous amount of effort into soliciting and selecting research papers with a balance of high quality, new ideas, and new applications. We hope that you enjoy reading and benefit from the proceedings of CWSN 2021.

October 2021

Li Cui
Xiaolan Xie

Organization

Conference Chairs

Huadong Ma   CCF Internet of Things Special Committee, China
Mei Wang   Guilin University of Technology, China

Honorary Chair

Hao Dai   Chinese Academy of Engineering, China

Steering Committee Chair

Jianzhong Li   Harbin Institute of Technology, China

Program Committee Chairs

Li Cui   Institute of Computing Technology, Chinese Academy of Sciences, China
Xiaolan Xie   Guilin University of Technology, China

Program Committee Co-chairs

Liang Liu   Beijing University of Posts and Telecommunications, China
Xiaohui Cheng   Guilin University of Technology, China
Minggang Dong   Guilin University of Technology, China
Yun Deng   Guilin University of Technology, China

Outstanding Paper Award Chair

Xue Wang   Tsinghua University, China

Organization Committee Chairs

Xinbing Wang   Shanghai Jiao Tong University, China
Minggang Dong   Guilin University of Technology, China
Yun Deng   Guilin University of Technology, China

Organization Committee

Haiming Jin   Shanghai Jiao Tong University, China
Qirong Lu   Guilin University of Technology, China

De Meng	Guilin University of Technology, China
Qiong Jiang	Guilin University of Technology, China
Hong Jin	Guilin University of Technology, China
Qin Yang	Guilin University of Technology, China
Yanqing Ma	Guilin University of Technology, China

Publicity Committee Chairs

| Yunqing Jiang | Guilin University of Technology, China |
| Xiaohui Cheng | Guilin University of Technology, China |

Program Committee

Guangwei Bai	Nanjing Tech University, China
Ming Bao	Institute of Acoustics, Chinese Academy of Sciences, China
Qingsong Cai	Beijing Technology and Business University, China
Shaobin Cai	Huaqiao University, China
Bin Cao	Harbin Institute of Technology, China
Deze Zeng	China University of Geosciences, China
Fanzai Zeng	Hunan University, China
Hong Chen	Renmin University of China, China
Wei Chen	Beijing Jiaotong University, China
Xi Chen	State Grid Information and Telecommunication Co., Ltd., China
Xu Chen	Sun Yat-sen University, China
Guihai Chen	Nanjing University, China
Haiming Chen	Ningbo University, China
Honglong Chen	China University of Petroleum, China
Jiaxing Chen	Hebei Normal University, China
Liangyin Chen	Sichuan University, China
Xiaojiang Chen	Northwestern University, China
Yanjiao Chen	Wuhan University, China
Yihong Chen	China West Normal University, China
Yongle Chen	Taiyuan University of Technology, China
Zhikui Chen	Dalian University of Technology, China
Xiuzhen Cheng	Shandong University, China
Hongju Cheng	Fuzhou University, China
Saiyao Cheng	Harbin Institute of Technology, China
Kaikai Chi	Zhejiang University of Technology, China
Li Cui	Institute of Computing Technology, Chinese Academy of Sciences, China
Xunxue Cui	PLA Army Service Academy, China
Haipeng Dai	Nanjing University, China
Xiaochao Dang	Northwest Normal University, China
Wei Dong	Zhejiang University, China

Zhenjiang Dong	Gosuncn Technology Group Co., Ltd., China
Hongwei Du	Harbin Institute of Technology, China
Juan Fang	Beijing University of Technology, China
Xiaolin Fang	Southeast University, China
Dingyi Fang	Northwest University, China
Guangsheng Feng	Harbin Engineering University, China
Xiufang Feng	Taiyuan University of Technology, China
Hong Gao	Harbin Institute of Technology, China
Ruipeng Gao	Beijing University of Posts and Telecommunications, China
Deyun Gao	Beijing Jiaotong University, China
Jibing Gong	Yanshan University, China
Zhitao Guan	North China Electric Power University, China
Songtao Guo	Chongqing University, China
Zhongwen Guo	Ocean University of China, China
Guangjie Han	Hohai University, China
Jinsong Han	Zhejiang University, China
Yanbo Han	North China University of Technology, China
Zhanjun Hao	Northwest Normal University, China
Yuan He	Tsinghua University, China
Daojing He	East China Normal University, China
Shiming He	Changsha University of Science and Technology, China
Shibo He	Zhejiang University, China
Chengquan Hu	Jilin University, China
Pengfei Hu	Shandong University, China
Qiangsheng Hua	Huazhong University of Science and Technology, China
He Huang	Soochow University, China
Liusheng Huang	University of Science and Technology of China, China
Jie Jia	Northeastern University, China
Nan Jiang	East China Jiaotong University, China
Hongbo Jiang	Huazhong University of Science and Technology, China
Xianlong Jiao	Air Force Engineering University, China
Qi Jing	Peking University, China
Bo Jing	Air Force Engineering University, China
Zhoufang Kuang	Central South University of Forestry and Technology, China
Chao Li	Institute of Computing Technology, Chinese Academy of Sciences, China
Fan Li	Beijing Institute of Technology, China
Feng Li	Shandong University, China
Jie Li	Northeastern University, China
Zhuo Li	Beijing Information Science and Technology University, China

Deying Li	Renmin University of China, China
Fangmin Li	Wuhan University of Technology, China
Guanghui Li	Jiangnan University, China
Guorui Li	Northeastern University, China
Hongwei Li	University of Electronic Science and Technology of China, China
Jianqiang Li	Shenzhen University, China
Jianbo Li	Qingdao University, China
Jianzhong Li	Harbin Institute of Technology, China
Jinbao Li	Heilongjiang University, China
Minglu Li	Shanghai Jiao Tong University, China
Renfa Li	Hunan University, China
Xiangyang Li	University of Science and Technology of China, China
Yantao Li	Chongqing University, China
Yanjun Li	Zhejiang University of Technology, China
Zhetao Li	Xiangtan University, China
Wei Liang	Shenyang Institute of Automation, Chinese Academy of Sciences, China
Hongbin Liang	Southwest Jiaotong University, China
Jiuzhen Liang	Changzhou University, China
Feng Lin	Zhejiang University, China
Chi Liu	Beijing Institute of Technology, China
Kai Liu	Chongqing University, China
Liang Liu	Beijing University of Posts and Telecommunications, China
Min Liu	Institute of Computing Technology, Chinese Academy of Sciences, China
Peng Liu	Hangzhou Dianzi University, China
Jiajia Liu	Xidian University, China
Xingcheng Liu	Sun Yat-sen University, China
Yunhao Liu	Tsinghua University, China
Zhouzhou Liu	Xian Aeronautical University, China
Xiang Liu	Peking University, China
Juan Luo	Hunan University, China
Chengwen Luo	Shenzhen University, China
Hanjiang Luo	Shandong University of Science and Technology, China
Junzhou Luo	Southeast University, China
Zicheng Lv	Chinese University of Hong Kong, China
Li Ma	North China University of Technology, China
Huadong Ma	Beijing University of Posts and Telecommunications, China
Lianbo Ma	Northeastern University, China
Mingxuan Ni	Hong Kong University of Science and Technology, China
Jianwei Niu	Beihang University, China

Qingshan Wang	Hefei University of Technology, China
Ruchuan Wang	Nanjing University of Posts and Telecommunications, China
Xiaoming Wang	Shaanxi Normal University, China
Xiaodong Wang	National University of Defense Technology, China
Xiaoliang Wang	Hunan University of Science and Technology, China
Xinbing Wang	Shanghai Jiao Tong University, China
Yiding Wang	North China University of Technology, China
Yuexuan Wang	Tsinghua University, China
Zhibo Wang	Wuhan University, China
Wei Wei	Xi'an University of Technology, China
Liansuo Wei	Qiqihar University, China
Hui Wen	Institute of Information Engineering, Chinese Academy of Sciences, China
Zhongming Weng	Tianjin University, China
Xingjun Wu	Tsinghua Tongfang Microelectronics Co., Ltd., China
Hejun Wu	Sun Yat-sen University, China
Xiaojun Wu	Shaanxi Normal University, China
Chaocan Xiang	PLA Army Service Academy, China
Fu Xiao	Nanjing University of Posts and Telecommunications, China
Liang Xiao	Xiamen University, China
Ling Xiao	Hunan University, China
Deqin Xiao	South China Agricultural University, China
Kun Xie	Hunan University, China
Lei Xie	Nanjing University, China
Mande Xie	Zhejiang Gongshang University, China
Xiaolan Xie	Guilin University of Technology, China
Yongping Xiong	Beijing University of Posts and Telecommunications, China
Jia Xu	Nanjing University of Posts and Telecommunications, China
Zhiwei Xu	Chinese Academy of Sciences, China
Chenren Xu	Peking University, China
Guangtao Xue	Shanghai Jiao Tong University, China
Zhan Huan	Changzhou University, China
Geng Yang	Nanjing University of Posts and Telecommunications, China
Zheng Yang	Tsinghua University, China
Guisong Yang	University of Shanghai for Science and Technology, China
Hao Yang	Yancheng Teachers University, China
Weidong Yang	Henan University of Technology, China
Weidong Yi	University of Chinese Academy of Sciences, China
Zuwei Yin	Information Engineering University, China
Wei Yu	Rizhao Hi-Tech Industrial Development Zone, China

Ruiyun Yu	Northeastern University, China
Jiguo Yu	Qufu Normal University, China
Peiyan Yuan	Henan Normal University, China
Ju Zhang	Information Engineering University, China
Lei Zhang	Tianjin University, China
Lichen Zhang	Shaanxi Normal University, China
Lianming Zhang	Hunan Normal University, China
Shigeng Zhang	Central South University, China
Shuqin Zhang	Zhongyuan University of Technology, China
Yanyong Zhang	University of Science and Technology of China, China
Yunzhou Zhang	Northeastern University, China
Jumin Zhao	Taiyuan University of Technology, China
Junhui Zhao	East China Jiaotong University, China
Zenghua Zhao	Tianjin University, China
Jiping Zheng	Nanjing University of Aeronautics and Astronautics, China
Xiaolong Zheng	Beijing University of Posts and Telecommunications, China
Ping Zhong	Central South University, China
Huan Zhou	China Three Gorges University, China
Anfu Zhou	Beijing University of Posts and Telecommunications, China
Juejia Zhou	Tsinghua University, China
Ruiting Zhou	Wuhan University, China
Xiaobo Zhou	Tianjin University, China
Changbing Zhou	China University of Geosciences, China
Zheng Zhou	Beijing University of Posts and Telecommunications, China
Hongzi Zhu	Shanghai Jiao Tong University, China
Hongsong Zhu	Institute of Information Engineering, Chinese Academy of Sciences, China
Peidong Zhu	Changsha University, China
Yihua Zhu	Zhejiang University of Technology, China
Liehuang Zhou	Beijing Institute of Technology, China
Shihong Zou	Beijing University of Posts and Telecommunications, China

Contents

Security and Privacy Protection on Internet of Things

Fog Computing and Wireless Computing

MISC

Theory and Technology on Wireless Sensor Network

Key Nodes Evaluation in Opportunistic Networks Based on Influence Between Nodes

Jian Shu, Xiaoyong Zhan, Guilong Jiang, and Wanli Ma(✉)

Internet of Things Technology Institute, Nanchang Hang Kong University, Nanchang, Jiangxi, People's Republic of China

Abstract. In order to accurately evaluate the key nodes in opportunistic networks, a key nodes evaluation method based on influence between nodes is proposed by analyzing the time-varying characteristics of opportunistic network topology. This method uses a summary graph model to formulate opportunistic networks. According to the inverse-square law, the number of connections between a node and other nodes is taken as the intensity of the node and the shortest path is taken as the distance between a node pair to obtain the node-pair influence, so as to quantify the influence between nodes. Then, the total influence of nodes is determined by fixing the influence range to two hops. On this basis, taking the total influence and total connection time of nodes as the evidence source, a D-S evidence theory based method is built to evaluate the key nodes in opportunistic networks. In three real networks, the Susceptible-Infected epidemic model is used to evaluate the infection ability of key nodes. The experimental results show that the proposed method is feasible and effective on better evaluation performance.

Keywords: Opportunistic networks · Key nodes · Node-pair influence · D-S evidence theory

1 Introduction

An opportunistic network is a dynamic network that takes advantage of meeting opportunities brought by node movement to realize communication without the need for the complete the links between source and target nodes [1]. Compared with other networks, the special information transmission mechanism of opportunistic networks makes the networks high in fault tolerance rate and limited in delay tolerance [2], which leads to a good application prospect in some environments with bad radio channels and application scenarios with low real-time requirements. However, key nodes damaging in this special information transmission mechanism may lead to abnormal operation of the whole networks, or even paralysis. If the key nodes can be known or evaluated in advance, the reliability of the networks can be improved based on the information of the key nodes and the corresponding protection activities for them. Furthermore, when there are some

This paper is supported by the National Natural Science Foundation of China (62062050, 61962037, 61762065), the Jiangxi Provincial Natural Science Foundation (20202BABL202039), and the Innovation Foundation for Postgraduate Student of Jiangxi Province (YC2020121).

L. Cui and X. Xie (Eds.): CWSN 2021, CCIS 1509, pp. 3–16, 2021.
https://doi.org/10.1007/978-981-16-8174-5_1

network operation problems, the key nodes can be checked immediately to reduce the time and cost of network maintenance.

Therefore, it is of great significance to evaluate the key nodes in opportunistic networks. In this paper, by analyzing the influence between nodes in opportunistic networks, combined with Dempster-Shafer (D-S) evidence theory, we propose a novel key nodes evaluation method. Firstly, we use a summary graph model to formulate opportunistic networks. Secondly, based on the inverse-square law, we calculate node-pair influence by the number of connections and distance between nodes. Then, we obtain the total influence of a node by summing the node-pair influence values between the node and other nodes in its influence range. Finally, by taking the total influence and total connection time of nodes as the evidence source of D-S evidence theory, the final evaluation score of the nodes is calculated, and the key nodes can be selected in order of ranking. Our main contributions are as follows:

- Based on the inverse-square law, by considering the number of connections between a node and its neighbor nodes as the intensity of the node and the shortest path as the distance between nodes, we obtain the node-pair influence to quantify the influence between node pairs.
- In order to combine the multiple influences between nodes in opportunistic networks, we propose a novel method based on D-S evidence theory by using D-S evidence theory to fuse the total influence value and the total connection time of nodes.

The rest of the paper is organized as follows. The related work is introduced in Sect. 2. In Sect. 3, we introduce the background knowledge relevant to our research. In Sect. 4, we propose our key nodes evaluation method. Some experiments on three real network datasets are presented in Sect. 5 to show the effectiveness of our method. Conclusion is given in Sect. 6.

2 Related Work

Based on the main research ideas of this paper, we divide the research methods into methods based on single indicator and methods based on multi-indicators. Since opportunistic network is a dynamic network, the relevant methods in dynamic network are introduced in Sect. 2.3.

2.1 Methods Based on Single Indicator

Researchers have proposed several different evaluation methods for different research scenarios [3]. Traditional methods generally identify key nodes by their centrality, such as Degree Centrality (DC), Betweenness Centrality and Closeness Centrality (CC), etc. [4] selects the important nodes in social networks by DC and CC, takes these nodes as the center of the network graph, and changes the graph into uncertainty graph by changing the network structure of these nodes, so as to achieve the purpose of protecting the privacy of social networks. [5] identifies influential nodes based on the inverse-square law, the mutual attraction between different nodes has been defined in complex network, which is inversely proportional to the square of the distance between two nodes. Then, it defines the sum of mutual attraction between a node and other nodes in the network as the intensity of the node, which can be considered as the influence of the node. [6] constructs a citation network, based on the LeaderRank algorithm, focusing on the temporal attributes of nodes, it proposes a model for evaluating the current influence of nodes in a time-containing citation network.

2.2 Methods Based on Multi-indicators

The evaluation methods based on single indicator can effectively find out the key nodes, but they do not consider the node information from multiple angles, and cannot correctly reflect the node importance [7]. Therefore, in order to describe the importance of nodes comprehensively, researchers propose methods based on multi-indicators to evaluate the key nodes. In [8], on the basis of improving the neighborhood structure hole indicator, the Gini coefficient and Kendall coefficient are used to calculate the objective weights of the selected multiple indicators, which solves the problem that the positive and negative ideal solution vertical line nodes cannot be effectively distinguished in the TOPSIS method, and improves the accuracy of the evaluation results. Liu D et al. [9] proposed a D-2SN algorithm based on D-S evidence theory. This algorithm considers the degree of each node in the networks and the second-order neighbor information. The experiment results show that this method has a lower time complexity and a better evaluation effect. In the study of the importance of nodes in multi-relational social networks, [10] proposes a method to evaluate the importance of nodes by integrating various information, using D-S evidence theory to fuse node centrality, reputation and transferability information according to probability.

2.3 Methods in Dynamic Networks

At present, most related research on the evaluation of key nodes in dynamic networks improve the static network centrality indicator and apply them to dynamic networks, such as time series degree centrality, time series betweenness centrality, temporal K-shell decomposition [7, 11, 12]. Kim H et al. [13] connected different time slices with directed edges, and transformed the network into a one-way directed static graph along time. Thus, the degree centrality, medium number centrality and near centrality of the directed time series graph are defined. In order to study the changes of network topology brought by time attribute in dynamic networks, Xuan B et al. [14] defined the concepts of journey and distance in temporal networks for the first time. Borrego C et al. [15] obtained the node credibility by studying node characteristics in large social opportunistic networks to select key routes for network message transmission. [16] frames the optimization problem on temporal networks to a spreading process following the rules of the susceptible-infected-recovered model with temporal scale equal to the one characterizing, the nodes with the most influence in the networks are obtained by comparing the spread effect of different nodes.

Based on the above research, we take the idea of using the inverse square law for the research in [5] to calculate the influence between a node pair by measuring the number of connections between a node and its neighbors as the intensity of the node, and the shortest path as the distance between nodes. Then, due to the communication characteristics of opportunistic networks, we set the influence range of the nodes in opportunistic networks to two hops, the total influence of a node can be obtained by adding the node-pair influence values in its influence range. Finally, using D-S evidence theory to fuse the total influence and total connection time of nodes, the evaluation score of the nodes can be obtained and the key nodes are selected in rank order.

3 Background

The opportunistic networks modeling method summary graph is described in Subsect. 3.1. In Subsect. 3.2, we will introduce the D–S Evidence Theory.

3.1 Opportunistic Network Model

Summary Graph. An opportunistic network can be sliced into a series of ordered graphs based on the size of time window:

$$G = \{G_1, G_2, \cdots, G_T\}$$

where $G_t = (V_t, E_t)$ is the network snapshot under time t, V_t and E_t is the node set and edge set under the time t, $t \in T$, T is the total number of network snapshots.

The corresponding summary graph is represented as follows:

$$G = (V, E, W)$$
$$V = V_1 \cup V_2 \cup \cdots \cup V_T$$
$$E = E_1 \cup E_2 \cup \cdots \cup E_T$$

where W is the edge weight set of edges in E, which is determined by the proportion of the corresponding edge appearing in all network snapshots.

Summary Graph Edge Weight (W). In a summary graph $G = (V, E, W)$, the weight of an edge between two nodes is defined as the proportion of edges appearing in all snapshots. If edge e_i appears in k snapshots, the weight of edge e_i can be expressed as Eq. (1):

$$W_i = \frac{k}{T}, k \leq T \tag{1}$$

In addition, the connections between nodes may disappear or exist several times in a snapshot, we use C and φ to denote the number of connections and the total time of connections between nodes, respectively.

As shown in Fig. 1, the edge a between nodes 1 and 2 does not appear after the time appears. The number of time snapshots is 3, and the weight of a is 1/3. At the same time, node pairs 1 and 2 are connected five times at the time, that is C_1^{12} is equal to 5. By analogy, the weight W and connection times C of all edges in the network can be calculated by integrating all time snapshots.

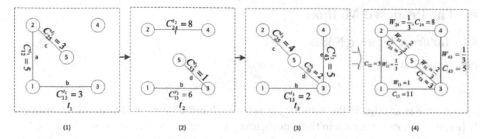

Fig. 1. The construction process of summary graph.

3.2 D-S Evidence Theory

D-S evidence theory is an imprecise reasoning theory proposed by Dempster and further developed by Shafer [17]. It provides uncertain reasoning based on incomplete information, with a complete evidence synthesis formulation, applicable to solving problems such as multi-attribute decision making and information fusion. Formally, the definitions of D-S evidence theory are as follows.

Identification Framework. Θ is called identification framework of variable X. It contains all possible assumption for the variable X, and the elements in Θ are mutually exclusive.

$$\Theta = \{H_1, H_2, \cdots, H_N\} \tag{2}$$

where N is the number of all possible assumptions for variable X. Further, using 2^Θ to represent the subset of set Θ.

Basic Probability Assignment (BPA). Function $m(A)$ indicates the support for assumption A from the selected source evidence, satisfies the following definitions:

$$\sum_{A \in 2^\Theta} m(A) = 1, 0 \le m(A) \le 1, m(\varnothing) = 0 \tag{3}$$

Dempster's Combination Rule. Given $m_1(A)$ and $m_2(A)$, which are the support for assumption A from evidence source 1 and evidence source 2. The Dempster's combination rule can be used to obtain combined support for assumption A by fusing the BPA of the two evidence sources. The combination rule is shown in Eq. (4):

$$\begin{cases} m(\varnothing) = 0 \\ m(A) = \frac{\sum_{B \cap C = A} m_1(B) m_2(C)}{1 - k} \end{cases}$$
$$k = \sum_{B \cap C = \varnothing} m_1(B) m_2(C) \tag{4}$$

where $k \in [0, 1]$ is called the conflict factor of evidence sources, which reflects the degree of conflict between evidence sources [17]. The closer to 1, it indicates that the conflict between evidence sources is greater. If $k = 1$, it means that the evidence sources are completely in conflict, and the Dempster's combination rule cannot be used to fuse the BPAs. And where B, C is the element in Θ.

4   The Proposed Method

4.1   Influence Between Nodes

For a temporal path:

$$J = \{(e_1, t_1), (e_2, t_2), \cdots, (e_T, t_T)\}$$

where e is an edge in the summary graph and T is the number of network snapshots. If $\{e_1, e_2, \ldots, e_T\}$ is a path in the topological structure of the summary graph, and edge e_t is satisfied to appear in snapshot G_t, J is called a path in the summary graph G. $J^*(i, j)$ are paths from node v_i to node v_j. Use d_{ij} to denote the shortest path from node v_i to node v_j.

$$d_{ij} = min(J^*(i, j)) \tag{5}$$

Average Connection Degree (AD). Giving a series of network snapshots of an opportunistic network $G = \{G_1, G_2, \cdots, G_T\}$, C_{ij}^t is the number of connections between node v_i and v_j in snapshot G_t, the average connection degree of node v_i can be calculated by Eq. (6):

$$AD_i = \frac{\sum_{t=1}^{T} \sum_{j \in \Gamma(i)} C_{ij}^t}{T} \tag{6}$$

Influence Node Set. The theory of complex network thinks the adjacent nodes within three hops of a node have a strong influence on the node [11]. Due to the sparse distribution of nodes in opportunistic networks, in this paper, the nodes in two hops of node v_i are taken as the set of nodes that can be influenced by node v_i, denoted as V_2^i.

Node-Pair Influence (NPI). Refer to the idea of the research in [5], we consider AD as the node intensity and the shortest path as the distance between two nodes for calculating the influence between a node pair with the inverse square law.

$$NPI_{ij} = \frac{AD_i \cdot AD_j}{|d_{ij}|^2} P, j \in V_2^i$$

$$NPI_{ij} = \frac{AD_i \cdot AD_j}{|d_{ij}|^2} P, j \in V_2^i \tag{7}$$

where v_j is a node in the influence node set of v_i, P is the product of the weights of all edges on the shortest path between v_i and v_j.

Total Influence (TI). The total influence value of a node in the network is obtained by summing the node pairs formed by node v_i and all the nodes in its influence node set.

$$TI_i = \sum_{j \in V_2^i} NPI_{ij} \tag{8}$$

Connection Time (CT). The total connection time is the sum of the time that node v_i is connected to other nodes in the network. It is calculated by Eq. (9):

$$CT_i = \sum_{j \in \Gamma(i)} \varphi_{ij} \tag{9}$$

where φ_{ij} is the total connection time between node v_i and its neighbor node v_j.

4.2 Key Nodes Evaluation Method

In order to integrate multiple influences between nodes, we apply D-S evidence theory to combine the total influence value TI and the total connection time CT. On this basis, we propose a novel key nodes evaluation method based on D-S evidence theory which is named DST. The concrete implementation steps of this method are as follows.

Assuming that nodes in an opportunistic network have two possible assumptions, namely, key node (h) and common node (l). The identification framework of nodes can be expressed as $\Theta = \{h, l\}$, and the subset is $2^{\Theta} = \{\varnothing, h, l, \{h, l\}\}$.

Step 1: Determining Positive and Negative Solutions.

Obtain maximum and minimum values of set TI and set CT.

$$TI_{max} = max(TI_1, TI_2, \ldots, TI_n)$$
$$TI_{min} = min(TI_1, TI_2, \ldots, TI_n) \tag{10}$$

$$CT_{max} = max(CT_1, CT_2, \ldots, CT_n)$$
$$CT_{min} = min(CT_1, CT_2, \ldots, CT_n) \tag{11}$$

where n is the number of nodes in the network.

Step 2: Constructing the BPA of evidence sources.

Create the BPA for TI by three cases: key node (h), common node (l), and unknown situation (θ).

$$TI_i(h) = \frac{|TI_i - TI_{min}|}{TI_{max} - TI_{min} + \Delta}$$
$$TI_i(l) = \frac{|TI_i - TI_{max}|}{TI_{max} - TI_{min} + \Delta}$$
$$TN_i(\theta) = 1 - TI_{max} - TI_{min} \tag{12}$$

where $\Delta \in (0, 1)$ is a regulating parameter, its function is to prevent the denominator to be 0, without affecting the final result.

Similarly, the BPA for CT can be created.

$$CT_i(l) = \frac{|CT_i - CT_{max}|}{CT_{max} - CT_{min} + \Delta}$$
$$CT_i(h) = \frac{|CT_i - CT_{min}|}{CT_{max} - CT_{min} + \Delta}$$
$$CT_i(\theta) = 1 - CT_{max} - CT_{min} \tag{13}$$

Using Eq. (15) to express the BPAs of TI and CT uniformly.

$$m_{TI}^i = \{TI_i(h), TI_i(l), TI_i(\theta)\}$$
$$m_{CT}^i = \{CT_i(h), CT_i(l), CT_i(\theta)\} \tag{14}$$

Step 3: Combining the BPA of evidence sources.

Use the Dempster's combination rule to fuse the BPAs of *TI* and *CT*. The combined support $m_i(h)$ and $m_i(l)$ can be obtained, $m_i(h)$ and $m_i(l)$ represent the probability of supporting the node as a key node and supporting the node as a common node respectively.

$$m_i(h) = TI_i(h) \oplus CT_i(h) = \frac{TI_i(h) \cdot CT_i(h) + TI_i(h) \cdot CT_i(\theta) + TI_i(\theta) \cdot CT_i(h)}{1 - k_i}$$

$$m_i(l) = TI_i(l) \oplus CT_i(l) = \frac{TI_i(l) \cdot CT_i(l) + TI_i(l) \cdot CT_i(\theta) + TI_i(\theta) \cdot CT_i(l)}{1 - k_i}$$

$$k_i = \sum_{A \cap B = \varnothing} m_{TI}^i(A) m_{CT}^i(B), \; A \text{ and } B \in \{h, l, \theta\} \tag{15}$$

where in the datasets used in this paper, the conflict factors k of *TI* and *CT* of the nodes are less than 1, and the specific results can be seen in Subsect. 5.2.

Step 4: Getting the final evaluation score.

The final evaluation score *DST* of node i is obtained by calculating its $m_i(h)$ and $m_i(l)$:

$$DST_i = m_i(h) - m_i(l) \tag{16}$$

Obviously, the higher the value of $m_i(h)$ the higher the probability of supporting the node as a key node. In contrast, the lower the value of $m_i(l)$ is, the higher the probability of supporting the node as a key node is. Thus, the larger the value of *DST*, the more likely the node is to be a key node, i.e. the key nodes can be selected according to the DST values.

5 Experiments and Analysis

We select three real network datasets and conduct the following two experiments. Experiment 1 calculates the conflict factors of the evidence sources (TI and CT of nodes) in each dataset. In experiment 2, the Susceptible-Infected (SI) epidemic model [18, 19] is used to compare our method with two well-known methods, including Temporal Degree Centrality (TD) [12], Influence Centrality (IF) [5].

5.1 Datasets

The basic information of the network datasets used in our experiments are shown in Table 1, where n is the number of nodes in the networks, C is the number of connections between nodes in the networks, and T is the duration of the networks.

In the datasets, Infocom2005 dataset is generated by Bluetooth devices carried by participants at a conference in Cambridge University, ITC dataset is derived from Cambridge University Students' life trajectory experiment, and Asturias dataset is extracted from vehicle GPS tracks collected by fire department in Asturias, Spain.

Table 1. Information of the three datasets

Opportunistic network	N	C	T
Infocom2005	41	22459	254150 s
ITC	50	6896	983109 s
Asturias	229	1200000	31619667 s

5.2 Conflict Factor of the Evidence Sources

In this paper, we use the Dempster's combination rule to combine the evidence sources: the total influence value (TI) and the total connection time (CT). The combination rule requires that the maximum conflict factor between the evidence sources less than 1, if there is a conflict factor of 1 between TI and CT of nodes in the selected dataset, the proposed method is no longer applicable to the dataset. Therefore, this experiment is designed to calculate the conflict factor of TI and CT, and results are shown in Fig. 2, 3 and 4.

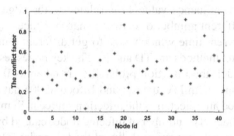

Fig. 2. The conflict factors in Infocom2005 dataset.

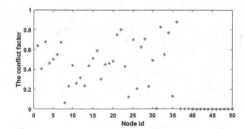

Fig. 3. The conflict factors in ITC dataset.

Figure 2 shows the result on Infocom2005 dataset, in the figure we can clearly see that the conflict factors of most nodes are between 0.2 and 0.6. It reflects that there is still a certain correlation between TI and CT, but the conflict is not significant. In Fig. 3 the ITC dataset, since nodes 37 to 50 have been never connected to any node, the conflict factors are 0, and the conflict factors of most other nodes are around 0.5. As Fig. 4

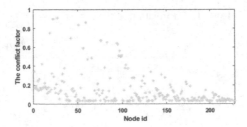

Fig. 4. The conflict factors in Asturias dataset.

shows, the conflict factors of most nodes in Asturias dataset are below 0.2, and there is no conflict factor equal to 1.

In summary, the conflict factor analyzing of the three datasets verifies the rationality of our method in selecting TI and CT as the evidence source, and the availability of the method.

5.3 Simulation Experiment

In our method, the total influence value TI is related to the edge weight of the summary graph, and the different number of network snapshot slices will produce different weights, so we set different time window size to get different number of slices in the datasets. The comparison methods are TD and IF. The key nodes result validation model is the SI epidemic model, the infection probability is taken as 0.15 [18]. Due to the different size of the datasets, in ITC dataset and Infocom2005 dataset the Top-2 nodes evaluated by each method are selected as the infection source in SI model, and in Asturias dataset it is the Top-5 nodes. The number of infected nodes caused by the nodes set as the infection source represents the infection ability of the key nodes. The larger the number, the better the method corresponding to these nodes. The results are shown in Fig. 5, 6, 7, 8, 9, 10, 11, 12 and 13.

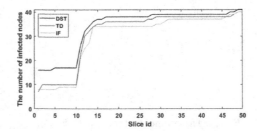

Fig. 5. The number of infected nodes in Infocom2005 dataset (50 slices).

As shown in Fig. 5, 6 and 7, because the nodes in Infocom2005 dataset are tightly connected and of short duration, there are a large number of connections in a short period, resulting in a nearly identical total number of infected nodes in the three methods. However, in early stage of the network, when the nodes start to active, the number of

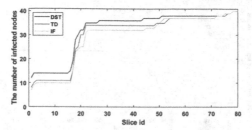

Fig. 6. The number of infected nodes in Infocom2005 dataset (80 slices).

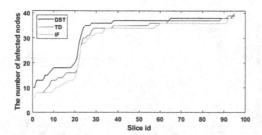

Fig. 7. The number of infected nodes in Infocom2005 dataset (100 slices).

infected nodes in DST is significantly higher than that in TD and IF, and the average number of infected nodes in each time slice is also higher than that of the other two methods. In other words, in Infocom2005 dataset, the infection ability of key nodes evaluated by DST is higher than TD and IF, which shows the superiority of DST.

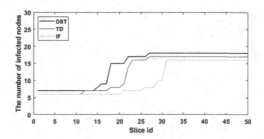

Fig. 8. The number of infected nodes in ITC dataset (50 slices).

Due to the sparse distribution of nodes in ITC dataset, the number of connections between nodes in the dataset is less. From the experimental results in Fig. 8, 9 and 10, we can see that there is almost no infection between nodes in the first half of the network. Compared with the experimental results in Infocom2005 dataset, when the nodes start to active in the network, the total number of infected nodes in DST is significantly larger than that in IF and TD. That is due to the high density between nodes in Infocom2005 dataset, and the values of TD and IF are changed by degree centrality and K-shell value. In dense networks, degree centrality and K-shell can provide a good reference for the evaluation of key nodes, but in sparse networks, just using the edge of nodes to evaluate

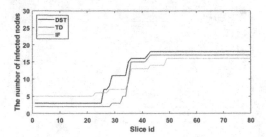

Fig. 9. The number of infected nodes in ITC dataset (80 slices).

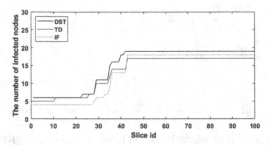

Fig. 10. The number of infected nodes in ITC dataset (100 slices).

key nodes is not enough. Compared with that, DST takes into the number of node connections, the time of node connections and the shortest path of nodes, it can provide a better reference for key nodes evaluation in sparse networks.

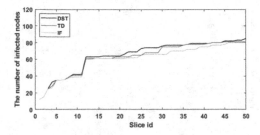

Fig. 11. The number of infected nodes in Asturias dataset (50 slices).

In the experimental results of Asturias dataset in Fig. 11, 12 and 13, it is obvious that IF is not suitable for sparse networks with long duration. Compared with TD, the number of infected nodes in DST is larger than that in TD in each network snapshot.

In summary, compared to the other two comparison methods, our proposed DST method performs better in the experimental evaluation of the SI model on all three datasets. More specifically, for the network with more closely distributed nodes, DST has the similar number of infected nodes as the other two methods, so it cannot rely on the total number of final infected nodes to determine whether the key nodes are accurate. Therefore, DST is more suitable for sparse networks.

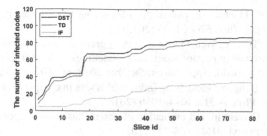

Fig. 12. The number of infected nodes in Asturias dataset (80 slices).

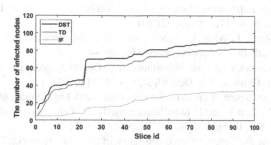

Fig. 13. The number of infected nodes in Asturias dataset (100 slices).

6   Conclusions

In order to evaluate the key nodes in opportunistic networks, we propose a key nodes evaluation method based on influence between nodes. The total influence TI takes into account the local topology of nodes, the message transmission path and the sparse distribution of nodes in opportunistic networks, which can better reflect the influence of nodes in opportunistic network. Using D-S evidence theory to combine two indicators (TI and CT) to evaluate key nodes in opportunistic networks, which takes more information into account than a single indicator, the evaluated key nodes are more reasonable and experiments on the SI model validate the superiority of the method in this paper.

The proposed method also has some limitations. Our method considers two evaluation indicators, there is still a lack of comprehensive consideration of the importance factors of nodes in opportunistic networks. In future work, we intend to optimize our evaluation method and propose a key node evaluation indicator that is more in line with the characteristics of opportunistic networks.

References

1. Xiong, Y.P., Sun, L.M., Niu, J.W., Liu, Y.: Opportunistic networks. J. Softw. **20**(1), 124–137 (2009)
2. Aung, C.Y., Ho, W.H., Chong, P.: Store-carry-cooperative forward routing with information epidemics control for data delivery in opportunistic networks. IEEE Access **5**(99), 6608–6625 (2017)

3. Bian, R., Koh, Y.S., Dobbie, G., Divoli, A.: Identifying top-k nodes in social networks: a survey. ACM Comput. Surv. **52**(1), 1–33 (2019)
4. Yan, J., Zhang, L., Tian, Y., Wen, G.: An uncertain graph approach for preserving privacy in social networks based on important nodes. In: Proceedings of 2018 International Conference on Networking and Network Applications, October 2018, pp. 107–111 (2018)
5. Fei, L., Zhang, Q., Deng, Y.: Identifying influential nodes in complex networks based on the inverse-square law. Phys. A **512**, 1044–1059 (2018)
6. Tan, L.J., Liu, X.: Current impact evaluation of papers based on temporal citation network. Chin. J. Sci. Tech. Period. **31**(4), 108–113 (2020)
7. Hossen, M.S.: DTN routing protocols on two distinct geographical regions in an opportunistic network: an analysis. Wirel. Pers. Commun. **108**(2), 839–851 (2019)
8. Lu, M.: Node importance evaluation based on neighborhood structure hole and improved TOPSIS. Comput. Netw. **178**, 107336 (2020)
9. Liu, D., Nie, H., Zhao, J., Wang, Q.: Identifying influential spreaders in large-scale networks based on evidence theory. Neurocomputing **359**, 466–475 (2019)
10. Luo, H., et al.: Research on node importance fused multi-information for multi-relational social networks. J. Comput. Res. Dev. **57**(5), 954–970 (2020)
11. Ren, Z.M.: Node influence of the dynamic networks. Acta Phys. Sinica **69**(4), 24–32 (2020)
12. Chen, S., Ren, Z.M., Liu, C., et al.: Identification methods of vital nodes on temporal networks. J. Univ. Electron. Sci. Technol. China **49**(2), 291–314 (2020)
13. Kim, H., Anderson, R.: Temporal node centrality in complex networks. Phys. Rev. E **85**(2), 26107 (2012)
14. Xuan, B.B., Ferreira, A., Jarry, A.: Computing shortest, fastest, and foremost journeys in dynamic networks. Int. J. Found. Comput. Sci. **14**(02), 267–285 (2003)
15. Borrego, C., Borrell, J., Robles, S.: Hey, influencer! Message delivery to social central nodes in social opportunistic networks. Comput. Commun. **137**, 81–91 (2019)
16. Erkol, Ş, Mazzilli, D., Radicchi, F.: Influence maximization on temporal networks. Phys. Rev. E **102**(4), 42307 (2020)
17. Xiao, F.: A new divergence measure for belief functions in D-S evidence theory for multisensor data fusion. Inf. Sci. **514**, 462–483 (2020)
18. Borrego, C., Borrell, J., Robles, S.: Efficient broadcast in opportunistic networks using optimal stopping theory. Ad Hoc Netw. **88**, 5–17 (2019)
19. Chen, F.H.: A susceptible-infected epidemic model with voluntary vaccinations. J. Math. Biol. **53**(2), 253–272 (2006)

A Novel Distance Estimation Model and Its Use to Node Localization

Yanyang Zhang and Xingcheng Liu[✉]

School of Electronics and Information Technology, Sun Yat-sen University,
Guangzhou, China
isslxc@mail.sysu.edu.cn

Abstract. To improve the positioning accuracy of anisotropic wireless sensor networks (WSNs), a range-free localization algorithm based on polynomial approximation and differential evolution (LA-PADE) is proposed. Firstly, the discrete value of hop count is converted into a more accurate continuous value, reducing the error in hop count calculation. A polynomial is then used to approximate the relationship between hop count and distance among nodes. Finally, the Dierential Evolution (DE) algorithm is applied to obtain the globally optimal solution of objective function corresponding to the estimated position of unknown node, in which the weights of anchor nodes are introduced to embody their importance in the calculation of the coordinates of the unknown nodes. Simulation results show that the proposed algorithm has higher localization accuracy compared to others in different networks.

Keywords: Wireless sensor networks (WSNs) · Node localization · Distance estimation · Polynomial approximation · Differential Evolution (DE)

1 Introduction

WSNs is a self-organising data processing network consisting of multiple sensor nodes deployed in monitoring areas. As modern intelligent networks, WSNs have been widely used in military, environmental monitoring, modern transportation and other fields. In the application, the data collected would be worthless without the relevant location information. Therefore, location technology is one of the hot spots in the research field of WSNs [1].

In WSNs, localization algorithms can mostly be divided into two phases: distance estimation and position estimation. In the distance estimation stage, according to whether a hardware device needs to be installed to directly measure the distance between transceivers, localization algorithms can be classified into

Supported by the Key Project of NSFC-Guangdong Province Joint Program (Grant No. U2001204), the National Natural Science Foundation of China (Grant Nos. 61873290 and 61972431), and the Science and Technology Program of Guangzhou, China (Grant No. 202002030470).

L. Cui and X. Xie (Eds.): CWSN 2021, CCIS 1509, pp. 17–29, 2021.
https://doi.org/10.1007/978-981-16-8174-5_2

Range-based [2–4] and Range-free [5–7]. Range-based localization algorithms estimate the distance between transceivers from the physical characteristics of the particular hardware device installed. There are four most commonly used, namely Time of Arrival (ToA) [8], Time Different of Arrival (TDoA) [9], Received Signal Strength Indicator (RSSI) [10] and Angle of Arrival (AoA) [11]. Range-free localization algorithms utilize the connectivity of the network to estimate the distance between nodes, such as the hop count of the shortest path. The low-cost range-free localization algorithm is more suitable for large-scale WSNs, because it does not require additional hardware devices to be installed on the sensor nodes.

Range-free positioning algorithms can also be classified into three categories: Geometrical Constraint Based [12], Hop-Progress Based and Machine Learning Based [13–15]. DV-Hop [6] is a hop-progress based localization method, in which anchor nodes calculate the Average Hop Progress (AHP) depending on the hop count and distance information collected by flooding, and then multiply it with the hop count to obtain the distance between nodes. But in anisotropic networks, AHP is inconsistent, and the positioning accuracy of DV-HOP is poor. LAEP [16] is a geometrically constrained localization method, which calculates the expected hop progress (EHP) based on the density of network nodes [17]. However, in the actual deployment environment, network topology is irregular, nodes are unevenly distributed, so the performance of LAEP is unstable. LSVM [7] and RANN [14] are machine learning-based localization algorithms that directly obtain the distance between nodes by regressing the hop count. Such algorithms demand sufficient datasets to train the model, however, the available information in WSNs is limited. Furthermore, the structure, parameters, and types of models have different effects on localization performance. That is, the machine learning localization algorithm lacks robustness.

In addition to the above algorithms, there are also range-free localization algorithms such as Convex [18], MDS-MAP [19], and RAPS [20]. Nevertheless, the localization accuracy of most algorithms is not ideal in anisotropic networks with coverage holes. In order to obtain satisfactory localization results, a novel localization algorithm based on polynomial approximation and differential evolution is proposed. The main contributions of this paper are listed as follows.

1. A new distance estimation method is proposed, firstly, the number of hops between nodes is serialised to get more reasonable hop counts; then the mapping model between hop count and distance is derived by polynomial approximation, and the distance estimation vector is obtained using the hop count vector as the model input.
2. In solving for the coordinates using the optimisation algorithm of differential evolution, improvements are made to the evaluation function. In this way, the different effects of different anchor nodes on the coordinate values are reflected when calculating the coordinates of unknown nodes, thus improving the localisation accuracy.

The remaining parts of this paper are organised as follows: Sect. 2 states the system model. The proposed algorithm is specified in Sect. 3. The conducted simulations and analysis of results are included in Sect. 4. Finally, the paper is concluded in Sect. 5.

2 Network Model

The proposed algorithm is used to localise nodes in WSNs without the assistance of hardware devices, and the details of the network model are as follows:

1. The nodes in the network are randomly deployed and the whole network is connected, which means that any two nodes in the network can communicate via single-hop or multi-hop links, and all nodes have the same communication radius.
2. Once deployed, the node's location does not change and the anchor node knows its location in advance, using the connectivity of the network to help locate unknown nodes.
3. The influence of anisotropic factors is considered during signal transmission.

3 Range-Free Location Based on Polynomial Approximation and Differential Evolution

The proposed algorithm can be divided into three stages: Continuity hop count process, building distance estimation model, locating the unknown nodes, and the specific procedure is described below.

3.1 Continuity Hop Count Process

Generally, when calculating the hop count, all nodes within the transmission radius are accumulated by one hop, and the estimated distance of nodes within one hop is equal to the communication radius. Obviously, this approach is not reasonable; the larger the communication radius, the greater the cumulative error of distance estimation. This phenomenon motivated us to find a more accurate method to calculate the number of hops. The specific steps are as follows.

Optimal Hop Count. Define H_{ij} as the theoretical optimal number of hops between anchor nodes,

$$H_{ij} = d_{ij}/R, \tag{1}$$

where d_{ij} is the true distance between anchor node i and anchor node j, R is the communication radius.

Anchor Node Hop Correction Factor. Set the proportion of the optimal number of hops is M_{ij},

$$M_{ij} = H_{ij}./h_{ij}, \tag{2}$$

where h_{ij} is the actual hop count between anchor node i and anchor node j. The hop correction factor of anchor node i is

$$\lambda_i = \bar{M}_{ij}, \tag{3}$$

where $i = 1, 2, ..., m$, $j = 1, 2, ..., m$, m is the number of anchor nodes.

Correct the Hop Count from Unknown Node to Anchor Node.
Unknown nodes choose the correction factor of the closest anchor node to correct
the hop count

$$\widetilde{h}_{ik} = \lambda_i * h_{ik}, \tag{4}$$

where h_{ik} is the actual minimum hop count from unknown node k to anchor
node i.

After obtaining the hop count of each pair of adjacent nodes, the shortest
path algorithm can be used to get the minimum hop count between all connected
nodes. Continuous hop count is acquired through the above method.

3.2   Polynomial Approximation

Establish Distance Estimation Model. In the stage of distance estimation,
this algorithm uses polynomial to approximate the complex non-linear relationship between hop count and distance. Assume that given the function $f(x_k, y_k)$,
$k = 1, \ldots, m$, here, x_k is the hop count between nodes, and y_k is the corresponding distance. When building the model, try to approximate the function $f(\cdot)$ by
the N degree polynomial $\phi(\cdot)$ in Eq. (5):

$$\phi(x) = a_0 + a_1 x + a_2 x^2 + \cdots + a_N x^N. \tag{5}$$

The goal is to find the coefficients $a_0, a_1, \ldots a_N$, which can be achieved by minimizing the objective function in Eq. (6):

$$LSE = \frac{1}{m} \sum_{k=1}^{m} (y_k - \phi(x_k))^2, \tag{6}$$

this can be regarded as a least square problem.

Choose the Degree of Polynomial. The distance between anchor node i and
anchor node j is expressed in Eq. (7):

$$d_{ij} = a_0 + a_1 h_{ij} + a_2 h_{ij}^2 + \cdots + a_N h_{ij}^N. \tag{7}$$

The choice of polynomial degree is determined by experimental data. In the
experiment, node density varied from 0.01 to 0.03, positioning errors of nodes
in S-shaped and Square-shaped networks were recorded and their average values
were statistically calculated. The results are shown in Table 1.

Analyzing the data in Table 1 leads to the following conclusions: as node
density increases, the localization error of the nodes in both networks decreases
significantly, regardless of the degree of polynomial, and then gradually stabilizes.
For the S-shaped network, as polynomial coefficient increases, the positioning
error of the node gradually decreases, reaches the minimum at the third degree,
then error begins to increase. For the Square-shaped network, as the polynomial
coefficients increases, the positioning error of the nodes gradually becomes larger,

Table 1. Positioning error with polynomial coefficient changing from 1th to 4th as node density varies.

Density	Degree							
	1th degree (m)		2th degree (m)		3th degree (m)		4th degree (m)	
	S	Square	S	Square	S	Square	S	Square
0.010	15.202	6.970	11.201	5.449	11.248	5.686	11.882	6.327
0.012	15.462	5.961	11.647	5.318	10.877	5.441	11.500	6.005
0.014	14.273	5.539	11.296	5.030	11.045	5.158	11.273	5.753
0.016	14.182	5.225	11.247	5.032	10.769	5.040	11.344	5.514
0.018	13.859	5.048	11.185	4.815	10.557	5.101	11.395	5.324
0.020	12.748	4.793	11.350	4.751	10.787	4.888	11.152	5.410
0.022	13.122	4.780	10.479	4.638	10.460	4.852	11.137	5.454
0.024	13.004	4.648	11.240	4.623	10.541	4.794	10.641	5.128
0.026	12.537	4.623	10.880	4.596	10.379	4.646	11.437	5.012
0.028	12.826	4.536	11.201	5.449	11.248	5.686	11.882	6.327
0.030	12.420	4.532	11.647	5.318	10.877	5.441	11.500	6.005
Means (m)	13.603	5.151	11.281	5.199	10.893	5.331	11.397	5.808

and the change is gentle, error increases significantly when the degree is increased to four. Based on the above analysis, it is reasonable to choose a third-degree polynomial to approximate the relationship between hop count and distance.

Choosing a third-degree polynomial to approximate can get a matrix of the following form:

$$
\begin{bmatrix} h_{i1}^3 & h_{i1}^2 & h_{i1} & 1 \\ h_{i2}^3 & h_{i2}^2 & h_{i2} & 1 \\ \vdots & & & \\ h_{in}^3 & h_{in}^2 & h_{in} & 1 \end{bmatrix} \begin{bmatrix} \alpha_3 \\ \alpha_2 \\ \alpha_1 \\ \alpha_0 \end{bmatrix} = \begin{bmatrix} d_{i1} \\ d_{i2} \\ \vdots \\ d_{in} \end{bmatrix},
\tag{8}
$$

where h is the hop count among anchor nodes, use the least square method to determine the optimal value of α,

$$
\alpha = \left(H^T H \right)^{-1} H^T D.
\tag{9}
$$

Broadcast Polynomial Coefficients. Each anchor node broadcasts a data packet containing its calculated polynomial coefficients in the network. When an unknown node receives this packet from its nearest anchor node (that is, the first packet that arrives), it calculates the distance between itself and anchor node according to Eq. (10):

$$
d_{ik} = \alpha_0 + \alpha_1 h_{ik} + \alpha_2 h_{ik}^2 + \alpha_3 h_{ik}^3,
\tag{10}
$$

where d_{ik} and h_{ik} are the distance and minimum hop count from the k_{th} unknown node to the i_{th} anchor node, respectively.

3.3   Differential Evolution Algorithm Locates Unknown Nodes

Differential evolution algorithm is a stochastic optimization algorithm based on population genetic evolution. Similar to other evolutionary algorithms, this algorithm also includes several genetic operations such as mutation, crossover and selection. The original vector X selected to perform mutation operation is called "target vector". The mutation vector V obtained after the differential mutation operation is called "donor vector". The new vector U generated by cross-combination of "target vector" and "donor vector" is called "trial vector". Finally, the algorithm selects the vector with better fitness from the target vector X and the test vector U by greedy selection to enter the next iteration. The following are the details of specific implementation.

Population Initialization. Assuming that the current population size is NP, the current population P_t can be described as follows:

$$P_t = \left\{ X_{i,t} \mid X_{i,t} = \left(X_{i,t}^1, X_{i,t}^2, \ldots, X_{i,t}^D \right)^T \right\}, i = 1, \ldots, NP,$$

where t represents the current evolutionary generation, $X_{i,t}$ represents the i_{th} individual vector in the population, which is also a D-dimensional feasible solution. The algorithm uses a random function conforming to uniform distribution to generate the initial solution. For example, the value of the j_{th} dimension of particle i can be generated by Eq. (11):

$$x_{i,0}^j = x_{\min}^j + \text{rand}(0,1) \times \left(x_{\max}^j - x_{\min}^j \right), \tag{11}$$

where $\text{rand}(0,1)$ is a uniformly distributed random decimal in the range of (0,1). $x_{\max}^j$ and $x_{\min}^j$ denote the maximum and minimum boundary values for an individual in the j_{th} dimension, respectively.

Mutation. Mutation refers to changing the value of a certain position through random perturbation. Differential evolution algorithm maintains the diversity of the population through mutation strategy in Eq. (12):

$$V_{i,t} = X_{r1,t} + F \times \left(X_{r2,t} - X_{r3,t} \right), \tag{12}$$

where $r1, r2, r3$ are the numbers of three random individuals in the population, and $r1 \neq r2 \neq r3$, so the size of population must satisfy $NP > 4$; $X_{r1,t}$ is the vector chosen to perform mutation operation, also known as "target vector"; $X_{r2,t}$ and $X_{r3,t}$ are two random vectors chosen to perform differential operation. Coefficient F is called scaling factor, which is used to control the overall impact of differential vector; the mutation vector $V_{i,t}$ obtained after the mutation operation is called "donor vector" of individual i.

Crossover. Through the previous mutation operation, donor vector $v_{i,t}$ is generated for individual i. At this point, the algorithm can generate test vector U_i by performing a crossover operation on the target vector X_i and the donor vector V_i according to Eq. (13):

$$u_{i,t}^j = \begin{cases} v_{i,t}^j, & \text{rand }_j(0,1) \leq CR \quad \text{or } j = j_{\text{rand}} \\ x_{i,t}^j, & \text{otherwise} \end{cases} \tag{13}$$

Selection. Differential evolution algorithm use greedy selection mechanism to select the target vector X_i, and the test vector U_i generated by mutation operation and crossover operation. The vector with better fitness is selected to enter the next generation population. Greedy selection according to Eq. (14):

$$\mathbf{x}_{i,G+1} = \begin{cases} \mathbf{u}_{i,G}, & f(\mathbf{u}_{i,G}) \leq f(\mathbf{x}_{i,G}) \\ \mathbf{x}_{i,G}, & \text{otherwise} \end{cases} \tag{14}$$

Realization of DE. After the unknown node k obtains the distance estimation vector $\hat{d}_k$, the following objective function is constructed:

$$e_k = \frac{1}{m} \sum_{i=1}^m w_{ki} \left(\sqrt{(\hat{x}_k - x_i)^2 + (\hat{y}_k - y_i)^2} - \hat{d}_{ki} \right)^2, \tag{15}$$

where $(\hat{x}_k, \hat{y}_k)$ are the estimated coordinates of unknown node k, (x_i, y_i) are the coordinates of anchor node i, $i = 1, 2, \ldots, m$, w_{ki} denotes the weight of anchor node i in the coordinate calculation process of unknown node k, which is calculated as follows:

$$w_{ki} = \frac{1/h_{ik}}{\sum_{i=1}^m 1/h_{ik}}, \tag{16}$$

where m is the number of anchor nodes, h_{ik} is the number of hops from unknown node k to anchor node i. The larger the h_{ik}, the higher the degree of tortuosity of the path from the anchor node i to the node to be located, resulting in greater errors. Therefore, the smaller the number of hops from the anchor node i to the unknown nodes, the greater the weight. Finally, differential evolution optimization algorithm is used to find the minimum of Eq. (15), and this solution is the estimated coordinates of unknown node k. The process is described by Eq. (17):

$$(\hat{x}_k, \hat{y}_k) = \text{argmin}_{(\hat{x}_k, \hat{y}_k)} e_k. \tag{17}$$

The pseudo-code of the proposed algorithm is shown in Fig. 1.

Algorithm 1 The procedure of LA-PADE

1: Initialization parameters, the number of nodes n, the number of anchor nodes m, communication radius R;
2: Generate network topology;
3: **for** $i = 1$ to m **do**
4:     **for** $j = 1$ to m **do**
5:         $d_{ij} = \sqrt{(x_i - x_j)^2 + (y_i - y_j)^2}$
6:         Set optimal hop count;
7:         $H_{ij} = d_{ij}/R$
8:         The ratio of the optimal hop count;
9:         $M_{ij} = H_{ij} \cdot /h_{ij}$
10:        The hop correction factor of anchor node i;
11:        $\lambda_i = \bar{M}_{ij}$
12:    **end for**
13: **end for**
14: Polynomial approximate distance estimation model;
15: Unknown node gets coefficient from nearest anchor node;
16: Estimate distance from unknown node to anchor node;
17: **for** $i = 1$ to $n - m$ **do**
18:     Create NP individuals with 2-D variables as Eq. (11);
19:     Evaluate every individual X_{it};
20:     Generation = 1;
21:     **if** Generation < Gmax **then**
22:         **for** $z = 1$ to NP **do**
23:             Mutation and Crossover operator;
24:             Generate mutation vector V_{it} as Eq. (12);
25:             **for** $j = 1$ to D **do**
26:                 Generate test vector U_{it} as Eq.(13);
27:             **end for**
28:             Evaluate test vector;
29:             **if** $f(\mathbf{u}_{i,G}) \leq f(\mathbf{x}_{i,G})$ **then**
30:                 $X_{i,G+1} = U_{i,G}$
31:             **else** $X_{i,G+1} = X_{i,G}$
32:             **end if**
33:         **end for**
34:         Generation=Generation+1;
35:     **end if**
36:     The best individual is the coordinate of unknown node.
37: **end for**

Fig. 1. Pseudocode of the proposed algorithm.

4   Simulations and Analysis

In order to evaluate the effectiveness of the algorithm, the experiment conducted simulations on two network models, Square-shaped network and S-shaped network, which are shown in Fig. 2 and Fig. 3. The normalized root mean square error (NRMSE) is introduced to evaluate the performance of the algorithm, which is calculated as follows:

$$NRMSE = \frac{\sum_{k=1}^{N_u} \sqrt{(\hat{x}_k - x_k)^2 + (\hat{y}_k - y_k)^2}}{N_u R}, \tag{18}$$

where N_u is the number of unknown nodes.

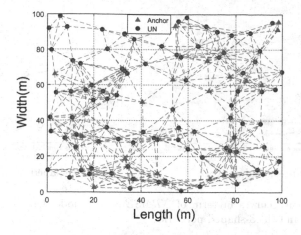

Fig. 2. Square-shaped network

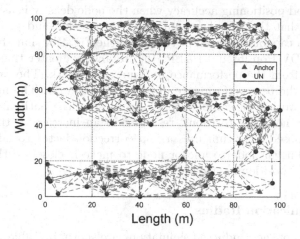

Fig. 3. S-shaped network

4.1   Node Density

The parameters of the conducted simulations are shown in Table 2. The performance curves corresponding to the node density are shown in Fig. 4.

Table 2. Parameters setting for different node densities.

Anchor	R	DoI	Monitoring area	Trials
20	20 m	0.05	100 m × 100 m	100

The NRMSE curves of the proposed algorithm are plotted in Fig. 4 as the node density varies from 0:01 to 0:03 in Squared and S-shaped networks, respectively. Figure 4(a) shows that the proposed algorithm has the best NRMSE performance among all investigated algorithm in Square-shaped networks. And it

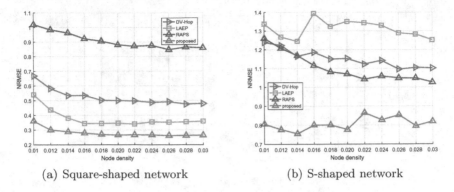

(a) Square-shaped network   (b) S-shaped network

Fig. 4. Performance curves in term of *NRMSE* versus node density in (a) Square-shaped network and (b) S-shaped network.

can achieve good positioning accuracy when the node density is as low as 0.012. The reason is that the DE algorithm converges quickly and has strong optimization search capability. It can be seen from the Fig. 4(b) that the positioning errors of both DV-Hop [6] and LAEP [16] are always greater than R, which is quite different from the performance in Squared network. The proposed algorithm also has the best performance in S-shaped networks. The main reason is that in the network with complex topology, most of the paths from unknown node to anchor node are tortuous, resulting in an increase in the number of hops. The proposed algorithm uses a hop correction factor to adjust the hop count from unknown node to anchor node to make it closer to the true value and improve the positioning accuracy.

4.2   Communication Radius

The parameters of the conducted simulations are shown in Table 3. The performance curves corresponding to the communication radius are shown in Fig. 5.

Table 3. Parameters setting for different radii.

Anchor	Density	DoI	Monitoring area	Trials
40	0.03	0.05	100 m × 100 m	100

The NRMSE curves of the proposed algorithm are plotted in Fig. 5, as the communication radius varies from 20 to 45 in square and S-shaped networks respectively. Figure 5(a) shows that the performance of LAEP [16] and RAPS [20] algorithms are extremely unstable and lack robustness. Although LAEP has good performance when the communication radius is 20, its localization error remains high since the communication radius increases to 25. The reason is that

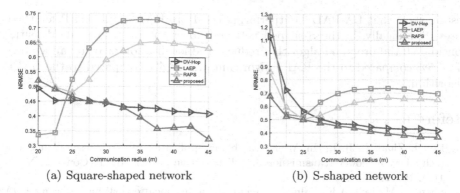

(a) Square-shaped network   (b) S-shaped network

Fig. 5. Performance curves in term of *NRMSE* versus communication radius in (a) Square-shaped network and (b) S-shaped network.

the algorithm estimates its distance to the anchor node directly based on the set communication radius, node density, and when the radius changes, the distance estimation error becomes larger, resulting in its poor localization performance. When the communication radius is less than 25, the proposed algorithm will be slightly inferior to the DV-Hop [6] algorithm, but as the communication radius increases, the superiority of the proposed algorithm become more and more evident. The reason is that with the increase of communication range, node can establish direct connection with more nodes, that is, there are more single-hop nodes. If it is directly recorded as an integer hop, the distance estimation error will increase. The proposed algorithm uses the hop count correction factor of the anchor node to make the hops between the unknown node and the anchor node continuous, in this way, the distance estimation error becomes smaller and the localization result is more accurate. In Fig. 5(b), the positioning error of the RAPS algorithm first decreases, and then gradually increases. In contrast, the localization errors of the DV-Hop algorithm and the proposed algorithm have been gradually decreasing, and the performance of the proposed algorithm is slightly better than that of the DV-Hop algorithm. It can be seen that the proposed algorithm has achieved good positioning accuracy no matter in a relatively simple network or a complex network, indicating the adaptability and stability of the proposed algorithm.

5   Conclusion

In this paper, a high-precision localization algorithm based on polynomial approximation and differential evolution called LA-PADE for WSNs is proposed. In LA-PADE, the hop counts are converted from discrete values to continuous values to make them more accurate. For further reducing the localization error, the DE algorithm is used to locate the unknown nodes, which defines the localization estimation process as an optimization problem. The extensive experiments are conducted in both S-shaped and Square-shaped networks. The experimental results show that LA-PADE outperforms DV-Hop, RAPS and LAEP for these cases. Specifically, in the S-shaped networks, over the range of node densities considered, the proposed algorithm reduces the localisation error by an average of 26.5% compared to the RAPS algorithm and 38.4% compared to the LAEP algorithm.

References

1. Liu, J., Zhao, Z., Ji, J., Hu, M.: Research and application of wireless sensor network technology in power transmission and distribution system. Intell. Converg. Netw. **1**(2), 199–220 (2020)
2. Shen, J., Molisch, A.F., Salmi, J.: Accurate passive location estimation using TOA measurements. IEEE Trans. Wirel. Commun. **11**(6), 2182–2192 (2012)
3. Shao, H., Zhang, X., Wang, Z.: Efficient closed-form algorithms for AOA based self-localization of sensor nodes using auxiliary variables. IEEE Trans. Signal Process. **62**(10), 2580–2594 (2014)
4. Liu, X., Su, S., Han, F., Liu, Y., Pan, Z.: A range-based secure localization algorithm for wireless sensor networks. IEEE Sens. J. **19**(2), 785–796 (2019)
5. Liu, X., Han, F., Ji, W., Liu, Y., Xie, Y.: A novel range-free localization scheme based on anchor pairs condition decision in wireless sensor networks. IEEE Trans. Commun. **68**(12), 7882–7895 (2020)
6. Niculescu, D., Nath, B.: DV based positioning in ad hoc networks. Telecommun. Syst. **22**(1), 267–280 (2003)
7. Tran, D.A., Nguyen, T.: Localization in wireless sensor networks based on support vector machines. IEEE Trans. Parallel Distrib. Syst. **19**(7), 981–994 (2008)
8. Xiong, H., Peng, M., Gong, S., Du, Z.: A novel hybrid RSS and TOA positioning algorithm for multi-objective cooperative wireless sensor networks. IEEE Sens. J. **18**(22), 9343–9351 (2018)
9. Vashistha, A., Law, C.L.: E-DTDOA based localization for wireless sensor networks with clock drift compensation. IEEE Sens. J. **20**(5), 2648–2658 (2020)
10. Bianchi, V., Ciampolini, P., De Munari, I.: RSSI-based indoor localization and identification for ZigBee wireless sensor networks in smart homes. IEEE Trans. Instrum. Meas. **68**(2), 566–575 (2019)
11. Zheng, Q., Luo, L., Song, H., Sheng, G., Jiang, X.: A RSSI-AOA-based UHF partial discharge localization method using MUSIC algorithm. IEEE Trans. Instrum. Meas. **70**, 1–9 (2021)
12. Singh, M., Bhoi, S.K., Khilar, P.M.: Geometric constraint-based range-free localization scheme for wireless sensor networks. IEEE Sens. J. **17**(16), 5350–5366 (2017)
13. Wang, L., Er, M.J., Zhang, S.: A kernel extreme learning machines algorithm for node localization in wireless sensor networks. IEEE Commun. Lett. **24**(7), 1433–1436 (2020)
14. Madagouda, B.K., Sumathi, R.: Analysis of localization using ANN models in wireless sensor networks. In: 2019 IEEE Pune Section International Conference, pp. 1–4 (2019)
15. Gharghan, S.K., Nordin, R., Ismail, M., Ali, J.A.: Accurate wireless sensor localization technique based on hybrid PSO-ANN algorithm for indoor and outdoor track cycling. IEEE Sens. J. **16**(2), 529–541 (2016)
16. Myint, T.Z., Lynn, N., Ohtsuki, T.: Range-free localization algorithm using local expected hop length in wireless sensor network. In: 2010 10th International Symposium on Communications and Information Technologies, pp. 356–361 (2010)

17. Wang, Y., Wang, X., Wang, D., Agrawal, D.P.: Range-free localization using expected hop progress in wireless sensor networks. IEEE Trans. Parallel Distrib. Syst. **20**(10), 1540–1552 (2009)
18. Doherty, L., Pister, K.S.J., El Ghaoui, L.: Convex position estimation in wireless sensor networks. In: Proceedings IEEE INFOCOM 2001. Conference on Computer Communications. Twentieth Annual Joint Conference of the IEEE Computer and Communications Society, vol. 3, pp. 1655–1663 (2001)
19. Wen, T., Zhang, B., Hu, Y., Long, Z.: Research on MDS-MAP location algorithm based on Floyd's shortest path. In: 2020 Chinese Automation Congress, pp. 5057–5060 (2020)
20. Lee, S., Koo, B., Kim, S.: RAPS: reliable anchor pair selection for range-free localization in anisotropic networks. IEEE Commun. Lett. **18**(8), 1403–1406 (2014)

UAV Task Allocation Method Using Swarm Intelligence Optimization Algorithm

Jiaqi Shi[1], Li Tan[1]([⊠]), Xiaofeng Lian[2], Tianying Xu[1], and Hongtao Zhang[1]

[1] School of Computer Science and Engineering, Beijing Technology and Business University,
Beijing 100048, China
`tanli@th.btbu.edu.cn`
[2] School of Artificial Intelligence, Beijing Technology and Business
University, Beijing 100048, China

Abstract. The multi-unmanned aerial vehicle (UAV) task allocation method has shortcomings such as long flight distance and long algorithm initialization time. In response to these problems, this paper proposes a UAV task allocation method based on Swarm Intelligence Optimization Algorithm (SIOA). The algorithm first compares the relationship between the number of UAVs and mission points when UAV is performing a task, and then introduces the idea of gradient descent to reduce the flying distance of UAV. Experimental results show that the SIOA method can effectively reduce the initialization time, shorten search distance of the UAV and the time UAV complete the task, and effectively solve the problem of high algorithm complexity.

Keywords: Task allocation · Swarm intelligence optimization algorithm · Algorithm complexity · Initialization time · Gradient descent

1 Introduction

With the rapid development of UAV technology and the increasingly complex mission environment of UAVs, coordinated control of multiple UAVs has become a very important research hotspot in UAV technology. And task allocation is the basis and guarantee for the coordinated control of multiple UAVs. The research on task allocation of multiple drones can ensure that multiple UAV complete tasks efficiently and safely, which is of great significance for search and rescue, inspections, and so on. Task allocation includes task allocation and path planning. This paper mainly studies the problem of task allocation.

Numerous researchers conducted relevant research on task allocation models. Alitappeh R.J. et al. [1] proposed a new deployment-based framework to solve the problem of task allocation in very large environment. They divided the problem into region partitioning and routing problem. Jin K. et al. [2] proposed a team-competition model, turn the allocation problem into how to assign tasks and the most suitable robot is selected to execute the most appropriate task. Xu S. et al. [3] proposed a mathematical model for UAVs task allocation in crowdsensing, and some algorithms are proposed to allocate

L. Cui and X. Xie (Eds.): CWSN 2021, CCIS 1509, pp. 30–40, 2021.
https://doi.org/10.1007/978-981-16-8174-5_3

tasks for the purpose of minimizing the incentive cost while ensuring the quality of sensing data. These methods mainly put forward the overall model of task allocation, and did not conduct research on specific algorithms.

At present, there are many researches on UAV task allocation using swarm intelligence algorithm. The swarm intelligence algorithm is a random search algorithm using swarms. By defining certain group behaviors and individual behaviors, the group has population evolution diversity and behavior orientation. Using these properties, it can be used to approximately solve some optimization problems that are difficult to solve directly. Therefore, swarm intelligence algorithm is an effective algorithm to solve the problem of multi-UAV task allocation. He W. et al. [4] used the time stamp segmentation model, and combining IPSO and MSOS to solve the multi-UAV cooperate path planning problem. Wang Y. et al. [5] used an improved max-min ant system to find the global optimal solution, and has a better performance on completion time and load balance. Yu X. et al. [6] combined the ant colony optimization and the A* algorithm, develops a two-layer algorithm ACO-A*. Ping K. et al. [7] proposed a cooperative path planning algorithm for multi-sprayer-UAVs based on the improved PSO, and divided the working area of each UAV. Cao Y. [8] transforms the minimum residence time into the shortest path combinatorial optimization, and discretizes heading angles, and through solving the model with genetic algorithm. Zhou X. et al. [9] integrated BA algorithm into the ABC algorithm, uses ABC to modify the BA and solves the problem of poor local search ability of BA. Huo L. et al. [10] proposed a hybrid differential symbiotic organisms search (HDSOS) algorithm by combining the mutation strategy of DE with the modified strategies of SOS. Liu W. et al. [11] proposed IACO to solve 3d multi-task programming under finite-time constraints, introduces the artificial preemptive coefficient matrix into the transfer probability formula. These algorithms have improved the swarm intelligence algorithm, but have not studied the complexity of the algorithm.

If the calculation time of the task assignment algorithm and the UAV flight distance is not taken into consideration, the efficiency of UAVs to complete tasks will be greatly reduced. So, for the purpose of solve these important problems, we focus on the complexity of the algorithm and the travel distance of the UAV, and proposes a UAV task allocation using swarm intelligence optimization algorithm (SIOA). The SIOA method can solve the high complexity of the algorithm and reduce the time and distance of the UAV to complete the task.

2 The SIOA Method

The SIOA method focuses on the optimization of the time complexity of the algorithm and the travel time and distance of the UAV to complete the mission. It should be noted that the situation in this article is considered in an ideal environment, and the existence of other obstacles is not considered.

The SIOA method compares the number of drones with the mission points' number. If the number of drones is less than or equal to mission points' number, each UAV will be assigned a task. On the contrary, only assign tasks to those closer UAV to the mission point.

Then introduce the idea of gradient descent to find the direction with the fastest decline relative to the existing position, so that the UAV can choose the next position in that direction.

The SIOA method will be explained in the ant colony algorithm, bat algorithm, and gray wolf algorithm.

In the Ant Colony Algorithm, the pheromone is first updated according to the pheromone calculation formula, and then the transition probability is calculated according to the pheromone.

When calculating the transition probability, according to the SOIA method, the calculation publicity is shown in Eq. (1)–(4).

There are two cases in the algorithm. The first case is that the ordinate belongs to *allowed$_k$*, as Eq. (1)–(2) shown.

$$p_{ij}^k = \frac{\tau_{ij}^\alpha(t)\eta_{ij}^\beta(t)}{\sum\limits_{k \in allowed_k} \tau_{ij}^\alpha(t)\eta_{ij}^\beta(t)}, j \in allowed_k \tag{1}$$

$$allowed_k = \{C - tabu_k\} \tag{2}$$

In Eq. (1) τ_{ij} is pheromone, *tabu$_k$* is the k-th UAV, α is the influence of the amount of information on UAV's selected path, β is the relative importance of visibility, η_{ij} is the expected degree of transition from node i to j.

The second case is that the ordinate not belongs to *allowed$_k$*, as Eq. (3) shown.

$$p_{ij}^k = 0, other \tag{3}$$

According to the idea of gradient descent, the path selected according to the selection probability is subjected to gradient descent processing. The processing process is shown in Eq. (4).

$$D_{min}(x, y) = \left(\frac{\partial D_S}{\partial x}, \frac{\partial D_S}{\partial y}\right) \tag{4}$$

In Eq. (4), D_{min} represents the current path selected according to the transition probability, $\frac{\partial D_S}{\partial x}$ and $\frac{\partial D_S}{\partial y}$ represent the gradient descent processing of the partial derivative of the currently calculated path.

In the Bat Algorithm, when updating the position of the UAV in the bat algorithm, the position and speed of the UAV will be updated at the same time. According to the SIOA method, the update of the UAV position is shown in Eq. (5)–(8).

First calculate the current UAV's position and flying distance, the calculation is as shown in Eq. (5)

$$x_i^t = x_i^{t-1} + v_i^t \tag{5}$$

In Eq. (5) $\left(x_{i_1}^{t-1}, y_{i_1}^{t-1}, z_{i_1}^{t-1}\right)$ is the coordinate of x_i^{t-1}, v_i^t is the time t's speed of the UAV, and its calculation is shown in Eq. (6)–(7).

$$v_i^t = v_i^{t-1} + \left(x_i^t - X_*\right) \times f_i \tag{6}$$

$$f_i = f_{\min} + (f_{\max} - f_{\min}) \times \beta \tag{7}$$

In Eq. (6)–(7) v_i^{t-1} is the flying speed of the UAV at the previous moment, X_* is the current local optimal solution of group position. f_i is frequency, $f_{\min}$ is a fixed frequency and $f_{\max}$ is the max frequency.

Then according to the idea of gradient descent, the current position of the UAV is processed by gradient descent, as shown in Eq. (8).

$$D_{\min}(x, y) = \left(\frac{\partial D_{x_i^t}}{\partial x}, \frac{\partial D_{x_i^t}}{\partial y}\right) \tag{8}$$

In Eq. (8), $D_{x_i^t}$ is the distance traveled by the current location of the UAV, $\frac{\partial D_{x_i^t}}{\partial x}$ and $\frac{\partial D_{x_i^t}}{\partial y}$ represent the gradient descent processing of the partial derivative of the currently calculated path.

In the Gray Wolf Algorithm, according to fitness, the wolves are divided into α, β, δ, ω, the SIOA method improves the surrounding and hunting phases in the gray wolf algorithm.

In surrounding the prey phase, wolves seek prey, and gradually approach and surround the prey, as shown in Eq. (9)–(10).

The distance is calculated as shown in Eq. (9).

$$D = C \circ X_p(t) - X(t) \tag{9}$$

In Eq. (9) t is the current moment, $\circ$ represents Hadamard product operation, C is coordinate coefficient vectors, Xp represents position vector of prey, $X(t)$ represents current position of wolf.

Then according to the idea of gradient descent, the current position of the UAV is processed by gradient descent, as shown in Eq. (10).

$$D_{\min}(x, y) = \left(\frac{\partial D}{\partial x}, \frac{\partial D}{\partial y}\right) \tag{10}$$

In Eq. (10), D_{min} represents the current path selected according to the transition probability, $\frac{\partial D}{\partial x}$ and $\frac{\partial D}{\partial y}$ represent the gradient descent processing of the partial derivative of the currently calculated path.

In hunting for prey phase, each iteration only the best three wolves in the current population, that is, three UAVs, are retained, and then the positions of other UAVs are updated based on the location information of the retained UAVs.

The SIOA method is optimized for location update, and the update process is shown in Eq. (11)–(13).

The calculation of the optimal position of the three UAVs is shown in Eq. (11)–(13):

$$D_\alpha = C_1 \circ X_\alpha - X \tag{11}$$

$$D_\beta = C_2 \circ X_\beta - X \tag{12}$$

$$D_\delta = C_3 \circ X_\delta - X \tag{13}$$

Then according to the idea of gradient descent, the current position of the UAV is processed by gradient descent, as shown in Eq. (14)–(16).

$$D_{\min 1} = \left(\frac{\partial D_\alpha}{\partial x}, \frac{\partial D_\alpha}{\partial y} \right) \tag{14}$$

$$D_{\min 2} = \left(\frac{\partial D_\beta}{\partial x}, \frac{\partial D_\beta}{\partial y} \right) \tag{15}$$

$$D_{\min 3} = \left(\frac{\partial D_\delta}{\partial x}, \frac{\partial D_\delta}{\partial y} \right) \tag{16}$$

In Eq. (14)–(16), $\frac{\partial D}{\partial x}$ and $\frac{\partial D}{\partial y}$ represent the gradient descent processing of the partial derivative of the currently calculated path.

Calculate the current position of the UAV based on the current distance value, as shown in Eq. (17)–(19).

$$X_1 = X_\alpha - A_1 \circ D_{\min 1} \tag{17}$$

$$X_2 = X_\beta - A_2 \circ D_{\min 2} \tag{18}$$

$$X_3 = X_\delta - A_3 \circ D_{\min 3} \tag{19}$$

In Eq. (17)–(19), A_1, A_2, A_3 are coordinate coefficient vectors and random vector in interval $[-a, a]$, linearly decreases throughout iterative process. When $A \in [-1, 1]$, the next moment position of UAV can be anywhere between current UAV and mission point.

Then calculate the position of the UAV at the next moment, as shown in Eq. (20).

$$X(t+1) = \frac{X_1 + X_2 + X_3}{3} \tag{20}$$

The specific SIOA method is as follows:

Input: task area's size *Boundary*, UAVs' number *N*, the number of targets *n*, initial positions of UAVs and targets

Output: final UAV roadmap, calculation time of the algorithm T, travel distance *D* and the flight time t

1） Set the maximum number of iterations *Maxloop*;

2） Set the groups in algorithm;

3） Set the speed of UAVs *v*;

4） Set the various parameters required by the currently used bionic algorithm;

5） Set i = 0;

6） Initialize the population number m,

7） update UAV positions X_{UAV}

8） If $N > n$: $I_{near} = 1$, $I_{far} = 0$;

9） While i < *Maxloop* do

10） Compute Ant Colony / Bat / Grey Wolf Algorithm D_S

11） Compute D_{th}

12） If $D_{th} < D_S$: $D = D_{th}$

13） End while

3   Simulation and Results Analysis

3.1   Simulation

The experimental environment is: AMD Ryzen 7 5800H CPU, the simulation environment of the experiment uses matlab simulation software. Set the experimental area to a three-dimensional space area of 100 m * 100 m * 100 m. The initial position of the UAV and the position of mission points are given. In this experiment, three UAVs and five mission points are set.

We choose the ant colony algorithm, the bat algorithm and the gray wolf algorithm in the swarm intelligence algorithm to verify the effectiveness of our proposed SIOA method. The roadmap of the algorithm is shown in Fig. 1–6. Figure 1, Fig. 3 and Fig. 5 are the result roadmaps of ant colony algorithm, bat algorithm and gray wolf algorithm respectively. Figure 2, Fig. 4 and Fig. 6 are the result roadmaps of ant colony algorithm, bat algorithm and gray wolf algorithm after using SIOA method respectively.

The initial position of the three UAVs in the experiment are [88, 6, 3], [92, 98, 16] and [69, 32, 12], The locations of the five mission points are [63, 87, 84], [22, 24, 100],

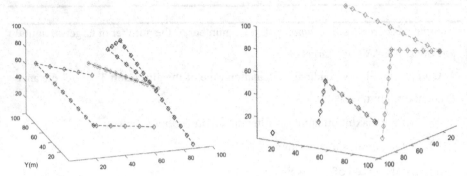

Fig. 1. Ant colony roadmap   **Fig. 2.** Ant colony SIOA roadmap

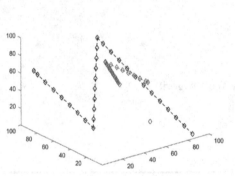
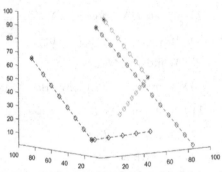

Fig. 3. Bat roadmap   **Fig. 4.** Bat SIOA roadmap

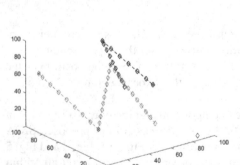
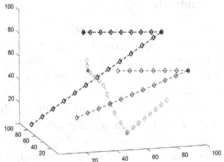

Fig. 5. Gray wolf roadmap   **Fig. 6.** Gray wolf SIOA roadmap

[74, 41, 51], [35, 56, 6] and [5, 89, 66]. In the figure the three colors line represents the three UAV's roadmap, and the red x represents the mission points. We can see from the figure that all the UAVs can finished the task and find the mission points.

3.2 Results Analysis

In the experimental analysis, we mainly judge whether the algorithm is effective by comparing the calculation time of the algorithm, the travel distance of the UAV and the flight time of the UAV.

The calculation time of the algorithm is the time complexity of the algorithm, the calculation time of the algorithm is compared to verify whether the method proposed in the article effectively reduces the time complexity of the algorithm. By comparing the travel distance of the UAV and the flight time of the UAV, it is tested whether the method proposed in the article can effectively reduce the energy consumption of the drone, so that the drone can complete the task more quickly. We randomly selected ten sets of experimental data, and verified the effectiveness of the algorithm by comparing three indicators.

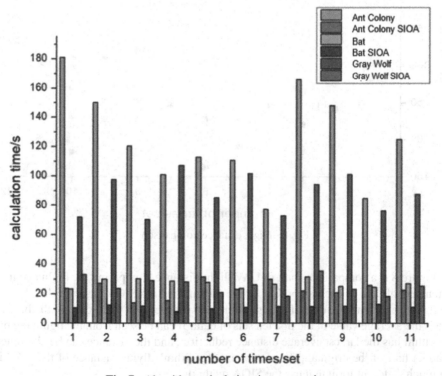

Fig. 7. Algorithm calculation time comparison

Figure 7 compares the calculation time before and after using SIOA in the ten groups of algorithms, and the 11th group is the average value of the first ten groups. In the figure,

Ant Colony, Bat and Gray Wolf represents the ant colony algorithm, bat algorithm and gray wolf algorithm, and Ant Colony SIOA, Bat SIOA and Gray Wolf SIOA represents the ant colony algorithm, bat algorithm and gray wolf algorithm after using the SIOA method. It can be seen from the Fig. 7. That calculation time of the ant colony algorithm is reduced the most, and the average is reduced to about one-sixth of the original. The bat algorithm and gray wolf algorithm respectively reduce the calculation time to about one-half and one-third of the original.

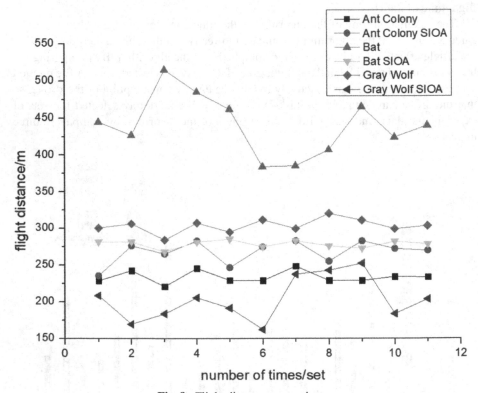

Fig. 8. Flight distance comparison

Figure 8 is a comparison chart of UAV flight distance, comparing the flight distance of ten sets of data of each algorithm before and after using SIOA. Each broken line in the figure represents the data of an algorithm, and the eleventh point data on the broken line is the average value of the first ten sets of data. It can be seen from the figure the bat algorithm has the largest average distance reduction, and the distance can be shortened to about half of the original. The ant colony algorithm's flying distance of the UAV is not much different form that use the SIOA method.

Figure 9 compares the flight time of drones. Each column of the histogram in the figure represents the travel time of the UAV corresponding to the algorithm on the abscissa, that is, the time required for the drone to complete the task. It can be seen from the figure that the UAV flight time of three algorithms has decreased to a certain extent

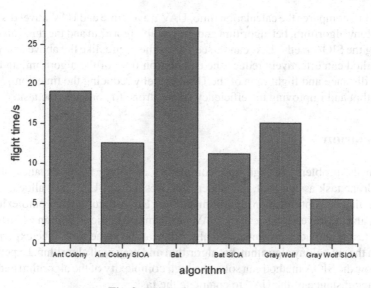

Fig. 9. Flight time comparison

after using the SIOA method. The ant colony algorithm has decreased by about 25%, the bat algorithm has decreased by about 60%, and the gray wolf algorithm has decreased by about 65%.

In summary, the SIOA method has improved the original algorithm in terms of algorithm calculation time, UAV travel distance and UAV flight time. It shows that the algorithm can reduce the time complexity of the algorithm and improve the efficiency of UAV to complete tasks. The overall comparison chart of the three evaluation standards is shown in Fig. 10.

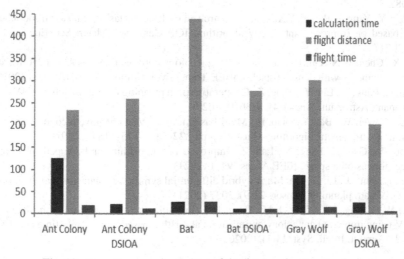

Fig. 10. Overall comparison chart of the three evaluation standards

Figure 10 compares the calculation time, UAV travel time and UAV travel distance of the ant colony algorithm, bat algorithm and gray wolf algorithm and the three algorithms after using the SIOA method. As can be seen from the figure, like the above analysis, the SIOA method can effectively reduce the calculation time of the algorithm, and reduce the travel distance and flight time of the UAV, thereby reducing the time complexity of the algorithm and improving the efficiency of the drone to complete the task.

4 Conclusion

Aiming at the problems of high time complexity and long flying distance of drones in multi-drone task assignment, this paper proposes a multi-UAV task allocation using swarm intelligence optimization algorithm (SIOA). SIOA focus on the complexity of the algorithm and the travel distance of the UAV, performs dynamic allocation when the UAV performs tasks, and adds a comparison algorithm at the same time. The experiment is verified in the ant colony algorithm, bat algorithm and gray wolf algorithm. Experimental results show the SIOA method can solve the high complexity of the algorithm and reduce the time and distance of the UAV to complete the task.

References

1. Alitappeh, R.J., Jeddisaravi, K.: Multi-robot exploration in task allocation problem. Appl. Intell. (2021). https://doi.org/10.1007/s10489-021-02483-3
2. Jin, K., Tang, P., Chen, S., Peng, J.: Dynamic task allocation in multi-robot system based on a team competition model. Front. Neurorobot. **20**(15), 674949 (2021)
3. Xu, S., Zhang, J., Meng, S., Xu, J.: Task allocation for unmanned aerial vehicles in mobile crowdsensing. Wirel. Netw. (2021). https://doi.org/10.1007/s11276-021-02638-7
4. He, W., Qi, X., Liu, L.: A novel hybrid particle swarm optimization for multi-UAV cooperate path planning. Appl. Intell. **51**(10), 7350–7364 (2021). https://doi.org/10.1007/s10489-020-02082-8
5. Wang, Y., Yang, R.R., Xu, Y.X., et al.: Research on multi-agent task optimization and scheduling based on improved ant colony algorithm. IOP Conf. Ser. Mater. Sci. Eng. **1043**(3), 11(2021)
6. Yu, X., Chen, W.N., Gu, T., et al.: ACO-A*: ant colony optimization plus A* for 3-D traveling in environments with dense obstacles. IEEE Trans. Evol. Comput. **23**(4), 617–631 (2019)
7. Kan, P., Jiang, Z., Liu, Y., Wang, Z.: Cooperative path planning for multi-sprayer-UAVs. Acta Aeronaut. Astronaut. Sin. **41**(4), 323610 (2020)
8. Cao, Y., Wei, W., Bai, Y., Qiao, H.: Multi-base multi-UAV cooperative reconnaissance path planning with genetic algorithm. Clust. Comput. **22**(S3), 5175–5184 (2019)
9. Zhou, X., Gao, F., Fang, X., Lan, Z.: Improved bat algorithm for UAV path planning in three-dimensional space. IEEE Access **99**, 1 (2021)
10. Huo, L., Zhu, J., Li, Z., Ma, M.: A hybrid differential symbiotic organisms search algorithm for UAV path planning. Sensors **21**(9), 3037 (2021)
11. Liu, W., Zheng, X., López, L.M., Garg, H.: Three-dimensional multi-mission planning of UAV using improved ant colony optimization algorithm based on the finite-time constraints. Int. J. Comput. Intell. Syst. **14**(1), (2020)

OP-RAW: A RAW Grouping Algorithm Based on Outage Probability for Industrial Internet of Things

Weifeng Sun[(✉)] [iD], Jianqiao Ding, Jia Cao, Kelong Meng, and Chi Lin

Key Lab Intelligent Control & Optimizat Ind Equip, Dalian
University of Technology, Dalian, China
{wfsun,c.lin}@dlut.edu.cn, {accelerator,
klmeng}@mail.dlut.edu.cn, caojxx0105@yeah.net

Abstract. IEEE 802.11ah is a wireless network protocol designed for large-scale Industrial Internet of Things (IIoT) scenarios. The restricted access window (RAW) mechanism introduced by IEEE 802.11ah assigns the nodes into different RAW groups to reduce conflicts between nodes. The original RAW mechanism randomly divides nodes into RAW groups with the same duration, which cannot meet the different requirements of different nodes. In order to reasonably divide the nodes into different RAW groups, a RAW grouping algorithm based on outage probability (OP-RAW) is proposed in this paper. Outage probability is introduced to evaluate the quality of data transmission in IIoT, and the influencing factors is analyzed. OP-RAW calculates the time slot duration of the nodes according to the load and outage probability of different nodes, and then groups the nodes with the same time slot duration requirements into the same RAW group. The simulation results show that, compared with the traditional RAW grouping algorithm and other RAW group optimization algorithm, the OP-RAW can increase the throughput by about 15% and effectively reduce the transmission delay.

Keywords: IIoT · IEEE 802.11ah · Restrict access window · Outage probability

1 Introduction

With the continuous development of wireless network technology, the number and coverage of nodes in Industrial Internet of Things (IIoT) are gradually expanding, including a variety of sensors. The IEEE 802.11ah is a wireless network protocol designed to support a large number of sensor access in IIoT [1]. In IEEE 802.11ah networks, an access point (AP) supports up to 8192 nodes to access. Efficiently organizing and managing so many nodes has become the key to ensuring the performance and stability of IIoT.

The restrict access window (RAW) mechanism is a key technology of the MAC layer introduced by IEEE 802.11ah to support large-scale sensers access [2]. RAW mechanism divides the accessed nodes into multiple groups, namely RAW group, and sets a RAW slot for each group. RAW slot is divided into multiple time slots internally, and the nodes in the RAW groups are evenly allocated to the time slots [3]. Each RAW slot occupies

© Springer Nature Singapore Pte Ltd. 2021
L. Cui and X. Xie (Eds.): CWSN 2021, CCIS 1509, pp. 41–54, 2021.
https://doi.org/10.1007/978-981-16-8174-5_4

the channels in turn, as shown in Fig. 1. RAW mechanism combines deterministic and random channel access, which reduces conflicts and ensures fair competition between nodes for channels.

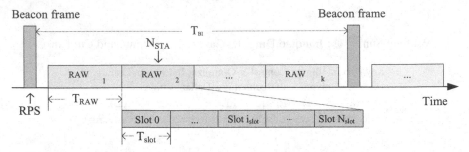

Fig. 1. Schematic diagram of RAW grouping mechanism in IEEE 802.11ah protocol.

The performance of RAW grouping strategy has an impact on the channel utilization, throughput and delay of the networks. For original IEEE 802.11ah, the nodes connected to the AP are randomly assigned to each RAW groups on average. The number and the duration of time slots in each RAW slot are fixed and the same. Little attention has been paid to efficient grouping strategies. There are different types of sensors in IIoT, which usually have different load sizes and packet sending rates. In addition, due to the diverse channel conditions in IIoT [4], the data transmission quality of the nodes in IIoT may also be different. Nodes with poor data transmission quality may have more retransmissions due to bit errors. Therefore, sensors with different traffic demand or different channel conditions have different requirements for the time slot duration in order to complete data transmission.

The original RAW mechanism allocates nodes to multiple groups and sets the access window (RAW) for each group. The RAW is divided into multiple RAW timeslots, and each node in the RAW group is evenly allocated to each RAW timeslot. Therefore, each RAW group is isolated in the time domain, and each node is allowed to participate in the competing channel only in the access window of the RAW group to which it belongs. RAW combines deterministic channel access with random channel access, which not only reduces the competition and collision between nodes, but also ensures the fair competition between nodes. However, the original RAW grouping algorithm doesn't consider the load of the node and the quality of data transmission, which causes network performance degradation.

In order to solve the problem that the original RAW mechanism cannot group nodes as different nodes required, outage probability is used in this article to evaluate the quality of data transmission in IIoT. The factors affecting the outage probability are quantitatively analyzed. Based on outage probability, a RAW grouping algorithm is proposed in this article named OP-RAW, which group the nodes according to the load size, packet sending rate and outage probability. The main contributions of this article are as follows:

- Outage probability is innovatively used to evaluate the quality of data transmission in IIoT, and multiple affecting factors of outage probability are firstly quantitatively analyzed, such as transmission distance, transmit power, and so on.
- A RAW group optimization algorithm based on outage probability (OP-RAW) is novelty proposed, which can reasonably group the nodes into different RAW groups according to the service and data transmission quality of different nodes.

2 Related Work

Appropriate RAW group algorithm has a critical impact on network performance in terms of throughput, delay, and energy consumption [5]. The research of RAW mechanism mainly focuses on the RAW group optimization algorithm. In paper [6], Cheng et al. proposed a channel-aware RAW adaptive algorithm, which dynamically adjusted the access window according to channel interference and other conditions. In paper [7], Sheu et al. proposed a dynamic time slot allocation scheme in view of the large number and denseness of nodes in IIoT which allocates more active devices to less congested devices, thereby reducing device contention for the channel. In paper [8], Miriyala et al. formulated an optimization problem using the artificial neural network to find the optimal number of RAW slots and to improve network performance. The results showed that the proposed optimization problem improved the throughput of the RAW mechanism. Liborio et al. [9] explored the application of network slicing technology in SDN using the IEEE 802.11ah, using SDN to obtain the function and quality of service requirements of nodes, and realizing logical slicing in the context of RAW.

In summary, existing works show that the RAW grouping algorithm has a critical impact on network performance, in terms of throughput, delay, and energy consumption, most researches do not comprehensively consider the quality of data transmission, so that the RAW groups and channel resources do not match.

3 Outage Probability in IEEE 802.11ah Networks

Outage probability is an expression of channel capacity, indicating whether the channel can meet the requirements of data transmission. High outage probability means that the channel capacity cannot meet the requirements of data transmission, and the quality of data transmission is poor.

3.1 A Subsection Sample

Definition (outage probability). Outage probability is defined as the probability that the instantaneous signal to noise ratio (SNR) of the channels is less than the set threshold SNR which is set to maintain a certain channel capacity. Let P_{out} denote the outage probability. The outage probability is computed as

$$P_{out} = \int_0^{r_{th}} p(r)dr \tag{1}$$

Where r_{th} is the threshold SNR set to ensure the channel capacity, r is the instantaneous SNR, and $p(r)$ is the probability density function (PDF) of r.

In IIoT scenario, the channel fading model is generally the Rayleigh fading channel [10], and the instantaneous SNR in the channel is index distribution. That is $r\epsilon(\bar{r})$, where $\bar{r}$ is the average SNR of the channel. The PDF of the SNR at the receiver is shown as Eq. (2).

$$p(r) = \frac{1}{\bar{r}} e^{\frac{r}{\bar{r}}}$$ (2)

In IIoT, the relay node generally decodes and then re-encodes the received signal and sends it to the next hop node, which called regenerative relay. Therefore, the outage probability of the channels is independent. According to Eq. (1) and Eq. (2), the outage probability of the m-hop regenerative relay system P_{out}^{m-re} is shown as Eq. (3).

$$P_{out}^{m-re} = 1 - \prod_{l=1}^{m} \int_{r_{th}}^{\infty} p(r_l) dr_l = 1 - e^{-r_{th} \sum_{l=1}^{m} \frac{1}{\bar{r}_l}}$$ (3)

In our previous work [11], the outage probability expressions of the two-hop non-regenerative relay system are derived which is shown as Eq. (4).

$$p_{out} = 1 - \frac{2r_{th}}{\sqrt{\bar{r}_1 * \bar{r}_2}} * K_1 \left(\frac{2r_{th}}{\sqrt{\bar{r}_1 * \bar{r}_2}} \right) e^{-r_{th} \left(\frac{1}{\bar{r}_1} + \frac{1}{\bar{r}_2} \right)}$$ (4)

Where $\bar{r}_1$ and $\bar{r}_2$ respectively are average SNR from the source node to the relay node and from the relay node to the destination node. The Monte Carlo method is used to verify the expressions of outage probability in two-hop regenerative and non-regenerative relay systems. Let $\bar{r}_1$ and $\bar{r}_2$ be respectively the SNR of the first and second hop links. Let $\bar{r}_1 = \bar{r}_2$, m = 2 and $r_{th} = 15$. 10,000 r1 and r2 are randomly generated according to the exponential distribution as instantaneous SNR. The experimental results are shown in Fig. 2.

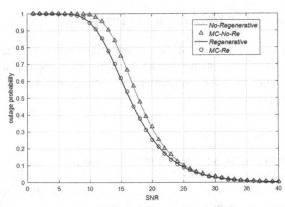

Fig. 2. The results of Monte Carlo method to verify the relationship between the probability of outage and the SNR.

In Fig. 2, the outage probability obtained by Monte Carlo method is basically consistent with that calculated by Eq. (3) and Eq. (4), which shows that the derived expressions are correct. As the SNR gradually increases, the outage probability gradually decreases. Moreover, the outage probability in the regenerative relay system is relatively lower, because the process of decoding and re-encoding corrects the error in the transmission.

3.2 Influencing Factors in IEEE 802.11ah Networks

The outage probability is directly related to the SNR at the receiver, which is affected by the receiver, which is affected by the received power P_r and the noise at the receiver N_0. P_r is as shown in Eq. (5).

$$P_r(dBm) = P_t(dBm) + G_t(dBi) + G_r(dBi) - L_{pf}(dB) \qquad (5)$$

Where P_t is the transmit power, G_t and G_r are the antenna gains of the sender and receiver, which are generally kept constant, and L_p is the path loss, which is usually different in different networks.

According to [12], the path loss model of the IEEE 802.1ah under the condition that the antenna length with 2m and 15m are as shown in Eq. (6) and Eq. (7) respectively.

$$L_p^{ah-2m} = 23.3 + 36.7 \log d \qquad (6)$$

$$L_p^{ah-15m} = 8 + 37.6 \log d \qquad (7)$$

According to Eq. (5), Eq. (6) and Eq. (7), the average SNR in IEEE 802.11ah networks with 2 m and 15 m antenna is respectively as shown as Eq. (8) and Eq. (9). Where $G_t = 3dBi$, $G_t = 0dBi$.

$$r_{ah-2m} = (P_t - 23.3 - 36.7 \log d)/N_0 \qquad (8)$$

$$r_{ah-15m} = (P_t - 5 - 37.6 \log d)/N_0 \qquad (9)$$

According to Eq. (3), Eq. (8) and Eq. (9), the outage probabilities for IEEE 802.11ah networks can be calculated from transmit power and transmission distance, according to Eq. (10) and Eq. (11), where P_t^l and d^l is transmit power and transmission distance of each hop.

$$P_p out^{ah-15m} = 1 - e^{-r_{th} \sum_{l=1}^m \frac{N_0}{\left(P_t^l - 37.6 \log d^l - 5\right)}} \qquad (10)$$

$$P_p out^{ah-2m} = 1 - e^{-r_{th} \sum_{l=1}^m \frac{N_0}{\left(P_t^l - 36.7 \log d^l - 20.2\right)}} \qquad (11)$$

Make $m = 1$ and $r_{th} = 15$ as an example to analyze the relationship between outage probability, transmit power and transmission distance. The results are shown in Fig. 3 and Fig. 4.

Outage probability can comprehensively reflect the influence of many factors on the channel quality, and evaluate the channel quality more comprehensively. Outage probability can be calculated through some simple parameters before the data transmission, and be used to guide the RAW grouping.

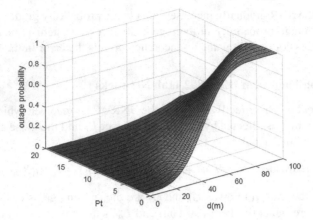

Fig. 3. The relationship between the probability of interruption and the power and distance of the IEEE 802.11ah protocol when the antenna height is 2 m.

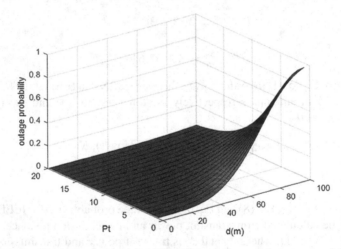

Fig. 4. The relationship between the probability of interruption and the power and distance of the IEEE 802.11ah protocol when the antenna height is 15 m.

4 Outage Probability Based RAW Grouping Algorithm

RAW slots should enable the nodes in the RAW groups to just complete the data transmission. In this section, a RAW grouping algorithm based on outage probability (OP-RAW) is proposed, which groups the nodes according to the load and data transmission quality.

4.1 Problems of Original RAW Grouping Algorithm

In large-scale IIoT, different types of sensors have different services, so the load size and the packets sending rate of different nodes are different. The time required to complete data transmission is also different. In addition, at the MAC layer of IIoT, IEEE 802.11ah provides data transmission without bit errors through cyclic redundancy check (CRC) technology. If the CRC detects error, the data frames will be retransmitted. The amount of bit error is related to the quality of data transmission. The Time to complete the data transmission is determined by the business and data transmission quality.

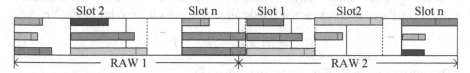

Fig. 5. Original RAW grouping strategy considering size of node payload and retransmission.

In original IEEE 802.11ah, the nodes are randomly assigned to several RAW groups and the number of time slots and the time slot duration in the RAW slot are the same, as shown in Fig. 5. The length of the rectangles in Fig. 5 represents time slot duration requirements of different nodes. The rectangles are divided into two parts, which respectively represent the time required to send the load and to retransmit the error frames. Some nodes don't fully utilize time slots, resulting in a waste of time slot. Some nodes' requirement for time slot duration is much greater than the assigned duration and occupies the next time slots, resulting in reducing throughput and increasing delay.

4.2 Slot Duration Calculation

For IEEE 802.11ah, the time slot in RAW slot is the same, so the RAW slot duration T_{RAW} is as Eq. (12).

$$T_{RAW} = N_{slot} * T_{slot} \tag{12}$$

Where N_{slot} and T_{slot} are the number and duration of time slots respectively. The time required to transmit each data packet is as shown in Eq. (13).

$$t_d = p/r \tag{13}$$

Where p is the size of load and r is the packet sending rate. Nodes within the time slot use distributed coordination function (DCF) to compete for the channels. Therefore, the packet transmission time is as shown in Eq. (14), where t_{DCF} is the time to wait for the channels to be idle and the counter to be zero when using DCF.

$$t_p = t_d + t_{DCF} \tag{14}$$

The time required to send the data packet is as shown in Eq. (15), where T_{BI} is the interval time of beacon frames, Δt is the packet sending interval.

$$T_p = t_p * T_{BI}/(r * \Delta t) \tag{15}$$

The outage probability is used as an index to directly evaluate the quality of data transmission and to correct the T_p so that the sensor can complete the retransmission. The corrected T_p is as shown in Eq. (16).

$$T_p^{P_{out}} = T_p/(1 - P_{out}) \tag{16}$$

Assuming the probability that the node doesn't collide is P_c, N_T, the time slot duration is as Eq. (17). Paper [13] has launched a detailed research on the value of P_c, N_T.

$$T_{slot} = N_T * T_p^{P_{out}}/P_{c, N_T}T \tag{17}$$

The slot counter in RAW is as shown in Eq. (18).

$$C = (T_{slot}(\mu s) - 500)/120 \tag{18}$$

For different nodes, the obtained C is generally different, and the time slot duration in the same RAW slot should be the same. Therefore, the nodes are grouped according to the interval where C is located.

4.3 Working Process of OP-RAW

OP-RAW calculates the suitable slot counter C for each node according to the load size, packet sending rate and outage probability. Then the nodes with similar C are regrouped into the same RAW group. Finally, the nodes are re-associated according to the grouping results.

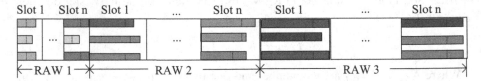

Fig. 6. OP-RAW algorithm group strategy.

The grouping strategy using OP-RAW algorithm is shown in Fig. 6. It can be seen that the OP-RAW algorithm allocates slot resources for nodes according to the service of nodes and quality of data transmission, which ensures the efficiency of data transmission and also improves the utilization of channel resources. The pseudo code of OP-RAW is shown in algorithm 1. The time and space complexity of the algorithm is O(n).

Algorithm 1 Local Search Based Algorithm

Input: T_{BI}, N_{slot} **Output:** RPS
1: Establish association;
2: //for STA
3: Send r^i and p_{size}^i to AP;
4: //for ap
5: Store r^i and p_{size}^i in list R and P_{size};
6: Calculate outage probability and store it in P_{out};
7: **while** there exists STAs ungrouped **do**
8:    Calculate t_p and T_p from p_{size}^i and r^i
9:    Calculate T_{slot} and C^{0i} from $P_{out}{}^i$;
10:    Map C^{0i} to C^i according to the interval where C^{0i} is located
11:    Store C^i in list C;
12: **end while**
13: Regroup the nodes according to list C;
14: Calculate T_{RAW};
15: Re-association and put result intop the RPS frame;

Firstly, the nodes establish association with the AP, the AP collects node information about the rate and size of data packets, and calculates the outage probability. Then the AP calculates a suitable slot counter C^i for each node according to r^i, p_{size}^i and P_{out}. The nodes with the same time slot counter are regrouped into the same RAW group. Finally, the AP calculates the RAW parameters based on the grouping results and writes the parameters into the RPS frame.

OP-RAW uses a single-layer loop to traverse the nodes associated with the AP, so the time complexity of the algorithm is $O(n)$. In addition, the algorithm contains a limited number of lists to store the information, so the space complexity of the algorithm is $O(n)$.

5 Evaluation

In this section, the OP-RAW algorithm is evaluated, compared with the TR-RAW algorithm, which groups nodes according to the services of different nodes [13]. The evaluation of NS-3 simulation shows that the regression-based model proposed in [13] is quite accurate, and their traffic perception grouping is outperforming other baseline methods, so tr-RAW algorithm is used in this paper for comparison. The simulation tool is NS3 extended by IDLab [14]. The operating system is Ubuntu 16.04 LTS.

5.1 Simulation Scenarios and Parameters

The network topology used in the simulation is shown in Fig. 7. In Fig. 7, in the circle with AP as the center and R as the radius, 40 STAs are uniformly distributed randomly. The nodes are divided into 3 categories according to packet sending rate and load size. Nodes with 128byte load and 100 ms packet sending interval are represented by red triangles, nodes with 128byte load and 500 ms packet sending interval are represented by green squares, and nodes with 512byte load and 100 ms packet sending interval are represented by blue circles. These nodes are evenly distributed in the network, and the transmitted power and noise in the environment remain the same. For nodes of the same type with the same data transmission quality, the required time slots are the same length. Other simulation parameters are shown in Table 1.

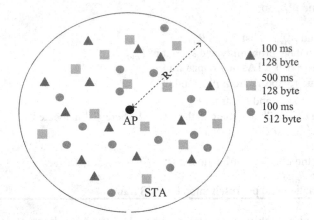

Fig. 7. IEEE 802.11ah network topology with different kinds of nodes.

Table 1. Simulation parameters

Parameter	Value
MAC layer Protocol	IEEE 802.11ah
Transport layer protocol	UDP
frequency	900 MHz
Simulation time	5s

5.2 Simulation Results and Analysis

When the transmit power is fixed at 10mW and the noise is 6.8 dB, using OP-RAW, TR-RAW and original RAW algorithm, the relationship between the transmission range and delay of the network are respectively as shown in Fig. 8. and the relationship between the throughput and delay of the network are respectively as shown in Fig. 9.

It can be seen from Fig. 8 that with the transmission range increasing, the throughput with the three algorithms is all decreasing. The throughput with OP-RAW algorithm is increased by about 6% compared with the TR-RAW algorithm, and about 12% compared with the original RAW algorithm. In the case of large transmission distances, the OP-RAW algorithm improves the throughput more obviously about 15%.

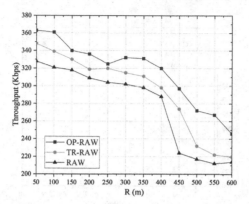

Fig. 8. Throughput under different transmission range using OP-RAW, TR-RAW and Original RAW algorithm.

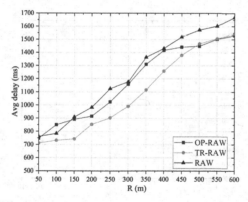

Fig. 9. Delay under different transmission range using OP-RAW, TR-RAW and Original RAW algorithm.

It can be seen from Fig. 9 that as the transmission distance increases, the delay of data transmission using the three algorithms keep increase. When the transmission range is $R \leq 500m$, the delay of using OP-RAW is always greater than using the TR-RAW, but smaller than using the original RAW algorithm. When the transmission range is $R \geq 500m$, the transmission delay using OP-RAW algorithm is the lowest.

When the transmission range is 500 m, the noise is 6.8 dB and using OP-RAW, TR-RAW and original RAW algorithm, the relationship between transmit power and delay is shown in Fig. 10 and the relationship between throughput and delay is shown in Fig. 11.

It can be seen from Fig. 10 that with the transmission power increasing, the network throughputs with the three algorithms are increasing. Using OP-RAW algorithm, the network throughput has a certain improvement compared with using TR-RAW and original RAW algorithm. Compared with the TR-RAW algorithm, the OP-RAW algorithm considers the retransmissions and appropriately extends the slot duration, which better improves the network throughput.

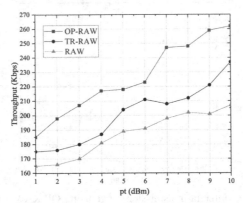

Fig. 10. Throughput under different transmit power using OPRAW, TR-RAW and Original RAW algorithm.

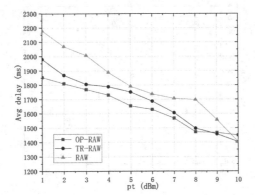

Fig. 11. The delay under different transmission power using OPRAW, TR-RAW and Original RAW algorithm.

According to Fig. 11, as the transmission power increases, the transmission delay with the three algorithms decreases. When $pt \geq 9mW$, the average delay is the lowest using OP-RAW algorithm. When $pt \geq 9mW$, the transmission delay of using OP-RAW algorithm is slightly higher than that of using the TR-RAW algorithm.

6   Conclusion

There are a great number of nodes in large-scale IIoT using IEEE 802.11ah. The original RAW grouping algorithm in IEEE 802.11ah doesn't consider the service of the nodes and the quality of the data transmissions. In order to group nodes reasonably, outage probability is used to evaluate the quality of data transmission. This article analyzes multiple factors affecting the outage probability, such as transmit power and transmission distance. Based on the outage probability, a RAW grouping algorithm named OP-RAW is proposed, which calculates the slot duration required according to the packet sending rate, load size and outage probability. The nodes with the same slot requirements are grouped into the same RAW group. Simulation results show that OP-RAW algorithm can optimize throughput and delay of the networks, and improve the utilization of time domain channel resources. Compared to TR-RAW, op-RAW algorithm better improves the network throughput and has advantages in the case of low transmission power, so it has high application value in related real scenario. In our future, the delay, priority and other requirements of the nodes will be considered comprehensively when regrouping the nodes.

Acknowledgment. This work is supported by the National Key R&D Program of China (2018YFB1700100), CERNET Innovation Project (NGII20190801) and the Fundamental Research Funds for the Central Universities (DUT21LAB115).

References

1. Wei, Y., Peizhao, H., Wenbo, W., Jiahui, W., Hongjian, Z.: FASUS: a fast association mechanism for 802.11ah networks. Comput. Netw. **175** (2020). https://www.sciencedirect.com/science/article/pii/S1389128619312083
2. Sangeetha, U., Babu, A.V.: Service differentiation in IEEE 802.11ah WLAN under restricted access window based MAC protocol. Comput. Commun. **172**, 142–154 (2021)
3. Ahmed, N., Hussain, M.I.: Periodic traffic scheduling for IEEE 802.11ah networks. IEEE Commun. Lett. **24**(7), 1510–1513 (2020)
4. Liu, C.-F., Bennis, M.: Data-driven predictive scheduling in ultra-reliable low-latency industrial IoT: a generative adversarial network approach. In: IEEE 21st International Workshop on Signal Processing Advances in Wireless Communications 2020, SPAWC, pp. 1–5. IEEE, Georgia (2020)
5. Yanjing, S., et al.: Raw online regrouping method in IEEE 802. 11ah protocol for industrial internet of things. Tongxin Xuebao/J. Commun. **41**(4), 92–101 (2020)
6. Yujun, C., Huachun, Z., Dong, Y.: CA-CWA: channel-aware contention window adaption in IEEE 802.11ah for soft real-time industrial applications. Sensors (Switzerland) **19**(13) (2019). https://www.mdpi.com/1424-8220/19/13/3002
7. Tsang-Ling, S., Pei-Hsun, C.: Dynamic slot allocations for m2m in IEEE 802.11ah networks. In: ACM International Conference Proceeding Series, pp. 13–18. IEEE, Poland (2020)
8. Mahesh, M., Harigovindan, V.P.: Throughput enhancement of IEEE 802.11ah raw mechanism using ANN. In: IEEE Delhi Section, India (2020)
9. Libório, P.P., Lam, C.T., Ng, B., Guidoni, D.L., Curado, M., Villas, L.A.: Network slicing in IEEE 802.11ah. In: 2019 IEEE 18th International Symposium on Network Computing and Applications, IEEE, NCA (2019)
10. Nasaruddin, N., Elizar, E., Ramzi, A.: Multi-relay orthogonal and non-orthogonal amplify and forward for two-way cooperative WLANs. Banda Aceh, Indonesia (2019)

11. Weifeng, S., Guanghao, Z., Yiming, Z., Rui, G.: An outage probability based channel bonding algorithm for 6G network. In: Wang, X., Leung, V.C.M., Li, K., Zhang, H., Hu, X., Liu, Q. (eds.) 6GN for Future Wireless Networks. 6GN 2020. Lecture Notes of the Institute for Computer Sciences, Social Informatics and Telecommunications Engineering, vol. 337, pp. 144–159. Springer, Cham (2020). https://doi.org/10.1007/978-3-030-63941-9_11

12. Zhao, L., Peng, L.: Ro-raw: run-time restricted access window optimization in IEEE 802.11ah network with extended kalman filter. Wireless Communications and Mobile Computing (2020)

13. Tung-Chun, C., Chi-Han, L., Kate Ching-ju, L., Wen-Tsuen, C.: Traffic-aware sensor grouping for IEEE 802.11ah networks: regression based analysis and design. IEEE Trans. Mob. Comput. **18**, 674–687(2019)

14. Tian, L., Ljivo, A., Santi, S., Poorter, E.D., Hoebeke, J., Famaey, J.: Extension of the IEEE 802.11ah ns-3 simulation module. In: ACM International Conference Proceeding Series, pp. 53–60, Surathkal, India (2018)

Application on Internet of Things

AcousticPose: Acoustic-Based Human Pose Estimation

Jinjiang Lai(✉) and Chengwen Luo

College of Computer Science and Software Engineering, Shenzhen University,
Shenzhen 518052, China
laijinjiang2018@email.szue.edu.cn, chengwen@szu.edu.cn

Abstract. In recent years, human pose estimation based on computer vision has become a popular research area. Conventional pose estimation systems usually require pre-deployed infrastructures such as cameras, WiFi, millimeter wave radar, etc. These external devices are usually expensive and difficult to deploy and are not feasible to track human poses continuously, e.g., when users are exercising outdoor. To tackle these challenges, in this paper we propose a human pose estimation system based on wearable and acoustic waves. The system utilizes wearable devices equipped with microphones and speakers and is easy to deploy. The acoustic waves are used to estimate the distances between each pair of wearable devices, and then the 2-dimensional structures of these devices are reconstructed as an estimation of the human pose. Our experiment results show that the proposed system can estimate different human poses accurately with an action recognition accuracy of 97.5%.

Keywords: Acoustic ranging · Human pose recognition · Signal processing

1 Introduction

Motivation. In recent years, human pose estimation technologies [1–3] have flourished due their wide application scenarios and the rise of machine learning technologies such as deep learning. However, the reconstruction of human pose based on vision inputs such as images has its limitations. First, complex background, occlusion, and changes in light will reduce the recognition accuracy of vision-based systems. In addition, due to privacy concerns, in some scenarios cameras are not proper to be deployed to collect images and videos. Therefore, many alternative technologies that use different data inputs have emerged for human pose recognition. For example, a novel deep neural network capable of reconstructing human full body pose in real-time from 6 Inertial Measurement Units (IMUs) worn on the user's body [4]. These devices can be configured on smart devices. In addition to using these sensors, a large number of smart devices

Supported by organization x.

are also equipped with microphones, speakers. There is a lot of work to realize the localization of objects through sound wave technology such as microphones, from two-dimensional positioning to three-dimensional positioning [5–11]. And it can be tracked after positioning [12–18]. In addition, there are many new and innovative applications, such as using a single microphone for positioning [19], using dual microphones for distance measurement [20], using acoustic recognition and tracking to recognize handwriting [21]. Based on the bottom-up method, the human pose estimation method is to first find out the key nodes of the human pose and then connect to construct the human pose, and the acoustic is used for positioning and tracking. Therefore, the acoustic can be used to locate and track the human pose node. The use of acoustic technology for human pose estimation and tracking has created the possibility.

Prior Works and Limitation. In human pose estimation, a lot of work has been focused on image and video data [1–3,22,23], but on the one hand the image and video data will be affected by ambient light, Obstructions, etc., on the other hand, it also creates hidden dangers of privacy and security. Therefore, work that uses wireless signals for human pose estimation has emerged, such as RFID, WI-FI, mmWave radar,etc. However, such work requires more expensive equipment on the one hand, and requires specific deployment of the surrounding environment on the other.

In recent years, smart devices have experienced explosive growth, and microphones and speakers have been embedded in a large number of smart devices. Therefore, the acoustic signal has become a low-cost technology that can be promoted and used in a large area. Human pose estimation and tracking through the use of sound wave ranging has the advantages of low cost and privacy. However, in acoustic ranging, using the relative ranging method [13,16,24], you need to fix one anchor point and then perform ranging location tracking on the other device, so it cannot meet the two requirements. Ranging requirements for free movement between mobile devices. The use of traditional flight time for distance measurement faces three major challenges: (1) The propagation speed of sound waves is uncertain. (2) It is difficult to synchronize clocks between different devices. (3) The equipment sending and receiving processing time is uncertain. Using RTOF [25–29] and ETOA [20] for ranging can avoid clock synchronization, but the former The distance measurement is limited to a single device and cannot meet the distance measurement between multiple devices. The latter will inevitably lead to higher time delays due to the need for round-trip measurement time.

Our Solution. We propose AcousticPose, a robust human pose estimation and human action recognition system based on acoustic signals ranging by the smartphone and speaker, which achieves high recognition accuracy under difference scenarios. AcousticPose can estimation six human pose and six human action.

In our solution, we adopt chirp signal as acoustic to transmit and receive. On the one hand, we design the chip signal using high frequency can not easy to be disturbed by the environment. On the other hand, the chirp signal can easy recognition by auto-correlation. We propose two algorithms, pre-processing and post-processing can effectively reduce signal interference and increase the frequency of ranging.

Aiming at the limitation of the non-unique spatial solution of MDS, an improved MDS algorithm is proposed and prior knowledge is introduced to realize the human pose estimation, and the frame filling algorithm of human pose is designed to track the human pose. To address the challenge of lacking of training data, we collect a small amount of six human action data. Collect the distance information of the human body under different actions, and use deep learning to train and test the data. The experimental results show that the sound wave based distance measurement can effectively track the human body posture and recognize the human body movement.

The main contributions of this paper are summarized as follws.

- To the best of our knowledge, this is the first work for human pose estimation using acoustic in smart devices, which can effectively promote the continuous development of the theory of human-computer interaction methods.
- Based on ETOA, We propose the design of Dynamic Range, a multi-devices ranging system. Dynamic Range addresses practical challenges such as multipath effect, hardware diversity, ranging slow, etc.
- We implements a human pose reconstruction and action recognition system based on acoustic wave distance measurement. On the one hand, it uses the MDS algorithm to construct a two-dimensional relative position based on the distance information. On the other hand, by collecting a large number of human pose distance information in six kinds of motion states, using deep learning model training, finally achieve the classification of human pose movements.

In the following, we present our system architecture in Sect. 2. We present our prototype system evaluation in Sect. 3. We review related work in Sect. 4 and conclude this paper in Sect. 5.

2   System Design

2.1   Overview

Figure 1 illustrates the overview of AcousticPose. AcousticPose consists of two main components,which are *Transceiver Ranging* and *Human Pose Identifier*. Transceiver Ranging uses adaptive debounce filtering and post-processing algorithm, the principle of distance measurement based ETOA. Human Pose Identifier consists of two parts, one part uses MDS to realize human pose estimation and tracking, and the other part uses deep learning to realize human action recognition.

2.2   Dynamic Ranging

Data Pre-processing. In actual sampling, due to the influence of the surrounding environment, a lot of noise data will inevitably appear, such as thermal noise of machine operation, environmental noise, multipath effect, etc. And the noise caused by the vibration of the hardware itself and the suffix harmonics received by the microphone. In actual experiments, the acoustic signal data that has not been processed for noise reduction will contain a variety of noises, as shown in Fig. 3(a) is a typical acoustic signal data that has not been processed for noise reduction.

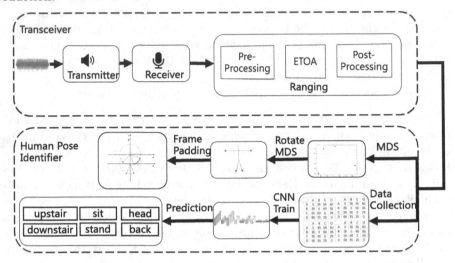

Fig. 1. Overview

Traditional filtering algorithms cannot achieve proper noise reduction effects. Therefore, this paper proposes an adaptive debounce filter method, the principle of which comes from the debounce filter method. The debounce filtering method is based on the noise data generated by the sensor jitter or jitter. By setting the filter counter, the value obtained by each sampling is compared with the threshold value. If it is invalid, it will be cleared, and if it is valid, it will continue to be processed. In actual use, the jitter amplitude of the sampled acoustic data is not unique, so the set threshold often needs to be adjusted manually. The adaptive debounce filtering method proposed in this paper can adaptively set the threshold size for the sampled acoustic data, so as to achieve the effect of noise reduction. The effect after pre-processing is shown in Fig. 2(b).

Post-processing. In the experimental setup, multi-threading is used for acoustic signal playback and recording, while the ETOA method is used for distance measurement. It is necessary to ensure the interlace of audio data and ensure that the acoustic signal data played by itself and the acoustic signal data played by the other party do not overlap to obtain the time difference. In order to calculate the distance. However, if the central control or other signal methods are used for synergistic acoustic signal, the time delay will be greatly increased, and better timeliness cannot be achieved. There are two main situations that cause the acoustic signal to calculate the time stamp abnormally. On the one

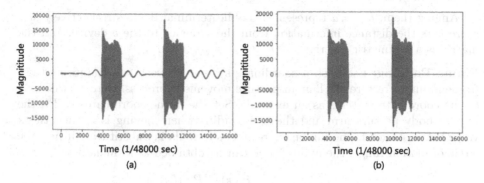

Fig. 2. (a) Original data. (b) Pre-processing data

hand, due to the influence of the surrounding environment or occlusion, the own device cannot capture the acoustic signal of the other device, and the acoustic signal is lost and cannot be calculated or the calculated time stamp is wrong. On the other hand, the time stamp calculation is abnormal because the microphone between the two devices receives its own acoustic signal and the acoustic signal of the other party overlaps. This paper proposes to use a detection algorithm on the received acoustic signal data. Once the acoustic signal overlap or there is no two audio data, insert a corresponding length of mute audio playback, so that the self-transmitted audio and the received audio can be interleaved.

2.3   Human Pose Identifier

Human Pose Tracking MDS Limitations. MDS can also be used for data visualization. Given the relative distance information of a set of specific points, the relative position of data points can be obtained. This algorithm has many advantages. On the one hand, it does not require prior knowledge and the calculation is relatively simple. On the other hand, the relative relationship of the data in the original space is retained, and the visualization effect can be obtained. In this article, the classic MDS algorithm is improved. On the one hand, it is necessary to give certain meaning to the data points. On the other hand, the prior knowledge of the human body posture can be added to it, so that the final human posture can get a better result. From the previous chapter, we can see that the distance between distance measurement is obtained by acoustic signal. In the previous section of this chapter, the distance measurement between multiple devices is also designed. In the actual experiment, 4 mobile terminal devices are used for distance measurement, so as to obtain $C_4^2 = 6$ distance information.

$$D = \begin{pmatrix} d_{aa} & d_{ab} & d_{ac} & d_{ad} \\ d_{ab} & d_{bb} & d_{bc} & d_{bd} \\ d_{ac} & d_{cb} & d_{cc} & d_{cd} \\ d_{ad} & d_{bd} & d_{cd} & d_{dd} \end{pmatrix} \qquad (1)$$

Among them, a, b, c, d represent 4 mobile terminal devices respectively. d_{ab} represents the distance information from the a device to the b device, and the matrix is a symmetric matrix.

Frame Padding: Establish a coordinate system between two frames and use frame filling to restore the human posture movement process. Here we take one of the coordinate systems as an example. Set the frame coordinates to Pi, the human body posture arm and the fixed radius when moving is r, then the x value between each frame can be expressed as formula 2. Substituting it into the circle of motion range, the filling frame can be obtained as formula 3.

$$x = P_{i-1}(x) + \frac{P_i(x) - P_{i-1}(x)}{K} \tag{2}$$

$$P_j(x,y) = (P_{i-1}(x) + \frac{P_i(x) - P_{i-1}(x)}{K}, \sqrt{r^2 - P_{i-1}(x) + \frac{P_i(x) - P_{i-1}(x)}{K}}) \tag{3}$$

Human Pose Action Recognition Data Processing: In the design of this section, the matrix is mainly used to collect distance information. The data format of each distance information is shown in Eq. 1. Each group of data collects 4 matrices for each action. A complete corresponding label data is D_i to D_{i+4}. Then the matrix information of 8×8 size can be formed by splicing. In the experiment, five experimenters were used for data collection. Each experimenter performed each of the six actions 30 times. The size of the data set is $5 \times 6 \times 30 \times 4 = 3600$ pieces of matrix distance information. Complete distance information is collected four times for each operation to form a complete training data.

Model Design: The deep learning convolutional neural network has a natural feature extraction advantage for matrix information. In this section, a three-layer convolutional neural network is designed to train the matrix distance information. The CNN input data of the system in this paper is to collect 4 matrix distance information Di at different times. The designed convolutional layer has a total of 2 layers, and each layer contains 2×2 convolution kernels for feature extraction, and a convolution with a step size of 2 is used to realize the function of the mean pooling layer. Finally, use the full connection and softmax function to output the final Di classification result. The designed model diagram is shown in Fig. 6.

3   Experiment

3.1   Experiment Setting

Parameter Setting: The sound wave parameter setting f_1 is 2000 and f_2 is set to 16k, as shown in the Fig. 2. The preprocessing algorithm sets the slope to be less than 1 to find the best threshold filter. In principle of distance measurement, the microphone and speaker of the device use the same position, so the distance

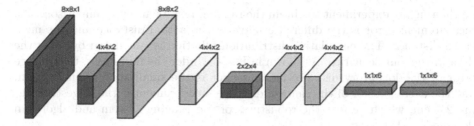

Fig. 3. Convolutional neural network design diagram

between the microphone and the speaker is ignored, that is, K is set to 0. In the post-processing algorithm, the difference point is set to 285, when sampling at $48kHz$ and calculating at a speed of $340\,\mathrm{m/s}$,

Data Collection: In the actual setting, we used four mobile devices (two Samsung Galaxy Note 4, one Xiaomi 6X, one oneplus 7pro). Among them, the speakers of Samsung mobile phones are on the back of the phone, and the speakers of Xiaomi and one plus are on the bottom of the side. We invited 5 volunteers (4 males and 1 female) to perform six actions and collect data. Each person collects 100 label data.

Model Training: The CNN input data of the system in this paper is to collect the distance information of four matrices at different times. The designed convolution layer has a total of 2 layers, each layer contains 2×2 convolution kernels for feature extraction, and the function of mean pooling layer is realized by using the convolution with step size of 2. Finally, the sorting result of the final D_I is output using the full connection and the *softmax* function.

First of all, in order to train the deep learning model and test the performance of the model at the same time. In this paper, the data set is divided into three parts: training set, verification set and test set. The training set is used for training, and the verification set is used for adjusting parameters to make the model converge. The test set finally evaluates the performance of the model. In this paper, 80%of 3000 sample data sets is taken as the training set, 20%as the verification set, and another 120 data are collected as the test set.

During the training initialization, random function is used to generate random numbers between 0 and 0.001 as the weight matrix after initialization. All the offset vectors are set to 0, and the objective function is the cross entropy. The traditional Adam gradient descent method was used to update the parameters. After the batch size was set to 32, the training began, and the number of training sessions was set to 100 rounds.

3.2 Evaluation

Ranging Evaluation. We uses the ranging accuracy error to measure the accuracy of the experimental results. Accuracy is defined as the straight-line distance between two smart devices. It is through the preset distance, and then carries on the ranging experiment to obtain the ranging results and its comparison. The measurement error is the difference between the actual distance and the measured distance. The cumulative distribution function is calculated by using the data in the four scenarios. As shown in Fig. 4, Under the four cases, the average error of the dormitory distance measurement is the smallest, reaching 1.3 cm, and the average error of the canteen distance measurement is the largest, reaching 2.4 cm, which verifies the robustness of the ranging system and algorithm designed in this paper.

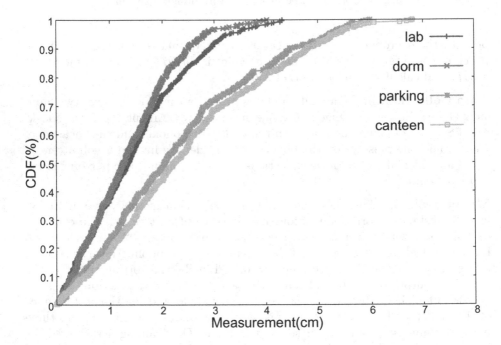

Fig. 4. Cumulative distribution function for the four test cases

Human Pose Tracking Evaluation. In the experiment of this section, we mainly combine mobile devices with human limbs to map human postures and movements. In this experiment, it is assumed that the initial body posture position is set, as shown in the Fig. 5. From left to right, from top to bottom in order: hands stretch, hands lift, right hand stretch, left hand stretch, natural relax, hands slightly lift.

Human Pose Action Recognition. The data set consisted of five experimenters, and each experimenter collected distance information of 100 groups of 6 movements. For each action, four distance information are collected continuously. When the convolution kernel size is 2, the batch size is 32, and the training

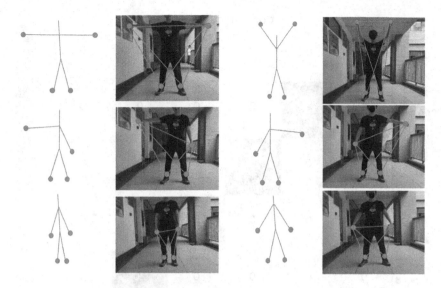

Fig. 5. Human pose actual comparison

iterations are 100 times. Finally, the CNN model was used to extract and classify the data features. The final results are shown in the Fig. 6. The average test accuracy is 97.5%.

4   Related Work

With the development of smart devices, microphones and speakers are embedded in a large number of smart devices(e.g., smartphones, smart watch, smart speaker), acoustic ranging has attracted wide attention in academia. Acoustic ranging is mainly divided into absolute ranging and relative ranging. Each distance information of absolute ranging needs to be measured again, while relative ranging is to update the position through the subsequent movement of the ranging target. The principle of absolute ranging mainly uses the time of flight (ToF: Time of Flight) to find the distance [30]. Due to the need for precise clock synchronization based on ToF ranging, there is a time difference of arrival (TDoA: Time Difference of Arrival) [31,32], of which Cricket [32] is the first sonic indoor based on TDoA The positioning system uses a combination of sound wave signals and radio frequency signals to perform distance measurement, but it cannot be widely deployed due to its high noise. Since then, acoustic ranging has been vigorously developed. The elapsed time between the two arrival times (ETOA: Elapsed Time between the two Time-of-Arrivals) [20] and the round-trip arrival time (RTOF: Round-Trip Time-of-Flight) [25–29] does not require clock synchronization and ranging and other related work. The main principle of relative ranging is based on Doppler effect, phase conversion and frequency modulation continuous wave technology. The paper [24] introduced the Doppler effect in 2012

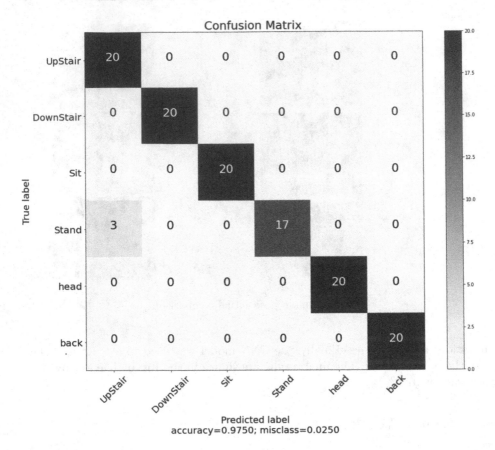

Fig. 6. Confusion matrix

to estimate the direction of motion. Swadloon [7] further combines the Doppler effect, uses phase conversion to achieve ranging, and achieves a maximum tracking error of 1.73 m on the 2000 m^2 plane. AAMouse [33] is based on Doppler effect ranging to track smart phones. FingerIO [5] uses phase conversion to solve the problem of unsynchronized distance measurement and positioning based on ToF. LLAP [13] and Stratavch516 expand on this basis, using only one microphone and two devices on the smartphone. Two speakers realize high-precision ranging and tracking.

In computer vision area, human pose estimation has lots of work are focused on 2D [1–3, 22, 23] ,and 3D human pose estimation with RGB-Depth cameras [34] and VICON system [35]. However,both require adequate lighting conditions and without bad illumination, occlusion and blurry, and may cause privacy issues. Recently, there are many wireless signals to solve the human pose estimation without camera. Wi-Fi signals are used to collect CSI data, combined with the image data collected by the camera and realize the human pose estimation [36,37]. In addition, there is also the use of RFID signals combined with deep learning technology to process them to obtain the human pose [38]. mmWave radar using forked CNN architecture was used to predict the real-world position of the skeletal joints in 3-D space, using the radar-to-image representation [39]. However, these wireless signals works are usually expensive and power-consuming, therefore are difficult to apply for daily and household use.

5 Conclusion

In this paper, we investigate the possibility of using acoustic signals to image the human body like a camera. Specifically, we propose a framework, named Acousti-Pose, that can construct 2D human pose using distance and recognize human activity. The proposed framework is able to implement a multiple device distance measurement system, and collect multiple distance information. Improved MDS can restore high-dimensional distance information to a two-dimensional position. Additionally, AcousticPose employs a convolutional neural network (CNN) to realize human activity recognition. The experimental results based on a real-world acoustic ranging testbed demonstrate that our proposed AcousticPose framework can construct 2D human pose and recognize human activity.

References

1. Toshev, A., Szegedy, C.: DeepPose: human pose estimation via deep neural networks. In: Proceedings of the IEEE Conference on Computer Vision and Pattern Recognition, pp. 1653–1660 (2014)
2. Cao, Z., Simon, T., Wei, S.-E., Sheikh, Y.: Realtime multi-person 2D pose estimation using part affinity fields. In: Proceedings of the IEEE Conference on Computer Vision and Pattern Recognition, pp. 7291–7299 (2017)
3. Guler, R.A., Neverova, N., Kokkinos, I.: DensePose: dense human pose estimation in the wild. In: Proceedings of the IEEE Conference on Computer Vision and Pattern Recognition, pp. 7297–7306 (2018)
4. Huang, Y., Kaufmann, M., Aksan, E., Black, M.J., Hilliges, O., Pons-Moll, G.: Deep inertial poser: learning to reconstruct human pose from sparse inertial measurements in real time. ACM Trans. Graph. (TOG) **37**(6), 1–15 (2018)
5. Nandakumar, R., Iyer, V., Tan, D., Gollakota, S.: FingerIO: using active sonar for fine-grained finger tracking. In: Proceedings of the 2016 CHI Conference on Human Factors in Computing Systems, pp. 1515–1525 (2016)
6. Wada, T., Ikefuji, D., Nakayama, M., Nishiura, T.: A study of 3D sound field localization system using parametric loudspeaker and indirect loudspeakers for reverberation reproduction. In: INTER-NOISE and NOISE-CON Congress and Conference Proceedings, vol. 249, no. 5, pp. 2909–2915. Institute of Noise Control Engineering (2014)
7. Huang, W., et al.: Accurate indoor localization using acoustic direction finding via smart phones. arXiv preprint arXiv:1306.1651 (2013)
8. Chen, X., Chen, Y., Cao, S., Zhang, L., Zhang, X., Chen, X.: Acoustic indoor localization system integrating TDMA+ FDMA transmission scheme and positioning correction technique. Sensors **19**(10), 2353 (2019)

9. Qiu, J., Chu, D., Meng, X., Moscibroda, T.: On the feasibility of real-time phone-to-phone 3D localization. In: Proceedings of the 9th ACM Conference on Embedded Networked Sensor Systems, pp. 190–203 (2011)

10. Herrera, J., Kim, H.S.: Ping-Pong: using smartphones to measure distances and relative positions. In: Proceedings of Meetings on Acoustics 166ASA, vol. 20, no. 1, p. 055003. Acoustical Society of America (2013)

11. Akiyama, T., Sugimoto, M., Hashizume, H.: SyncSync: time-of-arrival based localization method using light-synchronized acoustic waves for smartphones, pp. 1–9, October 2015

12. Hoflinger, F., et al.: Acoustic self-calibrating system for indoor smartphone tracking (assist), vol. 2015, no. 11, pp. 1–9 (2012)

13. Wang, W., Liu, A.X., Sun, K.: Device-free gesture tracking using acoustic signals. In: Proceedings of the 22nd Annual International Conference on Mobile Computing and Networking, pp. 82–94 (2016)

14. Wang, A., Gollakota, S.: MilliSonic: pushing the limits of acoustic motion tracking. In: Proceedings of the 2019 CHI Conference on Human Factors in Computing Systems, pp. 1–11 (2019)

15. Wei, T., Zhang, X.: mTrack: high-precision passive tracking using millimeter wave radios. In: Proceedings of the 21st Annual International Conference on Mobile Computing and Networking (2015)

16. Yun, S., Chen, Y.-C., Zheng, H., Qiu, L., Mao, W.: Strata: fine-grained acoustic-based device-free tracking. In: Proceedings of the 15th Annual International Conference on Mobile Systems, Applications, and Services, pp. 15–28 (2017)

17. Liu, Y., Zhang, W., Yang, Y., Fang, W., Qin, F., Dai, X.: PAMT: phase based acoustic motion tracking in multipath fading environments, pp. 2386–2394, April 2019

18. Zhang, Y., Wang, J., Wang, W., Wang, Z., Liu, Y.: Vernier: accurate and fast acoustic motion tracking using mobile devices. In: IEEE INFOCOM 2018-IEEE Conference on Computer Communications, pp. 1709–1717. IEEE (2018)

19. Murakami, H., Nakamura, M., Hashizume, H., Sugimoto, M.: 3-D localization for smartphones using a single speaker. In: 2019 International Conference on Indoor Positioning and Indoor Navigation (IPIN), pp. 1–8. IEEE (2019)

20. Peng, C., et al.: BeepBeep: a high accuracy acoustic ranging system using cots mobile devices. In: Proceedings of the 5th International Conference on Embedded Networked Sensor Systems (2007)

21. Du, H., Li, P., Zhou, H., Gong, W., Luo, G., Yang, P.: WordRecorder: accurate acoustic-based handwriting recognition using deep learning. In: IEEE INFOCOM 2018-IEEE Conference on Computer Communications, pp. 1448–1456. IEEE (2018)

22. Papandreou, G., et al.: Towards accurate multi-person pose estimation in the wild. In: Proceedings of the IEEE Conference on Computer Vision and Pattern Recognition, pp. 4903–4911 (2017)

23. Fang, H.-S., Xie, S., Tai, Y.-W., Lu, C.: RMPE: regional multi-person pose estimation. In: Proceedings of the IEEE International Conference on Computer Vision, pp. 2334–2343 (2017)

24. Nishimura, Y., Imai, N., Yoshihara, K.: A proposal on direction estimation between devices using acoustic waves. In: Puiatti, A., Gu, T. (eds.) MobiQuitous 2011. LNICST, vol. 104, pp. 25–36. Springer, Heidelberg (2012). https://doi.org/10.1007/978-3-642-30973-1_3

25. Graham, D., Simmons, G., Nguyen, D.T., Zhou, G.: A software based sonar ranging sensor for smart phones. IEEE Internet Things J. 2(6), 479–489 (2015)

26. Chen, H., Li, F., Wang, Y.: EchoLoc: accurate device-free hand localization using COTS devices. In: 2016 45th International Conference on Parallel Processing (ICPP), pp. 334–339. IEEE (2016)
27. Chen, H., Li, F., Wang, Y.: EchoTrack: acoustic device-free hand tracking on smart phones. In: 2017 IEEE Conference on Computer Communications. IEEE (2017)
28. Zhou, B., Elbadry, M., Gao, R., Ye, F.: BatMapper: acoustic sensing based indoor floor plan construction using smartphones. In: Proceedings of the 15th Annual International Conference on Mobile Systems, Applications, and Services, pp. 42–55 (2017)
29. Zhou, B., et al.: BatTracker: high precision infrastructure-free mobile device tracking in indoor environments. In: Proceedings of the 15th ACM Conference on Embedded Network Sensor Systems (2017)
30. Liu, Y., Yang, Z., Wang, X., Jian, L.: Location, localization, and localizability. J. Comput. Sci. Technol. **25**(2), 274–297 (2010)
31. Kaune, R.: Accuracy studies for TDOA and TOA localization. In: 2012 15th International Conference on Information Fusion, pp. 408–415. IEEE (2012)
32. Priyantha, N.B., Chakraborty, A., Balakrishnan, H.: The cricket location-support system. In: Proceedings of the 6th Annual International Conference on Mobile Computing and Networking, pp. 32–43 (2000)
33. Yun, S., Chen, Y.-C., Qiu, L.: Turning a mobile device into a mouse in the air. In; Proceedings of the 13th Annual International Conference on Mobile Systems, Applications, and Services, pp. 15–29 (2015)
34. Zhang, Z.: Microsoft kinect sensor and its effect. IEEE Multimed. **19**(2), 4–10 (2012)
35. Sigal, L., Balan, A.O., Black, M.J.: HUMANEVA: synchronized video and motion capture dataset and baseline algorithm for evaluation of articulated human motion. Int. J. Comput. Vis. **87**(1–2), 4 (2010)
36. Jiang, W., et al.: Towards 3D human pose construction using WiFi. In: Proceedings of the 26th Annual International Conference on Mobile Computing and Networking, pp. 1–14 (2020)
37. Wang, F., Zhou, S., Panev, S., Han, J., Huang, D.: Person-in-WiFi: fine-grained person perception using WiFi. In: Proceedings of the IEEE/CVF International Conference on Computer Vision, pp. 5452–5461 (2019)
38. Yang, C., Wang, X., Mao, S.: RFID-pose: vision-aided three dimensional human pose estimation with radio-frequency identification. IEEE Trans. Reliabil. (2020)
39. Sengupta, A., Jin, F., Zhang, R., Cao, S.: MM-pose: real-time human skeletal posture estimation using MMwave radars and CNNs. IEEE Sens. J. **20**(17), 10 032–10 044 (2020)

Smartphones-Based Non-contact Children's Posture Evaluation

Yue Li[1], Junhuai Li[1,2(✉)], Kan Wang[1,2], Ting Cao[1,2], and Huaijun Wang[1,2]

[1] School of Computer Science and Engineering, Xi'an University of Technology,
Xi'an 710048, China
1201210002@stu.xaut.edu.cn,
{lijunhuai,wangkan,caoting,wanghuaijun}@xaut.edu.cn
[2] Shaanxi Key Laboratory for Network Computing and Security Technology,
Xi'an, China

Abstract. Early detection of poor posture which might incur cervical spondylosis or lumbar vertebrae disease is of great significance to the healthy growth of children. Most of human body posture measurement methods require various sensors and wearable devices. However, devices are easily damaged and complicated to use, making these methods difficult to promote in daily life. In this paper, we propose a smartphones-based non-contact children's posture evaluation method based on computer vision, which is more convenient and accurate in contrast to sensor-based ones. First, we take children's standing posture images and record accelerometry data by smartphone at the same time. Then, the skeleton in the image is recognized through the children's skeleton keypoints recognition model, which is retrained in named children dataset by fine tuning of transfer learning. Next, the keypoints is corrected by the accelerometry data to solve the tilt problem in the smartphone shooting. Finally, the relations between keypoints, termed as Joint Angle, is used to evaluate the posture. Experiments results verify that the average accuracy rate of proposed method for evaluating a single part of body can reach 94.78%.

Keywords: Children's skeleton keypoints · Transfer learning · Posture evaluation · Smartphone

1 Introduction

Incorrect learning postures and overuse of electronic products typically incur poor posture in children. The long-term effects of repetitive strain injuries (RSI) on children are still unknown, but the impacts on spine or wrist development are doubtless. From [5,20], it follows that 80% of the respondents are affected by back pain in their lives, which is caused by long-term poor posture. Poor posture can cause a variety of health problems for children [3,9,17], which could result in

---

Supported by the National Natural Science Foundation of China 61971347.

L. Cui and X. Xie (Eds.): CWSN 2021, CCIS 1509, pp. 70–83, 2021.
https://doi.org/10.1007/978-981-16-8174-5_6

myopia and even cervical spondylosis. In particular, poor posture would typically take long-term negative effects on childhood and adolescence. If the body posture of a child or teenager is periodically examined and corrected throughout the growing years, then many diseases incurring body pain can be avoided.

Compared with the existing sensor-based posture evaluation methods, the computer vision-based methods [4] could extract human skeleton features from images to evaluate body posture without touching the body. Benefiting from the development of computer vision technology, many recent works emerge on image-based posture analysis [15,18,19]. Therefore, vision-based methods have significant advantages and would have great feasibility and universality in future promotion.

There is a certain difference between the skeleton structure of children and adults, and the skeleton will also change during growth and development [2]. The current skeleton evaluation models are feasible for adult, but still challenging for smaller somatotype children. Meanwhile, image distortion may be caused by tilting the phone. To solve these two challenges, under the premise of economics and universality, this paper proposes a smartphones-based non-contact children's posture evaluation method. We tried to study evaluation of children's body posture by taking image of standing posture, with the contributions of this work can be summarized as follows.

- Involving the difference between children's skeleton and adult, we collect children's images to constitute dataset named children dataset, including a training set of 90 pictures and a test set of 10 pictures.
- For improving the recognition effect of children, we propose a method of fine-tuning the openpose model to train children's skeleton keypoints recognition model through transfer learning.
- We propose to use accelerometer data to correct the image to eliminate the error caused by the tilt of the mobile phone, and to use the Joint Angle, characterizing the posture of various parts of the human body, to judge the bad posture.

The rest of this article is organized as follows. In Sect. 2, we briefly review the related works. In Sect. 3, we illustrate the proposed children's skeleton keypoints recognition model and the non-contact posture evaluation method. The experimental results and analysis are then provided in Sect. 4. Finally, Sect. 5 concludes our work.

2   Related Work

2.1   Body Posture Measurement

Body posture measurement is the basis of evaluation. Traditional intrusive methods and non-invasive methods often rely on various equipment and professionals, which are costly. However, due to sensors with lower cost and lower operating difficulty, numerous works have been used in this field [1,7,10]. Huijun Wang *et al.* [21] proposed to utilize Notch sensors to analyze user's sitting posture through the Euler angle and axis data of body parts. Guo *et al.* [9] used a Flex sensor placed on the neck to detect the user's neck posture. E. Sardini *et al.* [17] proposed to stitch the sensor into an elastic T-shirt and calculate the posture of the spine through the deformation on the T-shirt. Although aforementioned methods based on sensors and wearable devices could achieve good accuracy, they still pose some restrictions on users. Not only wearing the wearable device for a long time make users feel uncomfortable, but also some sensors may lose accuracy due to external factors.

Computer vision method is a new method of non-invasive methods, which could avoid the limitations of sensors. Worawat Lawanont *et al.* [12] proposed to mobile phone sensors and front-facing cameras to calculate neck posture intregrating the angle(the face relative to the mobile phone) with that(the mobile phone relative to the ground), with an error of no more than 4°.

2.2   Human Pose Estimation

Human pose estimation is the process of recovering human joint points from a given image. There are two kinds of pose estimation methods based on deep learning: top-down method and bottom-up method. On one hand, the basic principle of top-down method is to use the target detection algorithm [13] to detect the human target contour in the image or video, and then leveraging the human bone key point detection algorithm to identify the bone key points in the human body contour. On the other hand, the bottom-up human pose estimation method mainly includes two parts: bone key point detector and joint point connector. Xia *et al.* [6] proposed Part Segmentation to model the connection between human body parts and key points of bones to improve clustering efficiency and accuracy. Cao *et al.* [4] proposed the OpenPose model, using Part Affinity Fields (PAFs) with a convolutional attitude machine to model human limbs, simulating different limb structures of the human body, to a certain extent, and finally solving the key points of different human bones wrong connection problem.

2.3   Transfer Learning

Transfer Learning [23] has been used to solve the label issue in the training set, which could transfer the knowledge learned in the source domain to the target domain to improve the learning performance and learning effect of the target domain.

Fine-tune is a method of deep transfer learning, which modifies the network model structure and selectively loads pre-trained network model weights. In particular, it allows small data sets to achieve better training results. Yosinski *et al.* [22] show that general features are extracted from the lower layers of CNN and the higher layers are fine-tuned following the features of a target task. Therefore, for models that have been trained with large data sets, using fine-tuning can save a lot of computing resources and learning time, thus achieving higher learning efficiency. Many works have tried to improve the accuracy of deep convolutional neural network models through fine-tuning. Rusiecki *et al.* [16] combine fine-tuning in deep networks with elastic propagation algorithms to improve the accuracy of unsupervised learning. Noel Lopes *et al.* [14] fine-tuned the model by adding two additional layers, and improved the generalization performance of the pre-trained deep network by merging multiple layers.

3   Smartphones-Based Non-contact Children's Posture Evaluation

In the presented approach, we propose to use a skeleton with keypoints to represent the body posture following the existing evaluation standards, which could be characterized by several geometric features. For more accurate features, the skeleton keypoints recognition model and the image taken by smartphone are optimized. The framework of method is shown in Fig. 1.

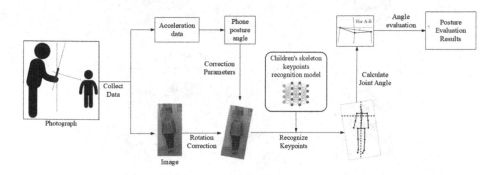

Fig. 1. Framework of smartphones-based non-contact children's posture evaluation.

Among them , the two most important parts of the framework are the children's skeleton keypoints recognition and the non-contact body posture analysis.

3.1   Skeleton Keypoints Recognition Based on Transfer Learning

Images are collected to constitute a children's skeleton keypoints dataset. Due to the small number and scale of images in the children dataset, training model directly on this dataset can not meet the accuracy. Therefore, fine tuning based on transfer learning is used to train a new children's skeleton keypoints recognition model.

The main process of model training is shown in Fig. 2. The OpenPose model [8,11] is trained on the COCO dataset, one of the commonly used skeleton keypoints dataset. The huge amount of data makes the OpenPose model learn a good recognition effect. We use it as a pre-training model and fine-tune the network structure by freezing convolutional layers. The first ten layers in the

OpenPose network are the feature extraction stage, which are used to extract the common feature F of the picture; its stages 1–6 are used for reasoning confidence set S and Part Affinity Fields set L. We respectively freeze the convolutional layers of several stages of the network. For example, in the first training, only the convolutional layer in the feature extraction stage is frozen; and in the second training, we freeze the convolutional layers of the feature extraction stage and stage 1, and so on. After freezing the convolutional layer, the model does not need to repetitively learn part of the knowledge, which could not only retain the original knowledge, but also enable the model to learn the features of new dataset.

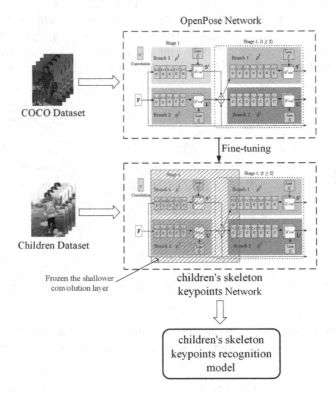

Fig. 2. Flowchart of children's skeleton keypoints recognition model.

3.2 Body Posture Analysis

Skeleton is the topological structure representing the body posture. In computer vision, only the skeleton keypoints are needed to get the skeleton. Whether a posture is poor posture can be judged by the relative position relationship between skeleton keypoints. As a necessity in modern life, smartphones can support image recognition. It is feasible to take children's standing posture images and to evaluate their body posture by extracting keypoints, with specific steps as follows.

Data Collection and Phone Posture Angle. A child's standing posture photo and acceleration sensor data G_{px}, G_{py}, G_{pz} are taken by smartphone. The angle between the x-axis of the smart phone is defined as X-angle, and the angle between the z-axis is defined as Z-angle. X-angle and Z-angle are collectively called the phone posture angle. Set the angle value to be negative when tilting to the left, and vice versa. The Z-angle is set to be negative when tilting forward, and positive when tilting backward. The calculation of the X-angle θ and the Y-angle φ are shown as (1) and (2). If the phone is not tilted, both θ and φ are 0. Nevertheless, θ and φ are usually not 0.

$$\theta = \arccos\left(\frac{G_{px}}{g}\right) - 90° \tag{1}$$

$$\varphi = \arccos\left(\frac{G_{pz}}{g}\right) - 90° \tag{2}$$

Photo Rotation Correction. When X-angle is not equal to 0 and the Z-angle is equal to 0, the phone rotates around the z-axis, and the photo plane also rotates, as shown in Fig. 3. When the coordinate system of mobile phone are not rotated, a point on the photo is $P(x, y, z)$. The X-angle is θ, and this point becomes $P'(x', y', z')$. P', which is obtained by rotating P. The calculation of point P are shown as (3) and (4).

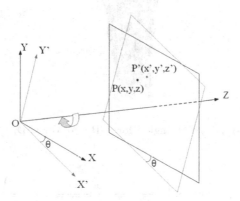

Fig. 3. Picture rotates around z-axis.

$$x = x' \cos\theta - y' \sin\theta \tag{3}$$
$$y = x' \sin\theta - y' \cos\theta \tag{4}$$

Joint Angle. The skeleton keypoints, namely joint points, can be obtained by identifying the corrected picture through the skeleton keypoints recognition model. We propose the Joint Angle, which is the one between the connection of two joint points and the horizontal or vertical line. The angle between the connection line of two joint points A(x_1,y_1), B(x_2,y_2) and the horizontal line is the horizontal Joint Angle recorded as Hor A-B. The angle between the connection line of two joint points C(x_3,y_3), D(x_4,y_4) and the vertical line is the vertical Joint Angle recorded as Ver C-D. Hor A-B and Ver C-D are shown in Fig. 4. Then the formulas for α_{AB} of Hor A-B and β_{CD} of Ver C-D are shown as (5) and (6), respecvtively.

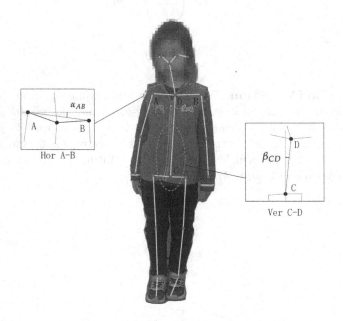

Fig. 4. Joint angle: Hor A-B and Ver C-D.

$$\alpha_{AB} = \arccos\left(\frac{x_2 - x_1}{\sqrt{(x_2 - x_1)^2 + (y_2 - y_1)^2}}\right) \tag{5}$$

$$\beta_{CD} = \arccos\left(\frac{y_4 - y_3}{\sqrt{(x_4 - x_3)^2 + (y_4 - x_3)^2}}\right) \tag{6}$$

Joint Angle Correction. When X-angle is equal to 0 and Z-angle is φ, the coordinates of phone rotates around the x-axis, and the photo plane also rotates, as shown in Fig. 5. When the coordinates of the mobile phone are not rotated, a point on the photo is P(x, y, z). The Z-angle is φ, and this point becomes P'(x', y', z'). The calculation of point P are shown as (7) and (8).

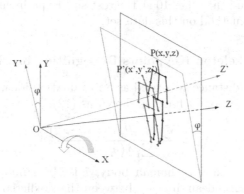

Fig. 5. Picture rotates around x-axis.

$$x = x' \tag{7}$$
$$y = -y' \sin \varphi + z' \cos \varphi \tag{8}$$

Bringing (7), (8) into (5), (6) to calculate the Joint Angle after correction. And the z values of the points on the same image plane are the same, and the Joint Angle formulas can be shown in (9) and (10).

$$\alpha_{AB} = \arccos \left(\frac{x'_2 - x'_1}{\sqrt{\left(x'_2 - x'_1\right)^2 + \left(-y'_2 \sin \varphi + y'_1 \sin \varphi\right)^2}} \right) \tag{9}$$

$$\beta_{CD} = \arccos \left(\frac{-y'_4 \sin \varphi + y'_3 \sin \varphi}{\sqrt{\left(x'_4 - x'_3\right)^2 + \left(-y'_4 \sin \varphi + y'_3 \sin \varphi\right)^2}} \right) \tag{10}$$

Joint Angle Evaluation. The smaller Joint Angle, the more standard the posture of the part. Conversely, when the joint angle is too large, the corresponding part will show a poor posture. We study the children's playground and consulted experts, and then decide to use the threshold to judge the angle. If the joint angle value is ε, the evaluation scheme is shown as (11).

$$f\left(\varepsilon\right) = \begin{cases} \text{perfect} & |\varepsilon| < 3° \\ \text{normal} & 3° \leq |\varepsilon| \leq 10° \\ \text{abnormal} & 10° < |\varepsilon| \end{cases} \tag{11}$$

If a joint angle is evaluated as abnormal, the part has a poor body posture, and the tester should be reminded to seek medical treatment as soon as possible for posture correction or treatment.

4   Experiment

We collecte 100 pictures of children playing on the Internet, randomly selecte 90 as the training set and the other 10 as the test set. Experiments are designed to verify the proposed method on this data set.

4.1   Children's Skeleton Keypoints Recognition Scoring Criteria

Weighted Euclidean distance is treated as an evaluation idea, with the recognition model evaluation score defined as shown as (12),

$$S_p = \frac{\sum_i (d_{pi}/l_p) \, \delta \, (v_{pi} = 2)}{\sum_i \delta \, (v_{pi} = 2)} \tag{12}$$

where, p is the number of human body, i is the number of the skeleton keypoint, d_{pi} is the Euclidean distance between the predicted keypoint position and marked position, l_p is the length of the human torso, v_{pi} is the state of the ith keypoint on the p, and $\delta(\cdot)$ is the kroneckerdelta function used to filter out points in visible status.

When the value of S_p is smaller, the distance between the predicted keypoint and labeled keypoint is smaller, and the accuracy of model is higher.

4.2   Experimental Result

Three sets of experiments are designed for different parameters of the model.

Frozen Convolution Layer. The convolutional layers in different stages of network model were frozen, and 7 network models are trained with the same number of iterations. The evaluation score of the result is calculated by (12), and the evaluation scores of each model are shown as Table 1.

Table 1. Evaluation scores of trained models.

	N layers before freezing	Pic1	Pic2	Pic3	Pic4	Pic5	Pic6	Average score
OpenPose model		0.455	0.077	0.145	0.028	0.149	0.044	0.150
Model 1	12	0.257	0.088	0.134	0.045	0.146	0.097	0.128
Model 2	17	0.260	0.086	0.134	0.045	0.146	0.064	0.123
Model 3	24	0.376	0.088	0.115	0.038	0.140	0.096	0.142
Model 4	31	0.455	0.086	0.260	0.046	0.151	0.094	0.182
Model 5	38	0.452	0.069	0.252	0.048	0.149	0.054	0.171
Model 6	45	0.422	0.065	0.118	0.030	0.146	0.048	0.138
Model 7	All layers	0.455	0.077	0.145	0.028	0.149	0.045	0.150

Among them, the original OpenPose model has the highest score, which means that its accuracy is the lowest. Fine-tuning has achieved better results. When the shallower convolutional layer is frozen, Model 2 has the lowest score. When the deeper convolutional layer is frozen, the Model 6 has the lowest score. Model 2, Model 6, and the original model are selected for comparison, and the model score results are shown in Fig. 6.

From Fig. 6, it is observed that the score of Model 6 is lower and the accuracy is higher.

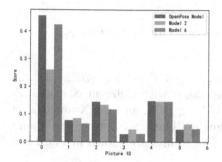

Fig. 6. Original model, Model 2, and Model 6 score results.

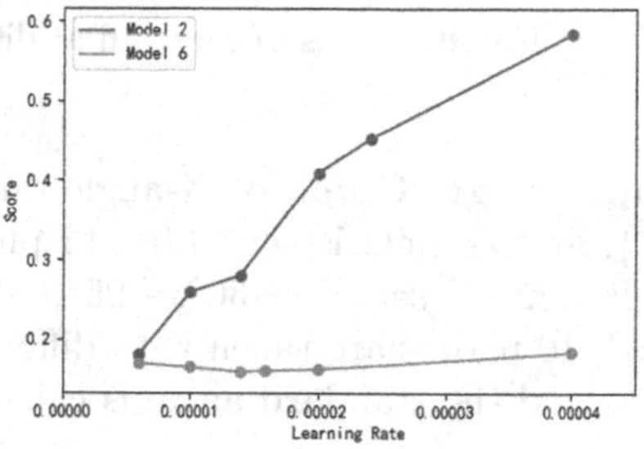

Fig. 7. Scores of Model 2 and Model 6 at different learning rates.

Learning Rate. Model 2 and Model 6 are trained with setting different learning rates, with the score shown as Fig. 7.

From Fig. 7, with the increase of the learning rate, the score of Model 6 don't change significantly, whereas the score of Model 2 increased. This indicates that Model 2 may have over-fitting due to the higher learning rate, and Model 6 still has a better recognition effect.

Iterations. Under different learning rates, Model 6 is trained with setting different learning rate and iterations, with score shown in Fig. 8.

As the iteration grows, the score shows a downward trend, that is, the accuracy of the model is getting increasingly higher. When the learning rate is between 0.000014 and 0.00002, the accuracy of the model is the highest.

It is observed that Model 6, trained by fine-tuning, has a better recognition effect than the OpenPose model.

4.3   Posture Evaluation

A child standing picture, with a posture evaluation sheet in the background, is used as a reference picture, and pasted on a vertical wall. The four joint angles of Ver head-neck (Ver H-N), Ver neck-coccyx (Ver N-C), Hor left shoulder-right shoulder (Hor LS-RS), and Hor left hip-right hip (Hor LH-RH) are calculated manually as the standard angles of the experiment as follows.

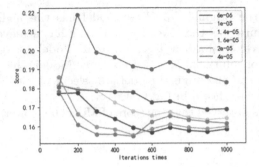

Fig. 8. Scores of Model 6 at different learning rates and iterations.

Single Angle Change. X-angle range is set to $\{-30°, -25°, -20°, -15°, ..., 30°\}$, and Z-angle is set to $0°$. 13 photos are taken with different X-angles. Z-angle range is set to $\{-30°, -25°, -20°, -15°, ..., 15°\}$, and the X-angle is set to $0°$. 10 photos are taken with different Z-angles. The error between each joint angle and the standard angle is calculated. The results are shown in Fig. 9 and Fig. 10.

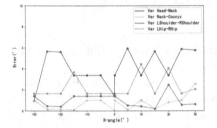

Fig. 9. The error with the X-angle.   **Fig. 10.** The error with the Z-angle.

When X-angle changes, the error of each joint angle has no obvious change. When the Z-angle is too large, the error becomes significantly larger. However, when the Z-angle range is between $-20°$–$15°$, the error of each joint angle has no obvious change.

Double Angle Change. Photos are taken with different Z-angles or X-angles, and error between each joint angle and the standard angle is calculated, with results are shown in Table 2.

It is observed that from Table 2 that the two joint angles of Ver neck-coccyx and Hor left shoulder-right shoulder have the highest accuracy, and the error probability of less than $5°$ is greater than 97%, and the evaluation accuracy is above 93%; the probability that Hor left hip-right hip error is less than $5°$ is 95.2%, but its evaluation accuracy is slightly lower, only 71.64%; the accuracy

Table 2. Errors of each joint angle

Joint angle	Error	Error less than 5°(%)	Accuracy
Ver H-N	3.668	69	51.49
Ver N-C	1.295	100	93.28
Hor LS-RS	1.492	97.6	94.78
Hor LH-RH	2.512	95.2	71.64

of Ver head-neck is the lowest, the error probability less than 5° is only 69%, and accuracy rate is only 51.49%. The main reason for the low accuracy of Ver head-neck and Hor left hip-right hip is that the recognition model still has certain errors in the recognition of the head center (nose), left hip, and right hip. The probability that the joint angle error of the three parts is less than 5° is greater than 95%, the evaluation accuracy rate is greater than 71%, and the accuracies of two joint angles is greater than 93%, thus proving high accuracy and feasibility of the proposed method.

5   Conclusions

In this paper, we have developed a smartphones-based non-contact children's posture evaluation method. This method based on computer vision uses smart phones to evaluate posture. Standing posture image and accelerometry data are collected by smartphone. The keypoints extracted from the image are corrected by the accelerometry data. Finally, the Joint Angle is calculated to evaluate posture. To improve the recognition accuracy of the model, we train the children's skeleton keypoint recognition model by transfer learning on children dataset. We have carried out experiments to verify the effectiveness of the proposed algorithm and model. The results demonstrated that fine-tuning the OpenPose network can make the model's recognition effect in the target domain more accurate, and the network after fine-tuning is better than the original network model. This method has high accuracy and feasibility. Compared with the existing body posture evaluation methods, the proposed method has the advantages of convenience and quickness.

References

1. Arjmand, N., Gagnon, D., Plamondon, A., Shirazi-Adl, A., Larivière, C.: A comparative study of two trunk biomechanical models under symmetric and asymmetric loadings. J. Biomech. **43**(3), 485–491 (2010). https://doi.org/10.1016/j.jbiomech.2009.09.032. http://www.sciencedirect.com/science/article/pii/S002192900900551X
2. Hamilton, W.J.: Textbook of Human Anatomy. Springer (1982)

3. Brienza, D., Chung, K., Brubaker, C., Wang, J., Kang, T., Lin, C.: A system for the analysis of seat support surfaces using surface shape control and simultaneous measurement of applied pressures. IEEE Trans. Rehabil. Eng. **4**, 103–113 (1996). https://doi.org/10.1109/86.506407

4. Cao, Z., Simon, T., Wei, S.E., Sheikh, Y.: Realtime multi-person 2D pose estimation using part affinity fields, pp. 1302–1310 (2017). https://doi.org/10.1109/CVPR.2017.143

5. Cassidy, J.D., Côté, P., Carroll, L.J., Kristman, V.: Incidence and course of low back pain episodes in the general population. Spine **30**(24), 2817–2823 (2005)

6. Xia, F., Wang, P., Chen, X.: Joint multi-person pose estimation and semantic part segmentation, pp. 6769–6778 (2017)

7. Faber, G.S., Chang, C.C., Kingma, I., Dennerlein, J.T., van Dieën, J.H.: Estimating 3D L5/S1 moments and ground reaction forces during trunk bending using a full-body ambulatory inertial motion capture system. J. Biomech. **49**(6), 904–912 (2016). https://doi.org/10.1016/j.jbiomech.2015.11.042. http://www.sciencedirect.com/science/article/pii/S0021929015006843

8. Gkioxari, G., Hariharan, B., Girshick, R., Malik, J.: Using k-poselets for detecting people and localizing their keypoints. In: 2014 IEEE Conference on Computer Vision and Pattern Recognition (CVPR), pp. 3582–3589 (2014)

9. Guo, Y., Zhang, X., An, N.: Monitoring neck posture with flex sensors. In: 2019 9th International Conference on Information Science and Technology (ICIST), pp. 459–463 (2019)

10. Hajibozorgi, M., Arjmand, N.: Sagittal range of motion of the thoracic spine using inertial tracking device and effect of measurement errors on model predictions. J. Biomech. **49**(6), 913–918 (2016). https://doi.org/10.1016/j.jbiomech.2015.09.003. http://www.sciencedirect.com/science/article/pii/S0021929015004790

11. He, K., Zhang, X., Ren, S., Jian, S.: Deep residual learning for image recognition. In: IEEE Conference on Computer Vision & Pattern Recognition, pp. 770–778 (2016)

12. Lawanont, W., Mongkolnam, P., Nukoolkit, C.: Smartphone posture monitoring system to prevent unhealthy neck postures. In: 2015 12th International Joint Conference on Computer Science and Software Engineering (JCSSE), pp. 331–336 (2015)

13. Liu, W., et al.: SSD: single shot multibox detector. In: Leibe, B., Matas, J., Sebe, N., Welling, M. (eds.) ECCV 2016. LNCS, vol. 9905, pp. 21–37. Springer, Cham (2016). https://doi.org/10.1007/978-3-319-46448-0_2

14. Lopes, N., Ribeiro, B.: Towards adaptive learning with improved convergence of deep belief networks on graphics processing units. Pattern Recogn. **47**(1), 114–127 (2014). https://doi.org/10.1016/j.patcog.2013.06.029. http://www.sciencedirect.com/science/article/pii/S0031320313002811

15. Ono, H., Suzuki, S.: Data augmentation for grossmotor-ActivityRecognition using DCGAN, pp. 440–443, January 2020. https://doi.org/10.1109/SII46433.2020.9026252

16. Rusiecki, A., Kordos, M.: Effectiveness of unsupervised training in deep learning neural networks. Schedae In. **24**, 41–51 (2015)

17. Sardini, E., Serpelloni, M., Pasqui, V.: Daylong sitting posture measurement with a new wearable system for at home body movement monitoring. In: 2015 IEEE International Instrumentation and Measurement Technology Conference (I2MTC) Proceedings, pp. 652–657 (2015)

18. Suzuki, S., Amemiya, Y., Sato, M.: Deep learning assessment of child gross-motor, pp. 189–194, June 2020. https://doi.org/10.1109/HSI49210.2020.9142684

19. Suzuki, S., Amemiya, Y., Sato, M.: Enhancement of child gross-motor action recognition by motional time-series images conversion, pp. 225–230, January 2020. https://doi.org/10.1109/SII46433.2020.9025833
20. Thiese, M.S., et al.: Prevalence of low back pain by anatomic location and intensity in an occupational population. BMC Musculoskeletal Disord. **15**, 283 (2014). https://doi.org/10.1186/1471-2474-15-283. https://europepmc.org/articles/PMC4153910
21. Wang, H., Zhao, J., li, J., Wang, K.: The sitting posture monitoring method based on notch sensor, pp. 301–302 (2019). https://doi.org/10.1109/ICII.2019.00058
22. Yosinski, J., Clune, J., Bengio, Y., Lipson, H.: How transferable are features in deep neural networks? In: Advances in Neural Information Processing Systems (NIPS), vol. 27, pp. 3320–3328 (2014)
23. Zhou, J.T., Pan, S.J., Tsang, I.W.: A deep learning framework for hybrid heterogeneous transfer learning. Artif. Intell. **275**(OCT.), 310–328 (2019)

Research on Military Application of Operating System for Internet of Things

Feng Li, Liang Chen[✉], Yaling Wang, and Xiarao Wang

Institute of Systems Engineering, Academy of Military Sciences, No. 2 on Fengti South Road, Beijing, China

Abstract. IoT OS is the core content of IoT applications. In this paper, the development of IoT OS is firstly overviewed, and the characteristics of terminal and server IoT OS are contrasted. Then the status of the global military IoT are analyzed, the military application scenarios of IoT OS are presented, and the technical requirements of IoT OS for military applications are summarized. Finally, we point out the difficulties of military applications of IoT OS and put forward some corresponding countermeasures and suggestions.

Keywords: IoT · Operating system · Military application

1 General Introduction

With the rapid development of sensor technology and communication technology, the Internet of Things (IoT) has become a hotspot in the global domain of science and technology and is evolving into an important supporting technology in the field of socio-economic and military reform. In 2020, the IoT was once again listed by Gartner as one of the top ten strategic technological trends in the world. According to the statistics of the Statista portal website, the number of IoT connected devices has reached 22 billion at the end of 2018 around the world, and expected to reach 50 billion by 2030 [1]. The massive number of IoT devices are affected by factors such as different manufacturers, diverse functions or complex deployment environments. As a result, related applications are mostly customized for functions, which brings about problems such as incompatible protocols, unsmooth data and difficult interactive sharing, restricting the large-scale promotion and unified management of the IoT. The operating system for IoT (IoT OS) can provide a unified calling interface for IoT applications by shielding hardware differences and better enhance the economic benefits and social value of IoT applications. Its military applications will provide more convenient basis of functional interoperability and data collaboration for battlefield environment monitoring, joint military training, modern military logistics, equipment monitoring and maintenance, and even the joint combat command, thereby enhancing the effectiveness of our military joint exercises, joint training and joint operation under the scenario of intelligent military transformation.

It is generally believed that the IoT OS is developed from an embedded operating system and is a software platform oriented to the IoT technology architecture and application scenarios [2]. Early IoT operating systems mainly included Tiny OS [3] of the

L. Cui and X. Xie (Eds.): CWSN 2021, CCIS 1509, pp. 84–96, 2021.
https://doi.org/10.1007/978-981-16-8174-5_7

University of California, Berkeley, Contiki of the Swedish Academy of Sciences [4], and the European IoT OS RIOT [5]. Tiny OS is specifically designed for low-power wireless devices. What requires to run it is only a few KB of memory space and tens of KB of encoding space, especially suitable for sensor memory or with appropriate scenarios. Contiki is completely developed in C language, which has better portability, accords with TCP/IP network and IPv6 protocol, supports multi-task operation and is suitable for devices with sufficient memory resources. Based on the microkernel architecture, RIOT is called Linux in the IoT. It supports multiple platforms and provides multiple communication protocol stacks and a complete real-time response solution. It is an important reference for the current mainstream IoT OS design.

With the innovation of IoT technology and the explosive growth of applications, Linux, ARM, Google, Huawei, Ali, etc. have all launched IoT operating systems with different characteristics [6]. For example: ARM Mbed OS supporting Cortex-M processor, lightweight IoT OS FreeRTOS, Linux Foundation's Zephyr, embedded VxWorks system, Google's Android Things, and China's RT-Thread OS similar to FreeRTOS, Alibaba's AliOS things, Huawei's LiteOS, TencentOS tiny and so on. The emergence of many IoT operating systems provides a solid foundation for the IoT to play a technical support role in modern military applications. However, due to major special requirements such as high confrontation, high security and high stability in the military field, the military application of the civil IoT OS still requires us to carefully investigate, analyze and propose corresponding countermeasures in advance. This article first analyzes the main features of the current IoT OS, then studies the business scenarios and technical requirements of the military IoT OS application, and then points out the main problems of the military IoT OS applications. Finally, specific countermeasures are proposed in conjunction with the development of global military IoT applications.

2   IoT OS Features

The IoT OS can usually be divided into two types according to whether it runs directly on the physical device. One is the terminal IoT OS. Most of these systems are based on an embedded architecture, run on the terminal IoT devices and drive the equipment directly to make it work normally. Early Contiki and RIOT mostly belong to this category. The other is the server-side IoT OS. Usually, the OS and the terminal device can be physically separated, mainly by hosting the OS on the server or the cloud, and supporting various applications to send commands or perform operation control to the terminal devices, such as a cloud camera, remote intelligent switch, etc. With the evolution of technology, these two classifications are not absolute, and there are overlapping and syncretic parts between them.

2.1   Features of Terminal IoT OS

From the perspective of application scenarios, the corresponding IoT OS also presents large differences with various types of devices, due to the differences in application fields and functional requirements of IoT terminal devices, or enterprises' protection of their own rights and interests. By analyzing the characteristics of 10 typical terminal

IoT operating systems, as shown in Table 1, this paper summarizes and analyzes the common characteristics of terminal IoT operating systems.

Table 1. Comparison of OS characteristics of IoT terminals.

OS name	Features
TinyOS [3, 7]	An open source OS designed for wireless sensor networks, which can quickly implement various applications with little code
Contiki [4, 8]	A small, open source and extremely portable multitasking OS, suitable for embedded systems and wireless sensors and a series of memory-constrained network systems
RIOT [5, 9]	Based on a micro-kernel structure, can run on multiple platforms, supports C and C++ languages to write applications, provides multiple communication protocol stacks, complete multi-threading and real-time response solutions
Android Things [10]	Suitable for low-configuration IoT devices, supports the machine learning library TensorFlow, and uses Weave's communication protocol to connect the device to the cloud and interact with services such as Google Assistant
RTOS [11]	An open source OS with safe, modular and connectable features which supports a variety of hardware architectures and development boards, and can run on systems as small as 8KB of memory
VxWorks [12]	Possesses important features such as reliability, high real-time performance, tailorability and synergy, and has good sustainable development capability, high-performance kernel and friendly user development environment
RT-Thread [13]	A kind of configurable, tailorable, reusable, expandable, portable and reliable operating system with small size, low cost, low power consumption, fast startup, high real-time performance and small resource consumption
ARM Mbed [14]	Designed for devices based on the ARM Cortex-M processor, uses an event-driven single-thread architecture and can be used for small-size, low-power IoT devices, and has the characteristics of simple development and wide application
LiteOS [15]	A lightweight IoT OS with zero configuration, ad hoc network, and cross-platform capabilities
AliOS things [16]	A simple operating system that can be developed with multiple components, provides system and chip-level security protection and supports the connection of terminal devices to Alibaba Cloud Link
TencentOS tiny [17]	A low power consumption, low resource occupancy, modular, safe and reliable operating system, which can be quickly transplanted to a variety of mainstream MCUs and module chips to support docking with cloud resources

High Adaptability. Many IoT operating systems adopt the open source method to further improve users' freedom and achieve the purpose of high adaptation capability. In addition, when designing the kernel of the terminal IoT OS, the kernel and the terminal firmware drivers are often adopted in the high separation architecture, so as to improve the hardware compatibility and increase the breadth of hardware adaptation capability of the OS.

Miniaturization and Low Energy Consumption. In order to meet the needs of different devices, the terminal IoT OS must be taken into account the terminal resource limitation and power consumption requirements. The miniaturized design compresses the volume to accommodate more terminal devices and reduces the energy consumption of the devices by performing less and more efficient computations to extend the use or maintenance cycle of the terminal devices.

Function Customization. Driven by the features of high adaptability, miniaturization and low energy consumption, terminal IoT operation systems often have features with customized functions, allowing the non-kernel modules of the OS to be tailored, expanded or optimized according to application scenarios or functional requirements. The volume of the same terminal IoT OS can be dozens of M or be cut to a few M under the condition of limited memory or storage. If necessary, it will turn off related functions that are not needed in order to save power consumption.

Collaboration and Cooperation. IoT terminal devices often need to perform a certain event through information transmission or functional collaboration. For example, the UAV cluster can perform information interaction and functional coordination through the built-up self-organizing network to jointly complete battlefield intelligence reconnaissance missions.

Safe and Stable. Often to be used continuously for months or years, massive IoT terminals are deployed in various indoor and outdoor environments. In addition to the low energy consumption attribute, maintenance-free is a realistic requirement for IoT terminal applications. The terminal IoT OS is the brain of the terminal equipment, and has higher security and stability requirements than the terminal itself. It must not only prevent sensitive data from leaking, but also resist all kinds of external interference or malicious intrusion. Moreover, it is also necessary to prevent the damage to the physical world after the system is controlled. At the same time, due to the external environment changes such as the temperature and humidity of the terminal device application scenario and internal software computing bugs, the terminal IoT OS must also have certain fault tolerance mechanisms and environmental adaptability to maintain high stability.

Trend towards Intelligence. With the improvement of the computing power and energy supply resources of the IoT terminals, as well as the continuous progress of lightweight algorithms, the terminal IoT OS will become more automated and intelligent. On the basis of reducing the maintenance by engineers, users' application intervention is further reduced. For example, the mode consistency of the operation behavior of the intelligent inspection program and the predefined behavior is supposed to improve the autonomous intrusion detection capability, automatically learn to record the operation frequency of an event, intelligently remind or help the user to automatically perform an operation, etc.

2.2 Features of Server-Side IoT OS

Another type of IoT OS is the server-side IoT OS that has gradually evolved with the development of communication technology and cloud technology. Compared with the terminal IoT OS, its definition is more broad and diverse, but basically all have the following main features.

Device Access and Management. The server-side IoT OS allows a large number of IoT terminals to access and implement basic operation and management of the terminals, including terminal access authentication, access, information reception and removal, which are the basic characteristics of all server-side IoT OS.

Feedback control. The OS can send basic control command functions such as startup, sleep, suspension, etc. It can detect the working status, feedback the perceived frequency of the IoT terminal, decide whether the terminal device should be upgraded or not, and can implement a series of personalized feedback control functions according to user needs.

Data Collection and Processing. The OS can receive all kinds of data information feedback from the terminal in a timely manner, including terminal operating status, business work data, and various log information generated by the terminal online. And can promptly collect, categorize and organize these information, even according to visual display of users' needs provides the basis for applications such as decision analysis or intelligent feedback control.

Calculation and Service. After a large number of IoT terminals are connected, the OS often needs to schedule and allocate various types of resources. It needs to perform efficient calculations according to different business logic, provide different types of algorithms and corresponding data or service call interface for business application layer software. The significant improvement in computing and service capabilities is a typical feature of the server-side IoT OS.

Extended Development. The server-side IoT OS is a platform software with complex and diverse functions. In order to improve terminal access capabilities and business support capabilities, it generally defines standard access specifications, interface development specifications, function expansion instructions and samples, and supports the access of non-native terminal equipment, the expansion of system application functions and the needs of different business logic operations.

Safe and Reliable. The server-side IoT OS is usually deployed in a professional service area in a centralized deployment manner and is hosted on a mature server OS. With professional and perfect safety protection measures, the comprehensive safety and reliability are high. But there are also potential security hazards such as terminal communication hijacking and information spoofing.

Intelligent and Autonomous. The access of massive terminal data provides the basis for artificial intelligence applications, and the applications of machine learning methods such as autonomous learning and enhanced learning make it possible for the server-side IoT OS to initially make autonomous decisions.

It is worth pointing out that with the continuous optimization and improvement of the IoT architecture, the proposal of the "cloud, pipeline, edge, terminal" model, and the development of edge computing models and technologies, the current IoT OS, whether it is a terminal or a server, has shown the characteristics of mutual integration development and collaboration, which jointly support the wide application of the IoT in different fields.

3   Military Application Requirements of IoT OS

3.1   Overview of Military Applications in the Global IoT

With the iterative upgrading of information and communication technology, artificial intelligence based on data, algorithms and computing power has risen rapidly, and the era of intelligent military revolution has arrived on the global scale. Emerging technologies represented by the IoT, artificial intelligence and 5G are catalyzing military reform and even changing the pattern of future global wars. The United States, Russia, China and other world powers have applied it to the military field since its early development.

The US military is the first country to apply IoT technology to the military field. Its IoT application areas are mainly concentrated in the following areas: the first is command, control, communication, computer, intelligence, surveillance and reconnaissance (C4ISR); the second is fire control system; the third is logistics management; the fourth is training and simulation. Among them, it has achieved outstanding results in the field of logistics management and has supported several US military operations.

Russia officially released the development roadmap for the IoT in 2016, started the development plan for the basic application technology of the IoT with a national strategy, and promoted the construction and development of the IoT system at the federal level from 2017. In 2019, Russian President Vladimir Putin also emphasized at the conference on the development of technologies in the field of artificial intelligence that Russia needs to ensure its technological dominance in such fields as the IoT and artificial intelligence, and said that it is the most important condition for promoting national security.

China is also one of the first country to apply the IoT technology in the military field. Public information shows that our military is currently mainly implementing a series of IoT applications in the field of military training, military logistics and equipment, including military warehousing and logistics based on barcode, RFID and Beidou technology, military support identification plate based on QR code and sensing chip technology, containerized multimodal transport based on the integrated technology of IoT application, and 5G-based remote medical treatment and other related researches. With the expansion of national defense missions and the continuous advancement of the strategy of revitalizing the military through science and technology, the IoT is gradually becoming one of the key frontier technologies of our military.

In addition, the "IoT Strategic Research Roadmap" and "Future IoT Strategy" released by the European Union provide a reference for the military application of the IoT. The NATO Scientific and Technical Organization and its Collaborative Support Office are leading the NATO's military applied research on the IoT through a trans-Atlantic defence cooperation approach. Japan, India, South Korea and other countries are also vigorously promoting the deployment of military applications of the IoT.

Just as the IoT has been rapidly warming up in the world in recent years and converging the focus on science and technology, its global military applications will also present a general trend of broader fields, wider scope, deeper applications, and faster advancement. The IoT OS as the IoT application hub will also be the key support for military applications of the IoT.

3.2 Military Application Scenarios of IoT OS

Combining the military activities of developed countries around the world, this paper analyzes the military application scenarios of IoT OS from the three dimensions of peacetime, wartime, and emergency, as well as war military operations and non-war military operations (rescue, disaster resistance, epidemic, etc.) [18]:

Usually Harsh Conditions. Including mountains, islands, caverns, and various types of IoT-related applications in frontier defense areas. Compared with civilian IoT applications, the more prominent fields of defense applications where communication conditions are pool, the natural environment is harsh, unforeseen factors are complex, and equipment maintenance costs are prominent put forward higher requirements on the power consumption, stability, security and maintenance-free nature of the terminal IoT device and OS, and on the communication reliability and security protection of the server-side IoT OS.

Battlefield of High Confrontation Conditions in Wartime. Including military operations such as joint military exercises, confrontational military training, and possible local conflicts. Due to the complexity, confrontation, mobility and unpredictability of the electromagnetic environment, it poses unprecedented challenges to the anti-damage, anti-interference, high availability, high security and high stability of terminal IoT devices and IoT OS.

Urgent Use of Temporary IoT Environment. Including non-military operations such as international humanitarian assistance, assistance in major natural disasters, and intervention in major public events, due to sudden events, sudden changes in natural conditions, social conditions, or human conditions, both terminal IoT devices and IoT OS are supposed to be quickly deployed, and has a high degree of debugging-free, maintenance-free, high compatibility and user-friendly features in order to reduce the difficulties of technical and application threshold caused by the rapid compression of preparation time.

Daily Military Applications and Combat Readiness. Including scenarios such as daily management of military barracks, routine combat readiness training, military material supply support, and security prevention and control of important military installations. It is similar to the civilian field, and the difference is mainly raise higher demand such as information security and confidentiality, more stable connection and more robust operational performance to the military application of the IoT OS.

Military-civilian Compatible IoT Applications. Whether it is a terminal or server-side IoT OS, it must consider the features of military-civilian compatibility in military applications to ensure that in all kinds of military or non-military operations. When there is a demand, they can fast deploy applications and carry various types of IoT application services to support the mutual cooperation between military IoT OSs.

3.3 Technical Requirements for the IoT OS

Through the analysis of the characteristics of the previous IoT OS and the overview of IoT military applications and scenarios, it is not difficult to see that the requirements and scenarios in the military field are quite different from the civilian field. And the military field has higher technical requirements for the IoT OS. In addition to the basic characteristics of the corresponding OS, we should pay more attention to the technical characteristics of the OS in the following five aspects: standard uniformity, anti-loss storage, maintenance-free and high availability, high security and stability, strong compatibility and scalability.

Unified Standards. Military operations are often accompanied by strong mobility characteristics, and the deployment of various types of terminal sensors and other equipment in the IoT often has the characteristics of deploying multiple applications at a time and can be used multiple times over a long period of time. No matter what type of IoT OS is selected, its military application should at least maintain highly uniform standards at the level of external information interaction, such as code identification, data transmission, protocol selection and service interface calling to support the rapid access of terminal devices in different types of military application scenarios.

Resistant to Loss. Due to legal and moral constraints in the civil field, there is relatively little intentional interference, sabotage, or malicious destruction of IoT terminals or servers, which is one of the challenges faced by the IoT applications in military operations. How to maintain a relatively high-level physical stability and stable system performance of terminal IoT devices and operating systems, i. e., overall resistance and persistence to damage, remains a long-term concern for military IoT operating systems.

Maintenance Free and High Availability. It is difficult to adjust the IoT OS in military applications once it is deployed, especially in wartime or emergency military operations. Because the time and space are very limited, the IoT OS must have highly maintenance-free and relatively strong self-bug repair or fault-tolerant ability. Otherwise, if the OS carrying the application fails, all the applications will inevitably fail synchronously. If it is physically difficult to intervene, the corresponding IoT hardware equipment will no longer be available and risk falling into the enemy's hand, causing the leakage of information.

High Security and Stability. The application of the IoT OS in civilian or commercial fields also has high requirements for security and stability, but it is still far from military applications. The military confrontation and its support to politics and economy determine its higher requirements for data security and communication security. The application of the IoT OS must consider its comprehensive security performance in an all-round way. In addition to supporting lightweight military encryption, it can resist partial security intrusions and maintain stable operating performance, it is also supposed to have the function of self-hiding irreversible self-destruction of key data when the conditions are triggered.

Strong Compatibility and Scalability. Military logistics support, daily management, barracks facilities and medical treatment both have typical characteristics of military-civilian integration. In the national defense mobilization or non-war military operations, the application of IoT will widely adopt civilian IoT terminals and equipments. In military applications, stronger compatibility and scalability must be considered. Under special conditions, a large number of civilian or commercial IoT equipment or facilities can be connected with less cost and investment, so as to create military-civilian compatible IoT applications.

4 Difficulties and Countermeasures of Military Application of IoT OS

4.1 Difficulties Faced by Military Applications of IoT OS

Self-Controllable Issues Throughout the Life Cycle. IoT OS life cycle management is the administration of a system from provisioning, through operations, to retirement. Every IoT OS, resource, and workload has a life cycle. Self-controllable management throughout the life cycle can 1) reliably create systems in an automated and scalable manner, 2) track and account for all systems, assets, and subscriptions, 3) ensure that systems are consistent across their life cycle, 4) decommission systems and resources when they are no longer needed. In the military field, due to the outstanding antagonism between the enemy and ourselves, the security requirements are relatively high. Subject to the impact of technological sanctions in developed countries and the implementation of the strategy of revitalizing the military, the application of civilian or commercial IoT OS in our military field should firstly solve the self-controllable issues throughout the life cycle, which can ensure that we have a clear pre-judgment on the OS architecture, code logic, possible risks and security issues, and have corresponding treatment plans.

The Structural Problems Arising from Damage Resistance. Architecture is the cornerstone for OS to support various characteristics. Civilian or commercial OS usually take an optimal approach in terms of function, performance, robustness, security, and scalability when designing architectures. However, it can be seen from the previous analysis of application scenarios that the military field puts the features of damage resistance, security and high stability in a relatively more important priority, which requires the OS selection or the design of architecture must be optimized according to these special requirements, and sometimes we even need to redesign the architecture.

Balance Between Closed Source and Terminal Adaptability. Because of the complexity and variety of IoT terminal devices, the IoT OS is often released in open source mode in order to adapt more terminals. But in the military field, in order to enhance the security of the system, closed-source methods are often used to release the software system when there is no absolute technical security advantage. This reduces the scope of application of the terminal IoT OS to a certain extent. How to strike a balance between closed source system or partially open source system and terminal adaptability is also a topic worth discussing of the Military IoT applications.

Functional High Degree of Freedom Configuration and Tailoring. In order to adapt to more application scenarios, the IoT OS generally allows users to autonomously configure their non-kernel-level functions, and even allows on-demand tailoring of functions to adapt as many resource-constrained terminals as possible or decrease the attack surface of system. That is, in addition to designing a highly compatible system, it can also provide the function to develop programs on the system. Military application scenarios are relatively more complex and diverse, and there are also large differences in the technical requirements of the OS. How to enhance the flexibility of functional custom configuration and functional tailoring without opening the source to users is also a challenge in the military specific practice of the IoT OS.

Support for Multiple Deployments and Heterogeneous Access. The military applications of the IoT in the wartime and emergency are quite different from those of civilian or commercial use, and they are characterized by centralized space, compact time, complicated environment, and may be accompanied by strong mobility. It has little impact to the terminal IoT OS, but it must be flexibly for the deployment of the server-side OS, which can support the access of heterogeneous terminal devices and even the data connection and coordination of non-military terminals or IoT services.

Due to the complexity of military application scenarios and the difference in requirements for the technical characteristics of the IoT OS, in addition to the above challenges, the current civilian or commercial IoT OS applications in the military field also have a series of similar difficulties or the directions that require in-depth research such as military information standards, military communication protocol compatibility, and the requirements of military security protection system. The related content is beyond the scope of this thesis and therefore will not be detailed.

4.2 Suggestions

Strengthen the Importance and Launch the Research on Military IoT OS as soon as Possible. Compared with developed countries such as the United States, China still has a large gap in terms of basic platforms and core key technologies. However, the gap is not large in the field of IoT. Both standard setting, technical research and application promotion are walking in the forefront of the world, and the research of IoT OS also has a place in the global realm. In terms of the military IoT OS, it should face the future military intelligent change, aiming at the military IoT OS to be fully autonomous and controllable. Just like attaching importance to the computer and Internet OS, we should plan and start research as early as possible, so as to avoid the problem of the basic platform being restricted by other countries as a result of the backwardness at the beginning.

Focus on the Foundation and Optimize the Architecture Design of the Military IoT OS. The application of Military IoT has broad prospects and rich scenarios. The terminal equipment and military requirements involved are complicated. At the same time, it needs to meet special technical requirements such as high security, anti-damage, flexible tailoring and customization of function. When selecting or designing the military IoT OS, it is necessary to deeply demonstrate the needs of military scenarios first, focus on the basic architecture of the OS kernel, and judge whether it is optimized or redesigned according to military application requirements, so as to meet various harsh conditions such as military confrontation.

Strengthen Standards, Improve the Compatibility of OS Interface on the Military-Civilian Combination. Under the further military-civilian integration strategy, a large number of commercial IoT terminal devices will be introduced into the military field. For these devices, the corresponding OS is mostly difficult to replace directly. Considering the integration of national defense mobilization resources in the course of military operations, it will also bring about the military-civilian compatible requirements of the military IoT OS. Therefore, in the process of military application or development of IoT OS, it is necessary to establish the concept of unified standards from the beginning to avoid the emergence of vast islands of information, so as to improve the compatibility of the Military IoT OS and various interfaces and protocols in peacetime, wartime or emergency.

Multi-Point Trial to Improve the Applicability of Various Military Scenarios of the OS. The IoT OS has a very close relationship with terminal devices, communication methods, protocol interfaces and deployment models. When selecting or designing an IoT OS, we should focus on battlefield intelligence reconnaissance, military exercise training, and logistics equipment support, medical treatment and protection for a variety of typical application scenarios. Combined with the characteristics of military IoT objects, communication mechanisms, technical requirements and network deployment, we should carry out a wide range of multi-round trials to ensure that the IoT OS can meet the needs of military applications to the greatest extent, and improve the economic and military benefits of research and application.

Keep Abreast of the Forefront and Focus on the Integration Trend of OS and New Technologies. With the continuous development and breakthroughs in technologies such as edge computing, artificial intelligence, 5G/6G, D2D, IPv6, blockchain, microservices and various lightweight encryption algorithms, the IoT OS is presenting the trend of integrative development of terminals and servers. The distributed IoT OS is gradually gaining more attention from researchers. When selecting and designing a military IoT OS, it should continuously improve the mass access, wide area distribution, multi-task coordination, multi-protocol compatibility, low energy consumption and other performance objectives, and then design the Military IoT OS for terminals and servers with an integrated approach.

5 Conclusion

This paper firstly outlines the current development situation of the IoT OS, selects and compares 10 common IoT OSs, and divides the IoT OS into the terminal IoT OS and the server-side IoT OS according to the coupling relationship with the device. The in-depth analysis summarizes the typical characteristics of each type of the IoT OS. On this basis, the application status of the IoT in the military field of major countries is summarized and the military application scenarios of the IoT OS are proposed. The typical technical requirements for the IoT OS in the military field are elaborated in detail in combination with the military characteristics. Combining the characteristics of the current IoT OS with military field application requirements, the problems and difficulties are given which are faced by the military application of the IoT OS and relative countermeasure suggestions.

The IoT OS is the core software platform for the development of IoT applications. It plays a key role as a bearing and information hub for the access, collaboration, and control of IoT objects. With the widespread application and in-depth development of the IoT military field, the military application of the IoT OS is bound to be an important research direction, and the related problems and difficulties are also the starting point of our next research.

References

1. Statista Research Department: IoT connected devices worldwide 2030. http://www.sta tista.com/statistics/802690/worldwide-connected-deviced-by-access-technology/(2020). Accessed 10 May 2021
2. Yu, B.Z., Hao, J.F.: Research on IoT OS. Aeronaut. Comput. Tech. **47**(03), 102–111 (2017)
3. Alkazemi, B.Y.: Middleware model for tinyos and contiki-based wireless sensor networks. In: 5th International Conference on Electronic Devices, Systems and Applications 2016, pp.1–4. IEEE Computer Society, Ras AI Khaimah, United Arab Emirates (2017)
4. Dunkels, A., Grnvall, B., Voigt, T.: Contiki-a lightweight and flexible OS for tiny networked sensors. In: 29th Annual IEEE International Conference on Local Computer Networks 2004, pp.455–462. IEEE Computer Society, Tampa, Florida, USA (2004)
5. Shalan, M., El-sissy, D.: Online power management using DVFS for RTOS. In: 4th International Design and Test Workshop 2009, pp. 1–6. IEEE Computer Society, Riyadh, Saudi Arabia (2009)
6. Amiri-Kordestani, M., Bourdoucen, H.: A survey on embedded open source system software for the IoT. In: Free and Open Source Software Conference 2017, pp. 27–32. Muscat, Oman (2017)
7. Levis, P., Madden, S., Polastre, J.: TinyOS: an operating system for sensor networks. In: Weber, W., Rabaey, J.M., Aarts, E. (eds.) Ambient Intelligence, pp. 383–396. Springer, Berlin, Heidelberg (2005). https://doi.org/10.1007/3-540-27139-2_7
8. Dunkels, A., Schmidt, O., Voigt, T.: Protothreads: simplifying event-driven programming of memory-constrained embedded systems. In: International Conference on Embedded Networked Sensor Systems 2006, pp.29–42. ACM, Boulder, Colorado, USA (2006)
9. D'Exploitations: RIOT-the friendly OS for the IoT-VIDEO. Genomics Inform. **10**(4), 249–255 (2012)
10. Pavelić, N.: Evaluation of android things platform. Undergraduate thesis, University of Zagreb, Faculty of Electrical Engineering and Computing, Zagreb (2017)

11. Inam, R., Maki-Turja, J., Sjodin, M.: Hard real-time support for hierarchical scheduling in FreeRTOS. In: 23rd Euromicro Conference on Real-Time Systems 2011, pp.51–60. IEEE Computer Society, Los Alamitos, California, USA (2011)

12. Wang, X.L.: Development and Application of Embedded VxWorks System, 1st edn. Posts and Telecommunications Press, Beijing (2003)

13. Qiu, W., Xiong, P.X., Zhu, T.L.: Embedded Real-time OS: RT-Thread Design and Implementation, 1st edn. Machinery Industry Press, Beijing (2019)

14. Zhang, X.: Research and implementation of key technology of IoT embedded system based on mbed. Master thesis, Institute of Computing Technology, Chinese Academy of Sciences, Liaoning (2018)

15. Cao, Q., Abdelzaher, T., Stankovic, J.: The lite os operating system: towards unix-like abstractions for wireless sensor networks. In: 7th International Conference on Information Processing in Sensor Networks 2008, pp. 233–244. IEEE Computer Society, St. Louis, Missouri, USA (2008)

16. AliOS Things [EB/OL]. https://iot.aliyun.com/products/aliosthings. Accessed 8 May 2021

17. TencentOS tiny [EB/OL]. https://cloud.tencent.com/product/tos-tiny. Accessed 10 May 2021

18. Ma, L.L., Yang, G., Ren, W.: IoT and Its Military Applications, 1st edn. National Defense Industry Press, Beijing (2014)

Application of Intelligent Traffic Scene Recognition Based on Computer Vision

XiaoChun Lei[1,2], Ren Li[1(✉)], and Kaihao Lin[1]

[1] School of Computer Science and Information Security, Guilin University of Electronic Technology, Guilin 541004, Guangxi, China
[2] Guangxi Key Laboratory of Image and Graphic Intelligent Processing, Guilin University of Electronic Technology, Guilin 541004, Guangxi, China

Abstract. The acceleration of urbanization has led to increasingly prominent traffic problems. In the context of the intelligent era, road traffic management is in urgent need of transformation and upgrading. The development of intelligent transportation is an important task for the construction of a modern city. The intelligent transportation system has the ability to automatically sense and analyze road conditions, which provides great convenience for traffic operation and management. Based on computer vision and deep learning technology, this paper designs and implements an intelligent traffic scene recognition system. The system processes the images taken by the traffic surveillance camera, and mainly realizes the intelligent recognition of two complex traffic scenes. One is the traffic statistics of passing vehicles at the intersection, and the other is vehicle speeding detection. The main process of system realization is divided into five steps. First, the YOLOv4 target detection algorithm is used to detect the vehicle. Second, use the SORT algorithm to track vehicles in real time, and then use the vector product-based virtual line counting method to achieve traffic flow statistics. Third, adopt the HyperLPR Chinese license plate recognition framework based on deep learning to recognize a wide range of license plates with high accuracy. Fourth, a two-line speed measurement method based on computer vision is designed to realize vehicle speeding detection. Finally, PyQT5 and WEB technology are used to realize the visualization of traffic recognition data.

Keywords: Intelligent traffic system · Traffic statistics · Overspeed violation detection · License plate recognition

1 Introduction

With the continuous innovation and breakthrough of artificial intelligence technology, the intelligent transportation system is the target trend of urban modernization. To realize the intelligent and automated operation of the traffic system, it is necessary to use computer vision technology to process a large amount of traffic information, such as license plate recognition, vehicle detection and traffic statistics, and vehicle violation detection [1]. Among them, traffic statistics are the basis for reducing traffic congestion and

© Springer Nature Singapore Pte Ltd. 2021
L. Cui and X. Xie (Eds.): CWSN 2021, CCIS 1509, pp. 97–110, 2021.
https://doi.org/10.1007/978-981-16-8174-5_8

improving traffic dispatch [2]. In addition, vehicle violation detection can improve people's awareness of maintaining traffic order, thereby reducing traffic accidents. Today's intelligent transportation systems are mostly composed of multiple subsystems, each responsible for different tasks [1]. But what this article realizes is a comprehensive system that integrates multiple functions into one application as much as possible, to better perform parallel computing and improve recognition efficiency.

Vehicle detection is the basis of traffic statistics and belongs to the category of target detection. The YOLO algorithm based on deep learning uses convolutional neural networks to automatically extract image features. The detection result of the target is determined by classification regression, which reduces the amount of calculation. Therefore, it has become a new trend of current target detection [2]. Traffic flow statistics are based on vehicle detection and vehicle tracking. The main purpose is to classify and count the cars, trucks, buses, and other vehicles on the road to provide data for traffic decision-making. In this process, the SORT multi-target tracking algorithm played an important role [2]. The realization of speeding violation detection is based on license plate recognition and speed detection. The HyperLPR Chinese license plate recognition algorithm uses a convolutional neural network to train the model of the classifier and recognize characters [3]. Speed detection uses two virtual lines to construct a speed measurement space and then calculates the speed through the mapping relationship between space and pixels.

This paper uses computer vision and deep learning technology to process the image data from the camera angle of public transportation intersections, and mainly realizes the intelligent recognition and analysis of two complex traffic scenes. One is the traffic statistics of passing vehicles at the intersection, and the other is vehicle speeding detection. At present, methods based on intelligent video detection have been widely used in intelligent transportation systems. Its advantages are as follows: 1) It does not install embedded devices under the road, so it does not damage the road, thereby reducing construction costs. 2) Obtain metadata through the ITS subsystem traffic video monitoring system.

2 System Architecture Design

2.1 Overall Architecture

The overall system architecture is shown in Fig. 1. First obtain data through traffic intersection cameras or local video files. Next, transfer the data to the data processing layer. The data is processed through machine learning and computer vision algorithm models and stored in the database. Finally, the front-end display module is realized through WEB and PyQt technology.

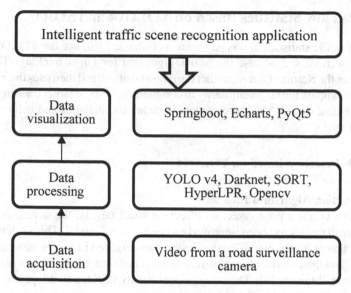

Fig. 1. Overall system architecture

2.2 Procedure Flow

See Fig. 2.

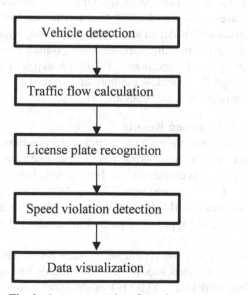

Fig. 2. System procedure flow chart

3   Vehicle Flow Statistics Based on YOLOv4 and SORT

The steps of traffic statistics in this paper are as follows: First, use the YOLOv4 model for target detection; second, use the SORT algorithm for target tracking. The SORT algorithm uses the Kalman filter to predict the target position, and then uses the Hungarian algorithm to compare the target similarity to complete the vehicle target tracking. Finally, the idea of virtual coils is used to complete vehicle flow statistics and achieve vehicle target counting.

3.1   Vehicle Detection Based on YOLOv4

Vehicle Detection Algorithm Idea

Although YOLO has a poor detection effect on small targets, the detection effect of YOLO on small targets has been improved on the YOLOv4 model. This system is based on the detection of highway traffic intersection surveillance video. The detection object is a vehicle, and the individual is relatively large. Therefore, the detection result is less affected by small targets [4]. Therefore, it was finally decided to adopt the YOLOv4 model as the target detection algorithm in this paper.

YOLOv4 Implementation Process

The target detection process of traffic intersection video using YOLOv4 can be divided into four steps [5]. First, the network information of each layer of YOLOv4 is obtained by loading the trained YOLOv4 model and its weight parameters. Second, read the video in the form of a picture, and reconstruct the size of the picture. In the next step, the reconstructed pictures are sent to the YOLOv4 feedforward network. YOLO model and Darknet algorithm are used to detect and calculate the category, confidence and bounding box. Then, a non-maximum value suppression algorithm is used to remove bounding boxes with a high degree of coincidence. The fourth step is to draw the detection results on the screen through the OpenCV method, and store the vehicle information, which will be used for subsequent target tracking [5].

Analysis of Vehicle Detection Results

The following figures show the effect of vehicle detection based on YOLOv4 under two different traffic intersection monitoring videos. It can be seen from the figures that the weather at intersection A is cloudy and the light is dark. But whether it is near or far, the confidence of the vehicle is around 98%. This model also has significant performance in the detection of intersection B. The confidence of vehicle detection is about 80%. The difference is that the main types of objects at intersection B are cars and motorcycles (Figs. 3 and 4).

In order to further verify the vehicle recognition performance of YOLOv4, the overhead traffic monitoring video was cut into 200 image test sets, and the Faster-CNN network, YOLOv3 model, and YOLOv4 model were tested. The performance of the algorithm was evaluated from three indicators: recognition accuracy, recall rate, and number of detected frames per second. The test results are shown in Table 1. According to the results, the YOLOv4 algorithm has greater advantages in detection accuracy and speed. It can meet the requirements of vehicle detection in traffic surveillance video.

Fig. 3. Vehicle detection effect of cloudy weather (intersection A)

Fig. 4. Vehicle detection effect of sunny weather (intersection B)

Table 1. The comparison of target detection algorithms

Detection algorithm	Accuracy (%)	Recall rate (%)	Frames per second (f/s)
YOLOv4	89.2	81.2	44
YOLOv3	88.3	83.5	31
Faster-CNN	88.9	84.0	5

3.2 Vehicle Tracking Based on SORT Algorithm

Vehicle Tracking Algorithm Idea

In order to achieve traffic flow statistics, after the vehicle target is detected, the front and rear frames of the vehicle need to be correlated. This requires designing a tracker that can track road vehicles in real time. By learning the existing multi-target tracking algorithm, we found that the SORT (Simple Online And Realtime Tracking) algorithm was fast and could meet the real-time tracking requirements of this system [7]. Compared with the DeepSORT algorithm, SORT does not need to obtain the apparent characteristics of the target. If the change tracking target does not need to be retrained, it is more versatile. Therefore, the SORT algorithm was selected as the multi-target tracker of this system.

Introduction to SORT Algorithm

The biggest feature of the SORT algorithm is that it greatly improves the speed of multi-target tracking by combining the Kalman filter algorithm and the Hungarian algorithm [6]. The tracker can achieve 260 Hz tracking. The simplified implementation flow chart of the SORT algorithm is shown in Fig. 5.

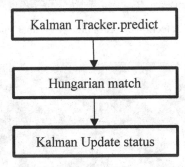

Fig. 5. SORT algorithm structure

SORT algorithm tracking can be divided into two steps:

1) The Kalman filter performs tracking prediction on the detected vehicle and obtains the tracking position and size of the corresponding target in the next frame [6].
2) The main function of the Hungarian algorithm is to match the detection information of the previous frame and the tracking estimation of the next frame [6].

3.3 Using Virtual Lines to Count Vehicles

The principle of the virtual coil vehicle counting method is to set one or more detection lines on the road in the video to detect passing vehicles [5]. By judging the position change between the vehicle and the virtual line, the number of vehicles passing the road is calculated [7].

The counting method of virtual lines is based on the vector product. The algorithm idea is to connect the center points of the detection frame front and rear the vehicle into a line segment AB. Assume that the detection line is CD. If the two line segments intersect, it indicates that the vehicle has passed the detection line, and the count is increased by one. As shown in Fig. 6, three vectors of AB, AC, and AD can be obtained, and then it can be judged whether the line segments intersect according to the result of the multiplication of the vectors. If the results of the vector product AB × AC and AB × AD are different, it indicates that the points C and D are on both sides of the AB line segment, and the line segments intersect.

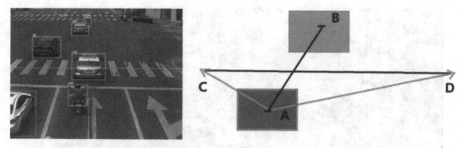

Fig. 6. Space mapping diagram of virtual lines

3.4 Analysis of Vehicle Flow Statistics Results

As shown in Fig. 7, the traffic flow detection was performed on the surveillance video of an intersection. A yellow virtual counting line was set up on the zebra crossing. Whenever the center point of the vehicle collided with the counting line, the traffic count increased by one. "In & Out" respectively represented the traffic statistics results of the forward lane and the reverse lane.

Fig. 7. Flow Statistics results

In order to further test the calculation ability of the algorithm at traffic intersections with heavy traffic, we selected a high-traffic road video for testing. As shown in Fig. 8, two yellow virtual lines were set up on the road to calculate vehicles in two lanes in different directions. The algorithm outputted the statistical results of the sub-vehicles on the picture. Compared with the actual traffic volume, the statistical accuracy rate was 94.84%.

Compared with the traditional road traffic statistics method based on machine vision, the SORT algorithm had higher recognition and tracking performance, and the vector product method was more accurate. In the case of large traffic volume, the detected traffic volume data was closer to reality. Therefore, we chose the high-traffic road video to test and compare different algorithms. The test results are shown in Table 2.

Fig. 8. Flow Statistics results in high-traffic road

Table 2. The comparison of traffic flow statistics

Algorithm	Real data	Test result	Accuracy (%)
Background subtraction method	194	143	73.71
YOLOv3 + SORT	194	181	93.29
YOLOv4 + SORT	194	184	94.84

4　License Plate Recognition Based on HyperLPR

The license plate recognition module uses the HyperLPR [3] algorithm, which is a lightweight Chinese license plate recognition framework. Deep learning technology is applied to character segmentation and character recognition. The biggest feature is that it can recognize many types of Chinese license plates.

4.1　Introduction to HyperLPR Algorithm

The implement process of license plate recognition is as follows [3]. First of all, rough positioning of the license plate contour is carried out through the Harr separator [8]. Second, determine the license plate boundary through image processing methods such as binarization and edge segmentation. Since the actual license plate photos cannot be guaranteed to be horizontal and vertical, the finely positioned license plate images need to be corrected to obtain the license plate images with the X-axis and Y-axis vertical [9]. Third, use the classification model trained by the convolutional neural network to segment the license plate characters. Finally, the segmented characters are passed to the character recognition network for recognition, and the license plate recognition result is obtained [9] (Fig. 9).

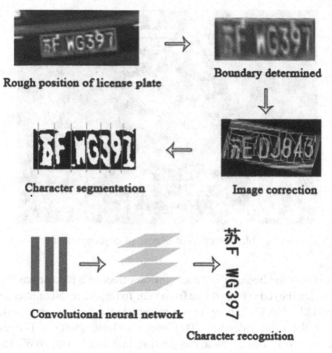

Fig. 9. The schematic diagram of HyperLPR algorithm

4.2 License Plate Priority Iteration

The vehicle recognizes the license plate from the first frame of the picture until the vehicle drives out of the picture. HyperLPR updates the license plate recognition result of each frame when the vehicle moves. When the vehicle approaches the camera, the target is larger and the recognition effect is stable. However, because the target is small when driving at a long distance, the license plate is changed frequently, thereby the confidence of the license plate is low.

In order to optimize the license plate detection of Hyperlpr in the video stream, this paper designs an iterative algorithm for optimizing license plate information. The idea is to store the id and license plate information of the vehicle in the dictionary car-NumberList. In the detection process, the license plate number with the highest confidence is output through continuous sorting and comparison. This improvement solves the problem of unstable and inaccurate long-distance license plate recognition of the original algorithm.

4.3 Analysis of License Plate Recognition Results

As shown in Fig. 10, for the two cars near the camera, the license plate recognition results are '川JG6128' and '川J1726W' respectively. After real video comparison, the detection result is consistent with the real license plate result.

Fig. 10. The effect of license plate recognition

Figure 11 shows the license plate recognition effect of a red car passing through an intersection. When the red vehicle drove from near to far, the result of license plate recognition remained "川 J66A16". In order to further test the performance of the algorithm, we decomposed the traffic video into 200 pictures to form a test set. The results showed that the accuracy rate of license plate recognition increased from 56.6% to 85.7%.

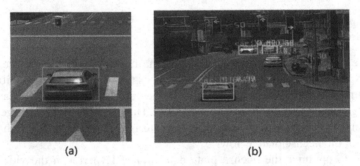

(a)   (b)

Fig. 11. The comparison of near and far license plate recognition

5   Vehicle Overspeed Violation Detection

Vehicle speeding violation detection is an important part of intelligent traffic monitoring system. At present, highway speed detection mainly adopts technical methods such as ultrasonic, infrared, and toroidal coils. However, these methods still have many limitations in the application of actual scenes [10]. For example, the toroidal coil method requires buried coils. As a result, the quality of roads has deteriorated, and maintenance costs have increased. In response to such problems, this paper will combine machine vision and image processing technology to achieve high-precision, low-cost and intelligent detection of speeding violations.

5.1 Two-Line Speed Measurement Method Based on OpenCV

The two-line speed measurement method is a method based on video speed measurement. The speed measurement area is determined by demarcating two virtual lines on the road on the video screen. Then, the time and distance are obtained by constructing the mapping relationship between the video pixel distance and the real space. Then the vehicle speed is obtained by the formula speed = distance/time (Fig. 12).

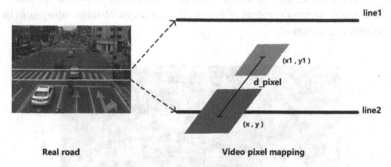

Fig. 12. Spatial mapping relationship\

In order to construct the relationship between a video image pixel and speed section length, a scalar ppm (pixel per meter) is proposed, which means the pixel length of the corresponding video per meter of road. The calculation publication of ppm is shown in Eq. (1), where line2-line1 represents the pixel length between the video speed measuring double lines, and linelong is the real road length, which can be estimated by Baidu map.

$$ppm = \frac{line2-line1}{linelong} \tag{1}$$

The previous target tracking has obtained the detection frame information of the two frames before and after the vehicle. The pixel length d_pixel between the front and rear frames can be calculated by the center point coordinates of the front and rear frames, that is, the pixel distance of the vehicle moving in one frame of video processing. Divide d_pixel by ppm to estimate the distance d_meter the vehicle travels on the road in the video frame. Because the frame rate of the video is 25 fps, the time to play one frame can be calculated as 1/25 s. The instantaneous speed of the vehicle, in m/s, can be obtained from the speed calculation formula, and can be converted to km/h by multiplying by 3.6. The calculation formulas are shown in formulas (2), (3) and (4).

$$d_{pixel} = \sqrt{(x - x1)^2 + (y - y1)^2} \tag{2}$$

$$d_{meter} = \frac{d_{pixel}}{ppm} \tag{3}$$

$$speed = d_{meter} * fps * 3.6 \tag{4}$$

Traffic laws require vehicles to pass through intersections or turn at traffic lights at a speed no more than 30 km/h. Therefore, the speed limit set by the system is 30 km/h. If the speed is greater than the speed limit, it is determined to be overspeed, and then the violation information is stored in the database.

5.2   Analysis of Vehicle Overspeed Detection Results

As shown in Fig. 13, when a vehicle with a license plate of "川J24A53" passed through the test area at a faster speed, the speed measurement module detected that its instantaneous speed was 40 km/s. The system judged it to be overspeed. Then, the system outputted the vehicle's violation information in real time at the bottom of the screen.

The system can monitor the speed of different vehicles in real time and accurately, record the information of illegal vehicles through the information stored in the database, and meet the requirements of the intelligent traffic monitoring system in terms of performance and function.

Fig. 13. Vehicle overspeed detection

6   Data Visualization

The visual application of the system, combined with WEB and PyQt5 technology, uses a friendly human-computer interaction interface and rich charts to display real-time traffic monitoring pictures, dynamic traffic flow, and dynamic violation information in a certain area [11]. Therefore, it provides better support for the integration of information resources for intelligent transportation operations. It also helps to predict the development trend of traffic roads, predict potential risks and make decisions in time (Fig. 14).

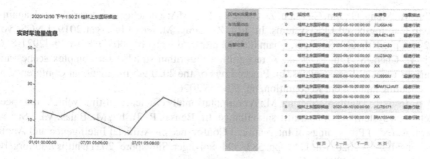

Fig. 14. Dynamic traffic flow and violation information on the website

7 Conclusion

This paper implements an intelligent traffic scene recognition application based on computer vision and other related technologies, which performs real-time vehicle detection, tracking, statistics and speed measurement on traffic video data. The vector product is also applied to the virtual line counting method to make the calculation of traffic flow more accurate. In addition, the HyperLPR license plate recognition algorithm is improved, and the optimal iterative algorithm for the license plate is added, which solves the problem of unstable license plate recognition and poor results when the vehicle is traveling far.

The above research shows that the application of computer vision and deep learning technology to process road traffic information has high accuracy, convenience and intuitiveness, can effectively assist traffic decision-making, and is of great significance to strengthening urban traffic supervision.

References

1. Qiu, L., Zhang, D., Tian, Y., Al-Nabhan, N.: Deep learning-based algorithm for vehicle detection in intelligent transportation systems. J. Supercomput. 77(10), 11083–11098 (2021). https://doi.org/10.1007/s11227-021-03712-9
2. Santos, M., Bastos-Filho, C.J.A., Maciel, A.M.A., Lima, E.: Counting vehicle with high-precision in Brazilian roads using YOLOv3 and deep SORT. In: 2020 33rd SIBGRAPI Conference on Graphics, Patterns and Images (SIBGRAPI), pp. 69–76 (2020)
3. Zhang, W., Mao, Y., Han, Y.: SLPNet: towards end-to-end car license plate detection and recognition using lightweight CNN. In: Peng, Y., et al. (eds.) PRCV 2020. LNCS, vol. 12306, pp. 290–302. Springer, Cham (2020). https://doi.org/10.1007/978-3-030-60639-8_25
4. Du, S., Zhang, P., Zhang, B., et al.: Weak and occluded vehicle detection in complex infrared environment based on improved YOLOv4. IEEE Access 9, 25671–25680 (2021)
5. Kumar, S., Vishal, Sharma, P., Pal, N.: Object tracking and counting in a zone using YOLOv4, DeepSORT and TensorFlow. In: 2021 International Conference on Artificial Intelligence and Smart Systems (ICAIS), pp. 1017–1022 (2021)
6. Wojke, N., Bewley, A., Paulus, D.: Simple online and realtime tracking with a deep association metric, pp. 3645–3649. IEEE (2017)
7. Chen, C., Liu, B., Wan, S., et al.: An edge traffic flow detection scheme based on deep learning in an intelligent transportation system. IEEE Trans. Intell. Transp. Syst. 22, 1840–1852 (2020)

8. Zha, M., Meng, G., Lin, C., Zhou, Z., Chen, K.: RoLMA: a practical adversarial attack against deep learning-based LPR systems. In: Liu, Z., Yung, M. (eds.) Inscrypt 2019. LNCS, vol. 12020, pp. 101–117. Springer, Cham (2020). https://doi.org/10.1007/978-3-030-42921-8_6

9. Li, Y., Chen, S., Liu, P., et al.: A recognition algorithm suitable for complex scenes and various types of license plates. In: Proceedings of the 2020 9th International Conference on Computing and Pattern Recognition, pp. 50–55 (2020)

10. Bhardwaj, R., Dhull, A., Sharma, M.: A computationally efficient real-time vehicle and speed detection system for video traffic surveillance. In: Bansal, P., Tushir, M., Balas, V.E., Srivastava, R. (eds.) Proceedings of International Conference on Artificial Intelligence and Applications: ICAIA 2020, vol. 1164, pp. 583–594. Springer, Singapore (2021). https://doi.org/10.1007/978-981-15-4992-2_55

11. Kujawski, A., Dudek, T.: Analysis and visualization of data obtained from camera mounted on unmanned aerial vehicle used in areas of urban transport. Sustain. Cities Soc. **72**, 103004 (2021)

eRRGe: Balancing Accuracy and Efficiency of Respiratory Monitoring Using Smart Watch by Combining Peak Detection and Regression Model

Fenglin Zhang, Langcheng Zhao, Anfu Zhou$^{(\boxtimes)}$, and Huadong Ma

School of Computer Science, National Pilot Software Engineering School,
Beijing University of Posts and Telecommunications, Beijing 100190, China
{zhang201105004,zhaolangcheng,zhouanfu,mhd}@bupt.edu.cn

Abstract. With the development of smart wearable devices, daily health care becomes a popular topic among mobile applications. As one of human body vital signs, respiratory rate monitoring is discussed in substantial number of recent work based on smart watch. Inertial Measurement Unit (IMU) and Photoplethysmograph (PPG) sensor on smart watch can obtain respiratory rate respectively through various algorithms. However, existing works is designed with complicated signal processing methods which are poor of efficiency and accuracy. Therefore, we propose eRRGe, a smartwatch-based respiratory rate monitoring system, which can balance efficiency and accuracy by using peak detection and regression model together in order to generate respiratory rate. The mean absolute error (MAE) of our system is 2.25 breaths/minute, which shows a better performance than other systems. Moreover, the memory usage of regression model and processing time of our system are lower than other similar systems. Make it compatible for actually deployment on smart watch.

Keywords: Respiratory rate monitoring · Smart watch · Accuracy and efficiency

1 Introduction

According to the survey in [15]: global smart medical wearable devices grow at a compound annual growth rate of about 5.6%, and in 2020, the total amount of smart medical wearable devices is around 15 billion, and it will continue rising in the future. Moreover, smartwatch which came in recent years is the most common device, it is also a kind of device which is the closest to our daily life.

Nowadays, body indicator monitoring on the smartwatch is getting popular. For example, heart rate estimation, pressure index measurement, sleep

The work is supported by National Key R&D Program of China (2019YFB2102202), NSFC (61772084, 61832010), the Fundamental Research Funds for the Central Universities (2019XD-A13).

L. Cui and X. Xie (Eds.): CWSN 2021, CCIS 1509, pp. 111–122, 2021.
https://doi.org/10.1007/978-981-16-8174-5_9

monitoring, and other functions can be realized on the watch. Researchers use multiple sensors on the smart watch to develop interesting and meaningful functions. For example, [22] uses accelerometer on the smart watch to get the data to judge whether the person got Parkinson's disease or not; [14] uses sensor under the skin to sense the skin deformation caused by the hand movement, obtaining user's action according to the sensor data.

Respiration is an important factor of human health. Specifically, many diseases can be reflected through respiratory rate monitoring, for example, if one person is exposed to inhalable particulate matter for a long time, his respiratory rate will badly change [13]; and chronic obstructive pulmonary disease (COPD) can be reflected in daily respiratory data [17], etc. Many researchers are focusing on respiratory rate monitoring on smart watch, and there are series of related work [6,7,10]. However, there are more or less some problems: Spectral analysis methods can not provide enough estimation accuracy [7]. Although deep learning based work [6,10] have reached the accuracy requirements for daily monitoring, for smart watches, their computing efficiency is generally low, so it is not realistic to deploy these systems on smart watch.

In order to solve this problem, we design eRRGe, a system contains two main modules which can balance efficiency and accuracy: First is the **signal pre-processing module** which contains linear interpolation; noise filtering; band-pass filtering and Fast Fourier Transform (FFT) in order to realize respiratory peak detection in frequency domain. Second is the **Random Forest Regression (RFR)** model to extract the final respiratory rate. The mean absolute error (MAE) is 2.25 breaths/min, which is adequate for daily monitoring. On this basis, our system can reduce the processing time to one tenth of the original. Compared with existing neural network methods, the model size is reduced to 1% of the original, which greatly improves the computational efficiency.

The main contribution of this paper is a novel design for respiratory rate monitoring which combines spectral signal processing with machine learning algorithm. So that our system can ensure accuracy and efficiency at the same time, making it compatible for smart watch.

2   Related Work

There are series of related works that focus on respiratory rate monitoring on smart watch. As a IMU-based approach, *WearBreathing* [10] uses accelerometer and gyroscope signal as input, employing a random forest regression model filter out bad quality signals, while qualified signal segments are feed into 1D-CNN model to extract respiratory rate. Another PPG-based work *RespWatch* [6] employs deep learning model, while it contains two routines in parallel, one method uses traditional signal processing methods to finish measurement, the other method uses 1D-ResNet to obtain respiratory rate. A special parameter called *EQI* is defined to judge which routine to choose. Existing deep learning works focus on raw signal, using complex neural networks to complete the task. However, the limited computing ability of the smart watch is a grim constraint, leading problems of real-time processing and battery life.

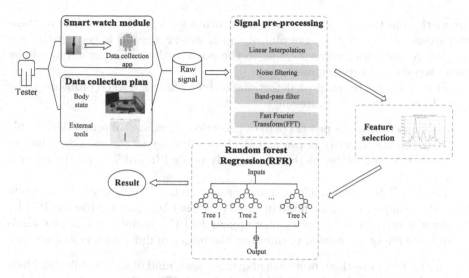

Fig. 1. Overview of the whole experiment design

Not all systems focus on using deep learning model to finish the task. *HeartPy* [7] mainly use traditional signal processing for estimation. The approach of is to generate heart rate firstly using PPG. Next, this system extract respiratory rate by processing heart rate variation (HRV) which is highly related to respiration through Respiratory Sinus Arrhythmia (RSA). This system is suitable for computing resource of smart watches. However, the respiratory rate obtained by that is not accurate enough, which is the primary reason why it cannot be applied to smart watches. Therefore, a respiratory rate monitoring system on smart watch which can balance result accuracy and computing efficiency is needed.

3 System Design

3.1 Overview of Experiment Design

In order to finish the task of respiratory rate monitoring, we need to design a signal processing flow. Figure 1 shows the overview of our respiratory rate monitoring system. After data collection, some kinds of raw signals will be collected, for different kinds of signals, signal pre-processing is needed in order to detect peaks which are related to respiratory rate. Then use some most related peaks which generated by signal pre-processing module as input of Random Forest Regression (RFR) model, the output of this model can be seen as result. In next two sections, these two modules are discussed in detail.

3.2 Signal Pre-processing

After collecting different kinds of raw signals, signal pre-processing module is needed to finish the task of peak detection. Some related work has used similar method in their respiratory rate monitoring work [6–8]. According to these researches, in our system, the aim of signal pre-processing is getting the frequency domain value corresponding to the point with the largest amplitude by using some pre-processing methods.

Since we want to use peak detection method, there are some problems to be solved about signal pre-processing:

- Although during the process of data collection, the data collection API is able to ensure the integrity of raw signal, there are more or less missing values in the signal, so a better method is urgently needed in order to fill the missing values.
- There will be some kinds of noise in raw signal. Small motion and body state changes may cause noise in accelerometer (ACC) and gyroscope (GYR) signals; more kinds of noises may appear in PPG signals, so different kinds of noise filters are needed to filter out the noises in different kinds of sensors.

In order to solve these problems above, for each kind of signal, different kinds of signal pre-processing flows should be designed. Figure 2 shows the processing flow of different kinds of signals. In the figure, ACC and GYR signal are use the same processing method, that is because this two kinds of signal have similar characteristics, in some related works, these two kinds of signal are used in parallel as input of the whole system. Therefore, these two kinds of signals can use same pre-processing method to process [8,10]. For each signal, there are some same signal pre-processing operations to be completed, including signal interpolation; noise filtering; band-pass filter; transfer from time domain to frequency domain.

Linear Interpolation. In order to solve the problem of signal period missing, linear interpolation is needed. According to the sensor parameters of the watch, the sampling frequency of the three signals are 100 Hz (PPG signal) and 50 Hz (ACC and GYR signal) [2]. To keep the integrity and make the later experiments more convenient,for each kind of signal, the interpolation frequency we set is 100 Hz.

Noise Filtering. There may be many kinds of noises in raw signals, especially for ACC and GYR signal, although we choose the data collection plan which can minimize the effect on motion, there still may be small motion noises. Fortunately, some different kinds of methods have been raised in some papers, a proper plan is using the modulus of ACC signal to judge it [8]. And a common Kalman filter [12,21] which has been used on similar tasks [19] will be used for noise filtering.

For PPG signal, although not as much affected by movement as other two kinds of signals, there are still some kinds of noises which may cause decrease of the quality of the signal. For example, some kinds of noises may cause mutations in the raw signal [4]. What's worse, compared with ACC signal and Gyr signal, PPG signal is more sensitive to noise, which improves the difficulty of noise

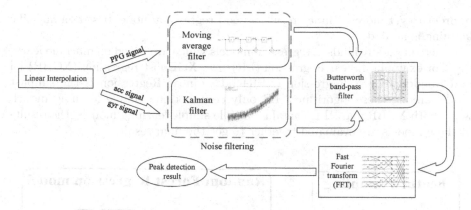

Fig. 2. Signal pre-processing flow for each kind of signal

processing of PPG signal. Moving average filter which mainly used for filtering mutation [9] will be compared. And the design of our moving average filter is shown below:

$$x'(i) = \begin{cases} x(i) & i \leq \frac{l-1}{2} \\ \frac{\sum_{i-\frac{l-1}{2}}^{i+\frac{l-1}{2}} x(i)}{l} & \frac{l-1}{2} < i \leq n - \frac{l-1}{2} \\ x(i) & n - \frac{l-1}{2} < i \leq n \end{cases} \tag{1}$$

In Eq. 1, $x(i)$ means raw signal; $x'(i)$ means the filtered signal; l means the fixed length of the slide window; n means the length of the raw signal. In other words, this is just a 1-D average filter. In our experiment, the window size we chose is 5.

Other Modules. After noise filtering, next step is band-pass filtering work. The aim of this part of job is filter out the data we are interested in. A 2-order Butterworth band-pass filter which is easily to achieve [18] will be used in our experiment, And the pass band is [0.083 Hz, 0.33 Hz], which is fit the range of normal respiratory rate (5 bpm to 20 bpm) we set in this experiment. Use Fast Fourier Transform (FFT) [16] which uses divide-and-conquer method to reduce the complexity to finish the task of spectrum conversion. Finally, we pick the highest peak(s) of different kinds of signals. These peaks may have relationship with respiratory rate. And we choose some of the most relevant peak characteristics of respiratory rate are used as input to regression models.

3.3 Regression Model

After signal pre-processing, since we have got some most related features, and to a certain extent, these features can be the respiratory rate by using some simple calculation methods, such as take the average of these values, take the most relevant feature, etc. However, the accuracy of this method is not so good, so in order to get more accuracy result, a good regression model based on machine learning is needed.

There are many kinds of regression models which are based on machine learning. For example, Linear Regression (LR) [20]; XGBoost regression (XGBR) [5] and Random Forest Regression (RFR) [11]. Linear Regression is the simplist model among these algorithms. LR only contains one simple learning model, while both XGBR and RFR contain multiple simple learning models, the results of these models are evaluated together to get the final result.

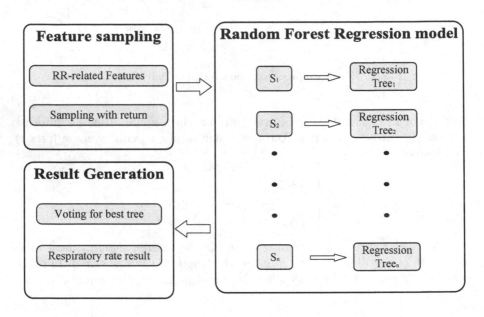

Fig. 3. Data flow of our system in random forest regression model

In our system, Random Forest Regression (RFR) model is chosen as the regression model we use. RFR model integrates multiple simple learning models in parallel. Figure 3 shows data flow of our system in random forest regression. Since we get some features which are related to respiratory rate (RR) by signal pre-processing, these features are the input of RFR model. Next, for all features, we use sampling with return method to sample n samples. Then, put all the samples into n individual trees. These trees may provide multiple respiratory rate results. Then, using a voting method to judge which tree can get the best result, finally give the respiratory rate as the output of this model. We implement this model by using *sklearn* library in Python. First, in order to make our regression model stable, we need to adjust n which means the number of simple learning models mentioned above. Then we need to adjust parameters which are related to the complexity of each simple learning model. The aim of this step is to find a best complexity with best accuracy and lower overfitting effect, there are many parameters related to this, here we use grid search and K-fold validation to ensure these parameters.

4 Evaluation

4.1 Evaluation Setup

In our system, we choose XiaoMi Watch to get raw signal periods including PPG; ACC and GYR signal. The raw signal dataset used in our system in this article includes nearly 200 pieces of data, and the respiratory rate corresponding to each piece of data is uniformly distributed in the interval of 5–20 breaths/minute (bpm). The time interval of the raw signal dataset is 2 min.

In order to facilitate measurement and reduce the noise of breathing, here we select the data of guided breathing, that is, use an external program [1] to control the respiratory rate. Testers sit stably and peacefully, wear smart watch correctly, breathing with the rhythm of external program. The state of data collection is shown in Fig. 4.

Fig. 4. The state of data collection, interface of the guided app is shown on the screen.

4.2 System-Level Results

Table 1 shows the comparison of our system and other respiratory rate monitoring systems, including *HeartPy*, CNN model in *RespWatch*, and the result obtained directly from the peak frequency of PPG signal which has the highest correlation with ground truth of the respiratory rate. In the table, mean absolute error (MAE) which can reflect the accuracy of the whole system, Model Size which can reflect the amount of parameters in the regression model, Processing

Time means the time of getting respiratory rate from raw signal. Model size and processing time are two important evaluation parameters about the efficiency of one system.

Table 1. Comparison of our method and other methods

Method	MAE (breaths/min)	Model size (KB)	Processing time (s)
eRRGe	2.25	310	0.015
Peak detection (PPG)	3.57	N/A	N/A
HeartPy [7]	2.64	3400	11
CNN (RespWatch) [6]	2.37	28467	0.198

Since the MAE of peak detection is too large ($MAE > 3$), so it is pointless to calculate processing time of this method. From the result in the table, it is obvious that our method can get more accuracy result with smaller model and shorter processing time. That means, our method can reduce the complexity of the algorithm while ensuring the accuracy of the premise, and improve the efficiency of extracting the breathing rate on the smart watch. It further proves that our method of extracting relevant features first and then performing regression processing on the features is more efficient.

4.3   Micro-benchmark Results

Feature Design. After signal pre-processing, in order to guarantee we can take hidden respiratory rate information from raw signal, we need to pick multiple frequencies which correspond to the peaks of the spectrum. The frequencies are the features we generated by signal pre-processing. However, not all of them contain respiratory rate information. Therefore, feature selection is needed. Here we take top-3 peak detection results of each signal, then choose some features which are most related to the ground truth. Figure 5 shows the correlation coefficients between them and ground truth value.

From the figure, we can clearly see that the correlation coefficient of the PPG signal peak extraction result is much larger than the correlation coefficient of the other two signals. It may be because we deliberately control the process of guided breathing. In addition to the movement of the wrist, the movement effect caused by breathing is weakened, so the extracted features are not so obvious.

In order not to affect the final respiratory rate extraction work, we choose top-3 peak values of PPG as input. At the same time, we can also draw a conclusion: In guided breathing scenario, there may be the closest relationship between PPG signal and respiratory rate.

What's more, we found another question about PPG signal. PPG signal appearing is obviously greater than the other two signals. We guessed that the PPG signal is an optical signal, and the optical signal consumes more energy.

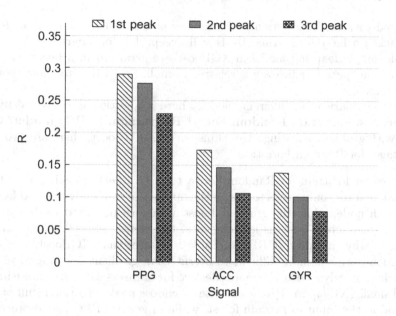

Fig. 5. Correlation coefficient between different signal peaks and the true value of respiratory rate

It is possible that the internal operating system settings make it unable to continuously perceive, which leads to this phenomenon. This is also a problem that needs to be solved in the future.

Regression Model Design. In our system, we choose RFR as the regression model since the relatively high accuracy and efficiency. In this section, we will compare the accuracy and efficiency of other regression models including RFR, LR, and XGBoost, all of them are implemented by using *sklearn* library. Table 2 shows the comparison between RFR and other regression models, including XGBoost and Linear Regression. The parameters in this table are the same with Table 1.

Table 2. Comparison of different regression models

Regression model	MAE (breaths/min)	Model size (KB)	Processing time (s)
RFR [11]	1.98(train)/2.25(test)	310	0.015
LR [20]	3.57	1	0.018
XGBoost [5]	2.19(train)/2.30(test)	43	0.041

From the result in the table, it is obvious that compare to other regression models, RFR has the most accuracy result of respiratory rate. Although compared with XGBoost, its model size may be a bit larger, but its model has not reached a large scale, this size is still acceptable for smart watches. Since multiple simple learning model in XGBoost are arranged in a linear way. The optimization space of efficiency is relatively small. So RFR is the best choice of our system.

After comparison of different models, here a question is raised: **Why we get the best result on Random Forest Regression (RFR) model?** Compared with gradient boosting algorithms such as XGBoost, there are two main advantages for Random Forest:

- It is easier for train for Random Forest than Gradient Boosting algorithms, Random forest only needs to design the number of randomly selected features on each node, while the gradient boosting algorithms need to design more super parameters, such as learning rate, tree depth, etc. [3], which can also explain why the speed of RFR in Table 2 is faster than XGBoost.
- Random forest is more difficult to overfit than gradient boosting algorithm, which indirectly leads to be more effective for datasets with large noise impact and small SNR [3]. In eRRGe, because we choose peak detection result of PPG signal as the input of random forest, while in general PPG signal processing process, respiratory signal is relatively weak, and the impact of respiration on PPG is generally treated as noise [7]. However, we extract this part of "noise signal" use similar method, which indirectly leads to low SNR in extracting respiratory related features from PPG.

Therefore, the performance of our feature data set on RFR is better than XGBoost. So if we want to improve the performance of our system, we can find another features related to respiratory rate which have higher SNR from different kinds of signals.

What's more, compared to other integrate learning method such as XGBoost, RFR also has an advantage in computational efficiency. Since the processes executed in different simple learning models will not interfere with each other. Therefore, the parallel computing principle can be used to optimize the computational efficiency of the regression model. What's more, this model has the same relatively strong generalization ability and strong anti-overfitting ability after reasonable parameter adjustment with XGBoost.

5   Conclusion

In conclusion, we raised a new method to get the respiratory rate from smart watch. That is, use simple digital signal processing method to get some features which related to respiratory rate from raw signal first. Then use some regression models to get the respiratory rate. In our experiment, we have proved this method is relatively accuracy and efficient. It can provide an idea for respiratory rate monitoring on smart watches. We hope that our research can provide some valuable references for future related research.

References

1. Guided breath program. https://github.com/ReinhardFink/Breath/, Accessed 20 May 2021
2. Xiaomi Mi Watch (China) black. https://vedroid.com/smartwatches/xiaomi/xiaomi-mi-watch-(china)-black.html/. Accessed 5 May 2021
3. Bernard, S., Heutte, L., Adam, S.: Influence of hyperparameters on random forest accuracy. In: Benediktsson, J.A., Kittler, J., Roli, F. (eds.) MCS 2009. LNCS, vol. 5519, pp. 171–180. Springer, Heidelberg (2009). https://doi.org/10.1007/978-3-642-02326-2_18
4. Chandrakar, B., Yadav, O., Chandra, V.: A survey of noise removal techniques for ECG signals. Int. J. Adv. Res. Comput. Commun. Eng. **2**(3), 1354–1357 (2013)
5. Chen, T., et al.: XGBoost: extreme gradient boosting. R package version 0.4-2 1(4) (2015)
6. Dai, R., Lu, C., Avidan, M., Kannampallil, T.: RespWatch: robust measurement of respiratory rate on smartwatches with photoplethysmography. In: Proceedings of the International Conference on Internet-of-Things Design and Implementation, pp. 208–220 (2021)
7. van Gent, P., Farah, H., van Nes, N., van Arem, B.: HeartPy: a novel heart rate algorithm for the analysis of noisy signals. Transp. Res. F Traffic Psychol. Behav. **66**, 368–378 (2019)
8. Hao, T., Bi, C., Xing, G., Chan, R., Tu, L.: MindfulWatch: a smartwatch-based system for real-time respiration monitoring during meditation. Proc. ACM Interact. Mob. Wearable Ubiquit. Technol. **1**(3), 1–19 (2017)
9. Lee, H.W., Lee, J.W., Jung, W.G., Lee, G.K.: The periodic moving average filter for removing motion artifacts from PPG signals. Int. J. Control Autom. Syst. **5**(6), 701–706 (2007)
10. Liaqat, D., et al.: WearBreathing: real world respiratory rate monitoring using smartwatches. Proc. ACM Interact. Mob. Wearable Ubiquit. Technol. **3**(2), 1–22 (2019)
11. Liaw, A., Wiener, M., et al.: Classification and regression by randomForest. R News **2**(3), 18–22 (2002)
12. Meinhold, R.J., Singpurwalla, N.D.: Understanding the Kalman filter. Am. Stat. **37**(2), 123–127 (1983)
13. Mu, L., et al.: Peak expiratory flow, breath rate and blood pressure in adults with changes in particulate matter air pollution during the Beijing Olympics: a panel study. Environ. Res. **133**, 4–11 (2014)
14. Ogata, M., Imai, M.: SkinWatch: skin gesture interaction for smart watch. In: Proceedings of the 6th Augmented Human International Conference, pp. 21–24 (2015)
15. Papa, A., Mital, M., Pisano, P., Del Giudice, M.: E-health and wellbeing monitoring using smart healthcare devices: an empirical investigation. Technol. Forecast. Soc. Chang. **153**, 119226 (2020)
16. Proakis, J.G.: Digital Signal Processing: Principles Algorithms and Applications. Pearson Education, London (2001)
17. Raupach, T., et al.: Slow breathing reduces sympathoexcitation in COPD. Eur. Respir. J. **32**(2), 387–392 (2008)
18. Selesnick, I.W., Burrus, C.S.: Generalized digital butterworth filter design. IEEE Trans. Signal Process. **46**(6), 1688–1694 (1998)

19. Sun, X., Qiu, L., Wu, Y., Tang, Y., Cao, G.: SleepMonitor: monitoring respiratory rate and body position during sleep using smartwatch. Proc. ACM Interact. Mob. Wearable Ubiquit. Technol. 1(3), 1–22 (2017)
20. Weisberg, S.: Applied Linear Regression, vol. 528. Wiley, New York (2005)
21. Welch, G., Bishop, G., et al.: An Introduction to the Kalman Filter. University of North Carolina at Chapel Hill, Chapel Hill (1995)
22. Wile, D.J., Ranawaya, R., Kiss, Z.H.: Smart watch accelerometry for analysis and diagnosis of tremor. J. Neurosci. Methods 230, 1–4 (2014)

A Calculation Time Prediction-Based Multiflow Network Path Planning Method for the AGV Sorting System

Ke Wang[1,2,3,4], Wei Liang[1,2,3]([✉]), Huaguang Shi[1,2,3,4], Jialin Zhang[1,2,3,4], and Qi Wang[1,2,3,4]

[1] State Key Laboratory of Robotics, Shenyang Institute of Automation, Chinese Academy of Sciences, Shenyang 110016, China
weiliang@sia.cn
[2] Key Laboratory of Networked Control System, Shenyang Institute of Automation, Chinese Academy of Sciences, Shenyang 110016, China
[3] Institutes for Robotics and Intelligent Manufacturing, Chinese Academy of Sciences, Shenyang 110169, China
[4] University of Chinese Academy of Sciences, Beijing 100049, China

Abstract. The Automatic Guided Vehicle (AGV) sorting system is a new way of sorting. Path planning is the key part to improve sorting efficiency of the system. In the existing methods, the multiflow network path planning method obtains optimal paths by transforming path planning problems into integer linear programming problems and solving them. However, due to the huge amount of calculation, it is hard to ensure the real-time performance and use the method in practice. In this paper, a Calculation Time Prediction-based Multiflow Network path planning method (CTPMN) is proposed to deal with the problem. Firstly, a new operating model is proposed, in which the time window of the AGV moving can be set according to the predicted calculation time of the path planning method. And then a support vector machine-based algorithm is used to learn the predicted calculation time based on the size of sorting area, number of sorting tasks and the maximum task distance. In addition, a task decomposition strategy is put forward to eliminate the constraint that the destination of any two tasks in the multi-flow network method cannot be the same. Finally, the effectiveness of the proposed method is verified by simulation experiments.

Keywords: AGV · SVM · Path planning · Predication

1 Introduction

As a new way of sorting, the Automatic Guided Vehicle (AGV) sorting system has high efficiency, flexible application, and good robustness. However, the multi-

Supported by the Special Fund for Strategic Pilot Technology of Chinese Academy of Sciences (XDC02020600), Liaoning Revitalization Talents Program (XLYC1902110), Liaoning Provincial Natural Science Foundation of China (2020JH2/10500002).

L. Cui and X. Xie (Eds.): CWSN 2021, CCIS 1509, pp. 123–135, 2021.
https://doi.org/10.1007/978-981-16-8174-5_10

AGV path planning problem is an NP-hard problem [1]. With the increasing of AGVs, multiple AGVs influence each other, so that it is difficult to plan the shortest paths for all AGVs. In addition, the path planning methods must ensure the generation of paths in time because of the real-time movement of AGVs. These problems pose great challenges to the design of path planning methods.

Many methods, which include static and dynamic methods, are used to solve the multi-AGV path planning problem. Researches on static methods are very extensive. The Conflict-Based Search (CBS) and its variants [2–6] divide the problem into two levels. The lower level plans specific path for each AGV, and the higher level solves conflicts among AGVs by a constraint tree. In the mathematical programming methods [1,7–11], path planning problems are transformed into Integer Linear Programming (ILP) problems and then solved by commercial solvers. The static methods focus on optimal solutions and do not pay much attention to reducing the solving time. Therefore, the optimality performance of the paths planned by static methods is good. Nevertheless, the static methods take a lot of calculation time for solving problems so as not to be suitable for practical industrial environment. For dynamic methods, more dynamic features are considered to increase the efficiency of path planning. Bnaya *et al.* [12] propose the Windowed Hierarchical Cooperative A* (WHCA*), in which a dynamic window is used to limit the search depth in order to spread computation during path planning process. But at the same time, the window reduces the success rate of path planning. Han *et al.* [13] propose the Diversified-path Database-driven Multi-robot path planning (DDM) algorithm, which is a decoupling-based planner. Some path diversification heuristics are used to plan evenly dispersed paths and facilitate the fast resolution of local path conflicts by optimal sub-problem solution databases. Compared with direct use of mathematical programming methods, it saves much solving time. Liu *et al.* [14] propose a hierarchical framework to solve the path planning problem. In the centralized prediction and planning level, a time-efficient traffic heat map is used to predict the distribution of AGVs and paths are generated based on the heat map. In the decentralized local coordination level, a variant of A* is used to generate local paths. Although the above dynamic methods consider the solving time, they only try to reduce the solving time without considering the actual influence of solving time on efficiency.

In this paper, we consider the influence of calculation time spent on path planning. In the above methods, multiflow network path planning method [1] has good optimality performance. But its calculation time is too long to be used in practice. Hence, we choose the multiflow network as the basic method and propose the Calculation Time Prediction-based Multiflow Network path planning (CTPMN) method to solve the path planning problem in the AGV soring system. The main contributions of this paper are summarized as follows:

- A new operating model, in which we set the AGV moving time by predicated calculation time, is proposed. And we use predicated calculation time instead of real calculation time to set the AGV moving time in each cycle.

- A Support Vector Machine (SVM)-based calculation time predication method which is used in above operating model is established. We select the size of sorting area, number of tasks, and maximum task distance as the independent variables and choose calculation time as the dependent variable. The SVM model is trained in advance and then used in the system.
- A task decomposition strategy is developed to eliminate the constraint that the destination of any two tasks in the mlutiflow network method cannot be identical.

The remainder of this paper is organized as follows. Section 2 describes the AGV path planning problem in the AGV sorting system. Section 3 introduces the multiflow network path planning method. Section 4 proposes the CTPMN method. Section 5 verifies the performance of the CTPMN method in comparison with the DDM method. Section 6 draws conclusions.

2 Problem Description

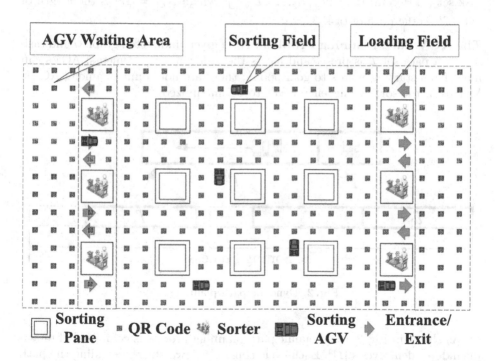

Fig. 1. Layout of the AGV sorting system.

Figure 1 shows layout of the AGV sorting system. In the sorting system, the sorting fields, the loading fields, and the AGV waiting areas are deployed from the middle to both sides. We use the sorting area to denote both the sorting field and the loading field. The Quick Response (QR) codes are used to locate the AGVs and the sorting panes are used to collect the express packages. In addition, the sorters are responsible for placing the express packages on AGVs. During the sorting process, the AGVs first pick up the express packages in the loading field, then go to the sorting field to put the packages into the sorting panes, and finally move to the AGV waiting area to wait for the next sorting.

The AGV sorting area can be modeled as an undirected graph $\mathcal{G} = (\mathcal{V}, \mathcal{E})$. Herein, $\mathcal{V} = \{v_1, v_2, \ldots, v_{N_{\mathcal{V}}}\}$, where $N_{\mathcal{V}} = |\mathcal{V}|$ is the number of vertexes in the sorting area, is the vertex set and $\mathcal{E} = \{(v_p, v_q)|v_p, v_q \in \mathcal{V}\}$ is the edge set in the sorting area. Usually, the AGV path planning is processed in the sorting area, so $\mathcal{G}$ just includes the sorting area. In addition, let $\mathcal{V}^I = \{v_1^I, v_2^I, \ldots, v_{N_{\mathcal{V}^I}}^I\}$ and $\mathcal{V}^O = \{v_1^O, v_2^O, \ldots, v_{N_{\mathcal{V}^O}}^O\}$, where $N_{\mathcal{V}^I} = |\mathcal{V}^I|$, $N_{\mathcal{V}^O} = |\mathcal{V}^O|$ and $(\mathcal{V}^I, \mathcal{V}^O \subset \mathcal{V})$, denote the entrance set and exit set, respectively.

Let $\mathcal{J} = \{J_1, J_2, \ldots, J_{N_{\mathcal{J}}}\}$, where $N_{\mathcal{J}} = |\mathcal{J}|$ is the number of tasks, be the task set. Herein, $J_i = (S_i, G_i)$ is a task including a starting point S_i and a goal point G_i.

Path set $\mathcal{L} = \{\mathcal{L}^1, \mathcal{L}^2, \ldots, \mathcal{L}^{N_{\mathcal{L}}}\}$, where $N_{\mathcal{L}} = |\mathcal{L}|$ is a feasible solution for task set $\mathcal{J}$. Herein, $\mathcal{L}^i = \{L_1^i, L_2^i, \ldots, L_{N_{\mathcal{L}^i}}^i\}$, where $N_{\mathcal{L}^i} = |\mathcal{L}^i|$ is the length of path $\mathcal{L}^i$, is the path of task J_i.

The AGV Path Planning Problem: For a given undirected graph $\mathcal{G}$ and task set $\mathcal{J}$, a path set $\mathcal{L}$ is preset and meets the following requirements: AGVs can move from starting points to goal points; there are not conflicts among AGVs. Moreover, the sorting efficiency needs to be maximized.

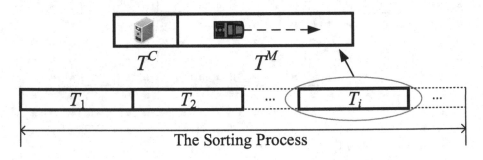

Fig. 2. Dynamic path planning.

As shown in Fig. 2, the dynamic path planning process is composed of multiple independent cycles [11]. Each cycle consists of two stages including the path planning stage T^C and the AGV moving stage T^M. In the path planning stage, the sever collects tasks information, solves the problem and then sends the paths information to AGVs by wireless networks. Subsequently, in the AGV moving stage, AGVs move according to their respective paths. Next, the above process repeats.

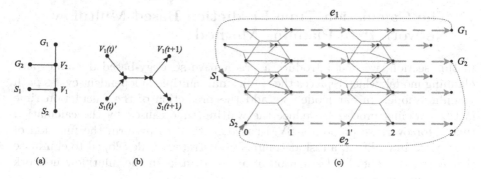

Fig. 3. Multiflow network path planning method. (a) Example of the sorting tasks. (b) Merge-split gadget. (c) The time-expanded version of example.

3   The Multiflow Network Path Planning Method

Yu *et al.* [1] propose a special multiflow network path planning method to model the path planning problem by time expansion. In this method, the undirected graph is transformed into a directed and time-expanded network by the merge-split gadget and links from a point to its time-expanded point. As shown in Fig. 3(a), a simple undirected graph with two tasks, i.e., $J_1 = (S_1, G_1)$ and $J_2 = (S_2, G_2)$, is given. Herein, V_1 and V_2 are points in the undirected graph.

As shown in Fig. 3(b), the merge-split gadget transforms edge (S_1, V_1) into a net model. The merge-split gadget shows the direction of flow in the network from t' to $t+1$, which represents the movement of the corresponding AGVs. For the gadget, all arcs are assigned unit capacity, which represents that only one AGV can pass (S_1, V_1). In addition, the method assigns unit cost to horizontal middle arc and zeros cost to other four arcs, which is used to calculate path cost.

As shown in Fig. 3(c), links from a point to its time-expanded points are added to the time-expanded network together with the merge-split gadget. There are two kinds of links including links from t to $t+1$ (the solid arrow) and links from t to t' (the dotted arrow). The former is assigned unit capacity and cost, and the latter is assigned unit capacity and zero cost. By this way, at most one AGV stays at a point. Furthermore, e_1 and e_2 are the loopback arcs, which connect the goal points and starting points, for task J_1 and J_2, respectively. The loopback arcs have unit capacity and zero cost. In addition, the length of the time-expanded network varies from small to large within $[\max_{J_i \in \mathcal{J}} D_{MT}(S_i, G_i), |\mathcal{V}|^3]$, where $D_{MT}(S_i, G_i)$ denotes manhattan distance from S_i to G_i. The optimal solutions are obtained when the solution is found for the first time.

Based on the multiflow network model, the path planning problem is transformed into a ILP problem. Then ILP solver is used to obtain the optimal solution. But for the same reason, it takes tremendous time to get paths. Therefore, it is hard to apply in practice because of the bad real-time performance.

4   The Calculation Time Prediction-Based Multiflow Network Path Planning Method

In this section, we first introduce a predicative strategy-based dynamic path planning model, which replaces the traditional multiple independent cycles path planning model. In our model, we add the prediction of the calculation time in the planning process to reduce the waiting time caused by the calculation time. Moreover, we propose a SVM-based method to perform the function of prediction. In addition, a task decomposition strategy is developed to eliminate the restriction that the destination of any two tasks in the mlutiflow network method cannot be identical.

4.1   The Predicative Strategy-Based Dynamic Path Planning Model

In practical operation, the calculation time of the system cannot be completely ignored. Therefore, we need to consider the influence of the calculation time on the system. The path planning process is executed on the server of the sorting system, and the AGV moving process is executed on AGVs in the sorting area. Hence the path planning process and the AGV moving process can be executed at the same time to a certain extent. Based on the above motivations, we propose a system operation model. As shown in Fig. 4, the upper part is the traditional operating model [11], and the lower part is the operating model we proposed. There are three consecutive cycles named as T_1, T_2, T_3 in both operating models, and we assume that tasks arrive randomly throughout the sorting process. Let T_k^C and T_k^M denote the path planning stage and the AGV moving stage, respectively. In the traditional operating model, paths of tasks arriving in T_1 are planned in T_2^C, and then AGVs move according to the paths in T_2^M. However, in our operating model, tasks arriving in T_1 are temporarily kept in the task queue. The above tasks and tasks carried by AGVs in the AGV sorting area at end of T_1 are planned in T_2. And in T_2, AGVs carrying express packages of tasks in the sorting area continue to move according to the planned paths. Herein, an important point is how far the AGVs move (i.e., how to set the value of T_2). In our operating model, a SVM-based predictive method (in Sect. 4.2) is used to determine T_2. Actually, the SVM-based predictive method is used to get the predictive value T_2^P of the calculation time T_2^C. And we set $T_2^M = T_2^P$ to make sure that AGVs move as far as possible while planning paths. Relying on the predicated T_2^M and planned paths, the location of AGVs at the beginning of T_3 (or end of T_2) are obtained. Together with tasks arriving in T_2, which are located at entrances of the sorting area, we can get the task set which is planned in T_3. Then, the above process is repeated in the subsequent cycles. In general, the tasks arriving in T_1 are planned in T_2, and then move in T_3.

Different from traditional operating model, we advance T_k^C so that T_k^C and T_{k-1}^M start at the same time. In traditional operating model, tasks arriving in T_{k-1} are planned in T_k^C. However, in our operating model, tasks arriving in T_{k-1} are planned in the T_k, and then move in T_{k+1}. Hence compared with the

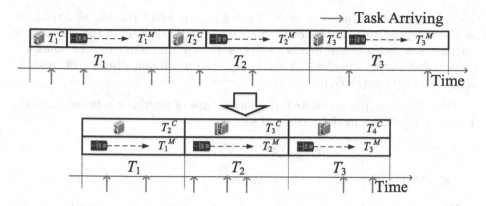

Fig. 4. The predicative strategy-based dynamic path planning model.

traditional model, the time when the tasks start to move (i.e., AGVs carrying the tasks start to move) in our model is delayed by one cycle. For a specific task, the delay of one cycle increases the time from tasks arriving to completing tasks. But for the entire system, the delay of one cycle only prolongs the running time of the system by about two cycles. When the system runs for long time, it does not reduce overall efficiency too much. And compared with the benefits brought by this method, the performance drop brought by the method is very small.

In operation, the duration of T_k is determined by T_k^M and T_{k+1}^C, and they meet the following conditions:

$$T_k = max(T_k^M, T_{k+1}^C). \tag{1}$$

In practical operation, our prediction cannot be completely accurate, so T_k^M and T_{k+1}^C are not exactly equal. On the one hand, if $T_k^M \geq T_{k+1}^C$, the AGVs are still walking when the calculation is completed. In this case, we only need to wait for the AGVs to continue moving to the preset goal points. Then seamlessly start the next cycle, and AGVs in the sorting area continue to move without stopping. On the other hand, if $T_k^M < T_{k+1}^C$, new paths have not been obtained yet when the AGVs have completed the panned paths. In this case, the AGVs need to stop at the preset goal points and wait for new path planning results before moving on.

4.2   The SVM-Based Predictive Method

In CTPMN method, the calculation time (i.e., solving time) of the multiflow network method needs to be predicated. We select SVM for building the prediction model.

In the multiflow network method, the ILP solver needs to traverse the entire solution space to find the optimal solution. Hence the solving time is closely related to the size of the established network flow model. Moreover, the size of the sorting area, the number of tasks and the maximum distance of tasks play decisive roles in the network scale. Therefore, we select the above attributes as the independent variables of the predication model. Herein, the size of the sorting area includes the number of rows R and the number of columns C; the number of tasks in the task set is $N_{\mathcal{J}}$; the maximum distance of tasks is $D_{max} = \max\limits_{J_i \in \mathcal{J}} D_{MT}(S_i, G_i)$.

Let T^P denote the predicated calculation time of multiflow network method. Then the predictive model is denoted as:

$$T^P = f_p(R, C, N_{\mathcal{J}}, D_{max}). \tag{2}$$

The establishment process of the SVM prediction model is given as follows:

1) We generate task sets based on random four independent variables on the computer.
2) These task sets are solved by multiflow network method on the computer and we record the solving time according to different task sets.
3) After finishing all the data recording, we use SVM to fit the relationship between the above four independent variables and solving time to get the predictive model $f_p(R, C, N_{\mathcal{J}}, D_{max})$.

During the system operation period, the predictive model is used to predict the calculation time to make the system run smoothly (in Sect. 4.1).

4.3   The Task Splitting Strategy

In the multiflow network method, any two tasks cannot have the same goal point in a solution. It is determined by the capacity constraints in the multiflow network method. When two tasks have the same goal point, a feasible solution to the problem cannot be obtained due to the conflict in the constraints. We are inspired by the Divide-and-Conquer Over the Time Domain method [1], and we can use task splitting strategy to solve this problem. The idea is to split the longer task in the conflicting task into two tasks. In the current cycle, only the first half of the tasks are completed, and the second half of the tasks are reserved for completion in the next cycle.

If a task set with goal point conflicts are solved by the multiflow network method, it will fail to solve the problem due to the constraint conflict. And then the multiflow network method increases the length of the time-expanded network (in Sect. 3) and solve it again. In the end, the algorithm infinitely increases the length of the time-expanded network but cannot get a feasible solution to the problem. For a single solution, this problem is difficult to solve. However, in actual operation, the path of a task needs to be planned many times during the transportation process. Hence, we split the longer task into two subtasks. The first subtask is added to the current task set, and the second subtask is added to the task set when the first subtask is completed. Example of the task splitting strategy is shown in Fig. 5. Herein, $J_1 = (S_1, G_1)$, $J_2 = (S_2, G_2)$, and $S_1 \neq S_2$, $G_1 = G_2$. We have the following situations:

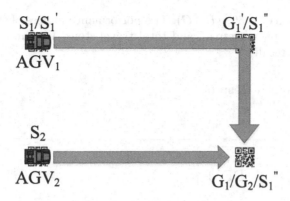

S_1/S_1' G_1'/S_1''

AGV_1

S_2

AGV_2 $G_1/G_2/S_1''$

Fig. 5. The task splitting strategy.

1) If $D_{MT}(S_1, G_1) > D_{MT}(S_2, G_2)$, then we create two subtasks $J_1' = (S_1', G_1')$ and $J_1'' = (S_1'', G_1'')$. We plan a path Pt^1 for J_1 by A* method, and select the point P^{mid}, which is $D_{MT}(S_2, G_2)$ units away from point S_1, on Pt^1. Then we set $S_1' = S_1$, $S_1'' = G_1' = P^{mid}$ and $G_1'' = G_1$. The subtask J_1' replaces the task J_1 and the subtask J_1'' is reserved. After J_1' is completed, J_1'' was add to the task set.
2) If $D_{MT}(S_1, G_1) < D_{MT}(S_2, G_2)$, we swap task 1 and task 2, and the rest is the same as situation 1.
3) If $D_{MT}(S_1, G_1) = D_{MT}(S_2, G_2)$, the distance between the two tasks is equal. In this situation, we choose the point P^{mid} that is $D_{MT}(S_1, G_1) - 1$ units distance away from S_1. The rest is the same as situation 1.

5   Performance Evaluation

In this section, we evaluate the performance of the CTPMN method through numerical simulations. The DDM method [13] is used for comparison.

5.1   Experimental Settings

In our experiment, to test the extreme performance of these methods, five tasks in each entrances are added to the task queues at the beginning. The tasks enter the sorting area at the beginning of each cycle. The speeds of AGVs are set to 2 units of distance per second. In addition, we change the size of the sorting area to test the performances of the above methods. The sizes of the sorting area include 14×14, 18×14, 22×18, 26×18, 30×22, and 34×22. With the size increasing, the numbers of entrances, exits, tasks are also increasing and it means increasing of the scale of the path planning problem. For the CTPMN method, we set a time limit of 1000s for a cycle. In addition, the calculation time of the DDM method is relatively short but deadlock may occur. Hence, for saving time, the experiment is regarded as a failure if the length of any path in the experiment exceeds $50 * (R + C)$. The performance indices of the experiment include success rate, makespan, and total travel steps. We run 50 experiments and average the results.

5.2 Experimental Results

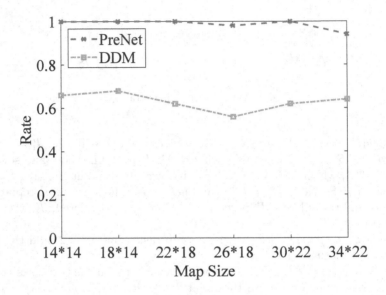

Fig. 6. The success rate versus map size.

The success rate determines the stability of the system, so it is the most important performance index. As shown in Fig. 6, the success rates of DDM method changes within $[0.56, 0.68]$, which cannot ensure the smooth operation of the system. In contrast, the success rates of the CTPMN method are close to 100%, which means the CTPMN method can solve most problems. The reason is that the multiflow network can obtain the optimal solution and our operating model can reduce the calculation time by limiting the number of AGVs to a certain extent.

The makespan is the length of time from the beginning of the experiment to the completion of the last task, and it reflects the efficiency of the system. The makespan values in Fig. 7 are the average value of successful tasks. It is shown that when the size of the sorting area is small, the makespan of the CTPMN method is relatively short. But the makespan increases accordingly and reach the level equivalent to the DDM method as the size increases. It is caused by increasing of the calculation time T_k^C for each calculation, which leads to increase in cycle T_k. Here, we must note that efficiency is the opposite of makespan. Therefore, on the whole, the efficiency of the CTPMN method is higher than that of the DDM method.

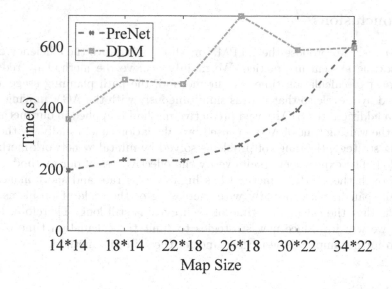

Fig. 7. The makespan versus map size.

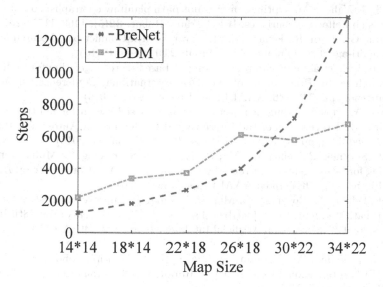

Fig. 8. The total travel steps versus map size.

The total travel steps is the sum of steps taken by all AGVs, and it represents the time taken by the AGVs from entering the sorting area to arriving the AGV waiting area. Therefore, the total travel steps reflects how fast a single task is completed, and it does not have a decisive impact on system efficiency. As shown in Fig. 8, the CTPMN method has fewer steps when the size is small, but the steps increase rapidly with increasing of map size. This is also caused by increasing of the calculation time T_k^C.

6 Conclusions

In this paper, we propose the CTPMN method to improve the efficiency of the AGV sorting system in practice. We mainly achieve the method by reducing the impact of calculation time. In our method, the path planning stage T_k^C is advanced by a cycle so that it runs simultaneously with the AGV moving stage T_{k-1}^M. In addition, the SVM-based predictive method is applied in our method to reduce the waiting time of AGVs caused by calculation time. Finally, by the task splitting strategy, the range of problems solved by mlutiflow network method is expanded. The experiment results verify the effectiveness of our method.

Although the CTPMN method has high success rate and short makespan, the makespan increases rapidly with increasing of the scale of problems. The reason is that the calculation time of each cycle is still long. Therefore, in the future, we will introduce new strategies to limit the calculation time of each cycle to further improve the performance of the CTPMN method.

References

1. Yu, J., LaValle, S.M.: Optimal multirobot path planning on graphs: complete algorithms and effective heuristics. IEEE Trans. Robot. **32**(5), 1163–1177 (2016)
2. Sharon, G., Stern, R., Felner, A., Sturtevant, N.R.: Conflict-based search for optimal multi-agent pathfinding. Artif. Intell. **219**, 40–66 (2015)
3. Boyarski, E., et al.: ICBS: improved conflict-based search algorithm for multi-agent pathfinding. In: Proceedings of the 24th International Conference on Artificial Intelligence, pp. 740–746. AAAI Press, Buenos Aires (2015)
4. Felner, A., et al.: Adding heuristics to conflict-based search for multi-agent path finding. In: Proceedings of the International Conference on Automated Planning and Scheduling, pp. 83–87. AAAI Press, The Netherlands (2018)
5. Li, J., Surynek, P., Felner, A., Ma, H., Kumar, T.S., Koenig, S.: Multi-agent path finding for large agents. In: Proceedings of the 33th AAAI Conference on Artificial Intelligence, pp. 7627–7634. AAAI Press, Hawaii (2019)
6. Li, J., Felner, A., Boyarski, E., Ma, H., Koenig, S.: Improved heuristics for multi-agent path finding with conflict-based search. In: Proceedings of the 28th International Joint Conference on Artificial Intelligence, pp. 442–449. AAAI Press, Macao (2019)
7. Yu, J., LaValle, S.M.: Planning optimal paths for multiple robots on graphs. In: the IEEE International Conference on Robotics and Automation, pp. 3612–3617. IEEE, Germany (2013)
8. Yu, J., LaValle, S.M.: Fast, near-optimal computation for multi-robot path planning on graphs. In: 27th AAAI Conference on Artificial Intelligence, pp. 155–157. AAAI Press, Washington (2013)
9. Murakami, K.: Time-space network model and MILP formulation of the conflict-free routing problem of a capacitated AGV system. Comput. Ind. Eng. **141**, 106270 (2020)
10. Nishi, T., Maeno, R.: Petri net decomposition approach to optimization of route planning problems for AGV systems. IEEE Trans. Autom. Sci. Eng. **7**(3), 523–537 (2010)

11. Nishi, T., Tanaka, Y.: Petri net decomposition approach for dispatching and conflict-free routing of bidirectional automated guided vehicle systems. IEEE Trans. Syst. Man Cybern. Syst. **42**(5), 1230–1243 (2012)
12. Bnaya, Z., Felner, A.: Conflict-oriented windowed hierarchical cooperative A*. In: 2014 IEEE International Conference on Robotics and Automation, pp. 3743–3748. IEEE, Hong Kong (2014)
13. Han, S.D., Yu, J.: DDM: fast near-optimal multi-robot path planning using diversified-path and optimal sub-problem solution database heuristics. IEEE Robot. Autom. Lett. **5**(2), 1350–1357 (2020)
14. Liu, Z., Wang, H., Wei, H., Liu, M., Liu, Y.H.: Prediction, planning, and coordination of thousand-warehousing-robot networks with motion and communication uncertainties. IEEE Trans. Autom. Sci. Eng. 1–13 (2020)

UACHR: Accurate CSI-Based Human Behavior Recognition Using Gaussian Goodness

Ying Liu(✉) [ID], Lu Chen [ID], Guoqing Li [ID], Jie Zhang [ID], Shenghua Dong [ID], and Zhiyong Tao [ID]

School of Electronic and Information Engineering, Liaoning Technical University, Huludao 125105, Liaoning, China

Abstract. Human motion and behavior analysis has become a new research field in pervasive computing, in which the feature modeling of behavior is particularly critical. This paper proposes an accurate CSI-based human behavior feature modeling method using Gaussian goodness. Firstly, this paper starts from the data distribution of CSI to find the difference between the still and action stages of the human body. By introducing Gaussian goodness of fit R-square, the degree of Gaussian fit of different stages is measured quantitatively, and the stage of action occurrence is extracted effectively. Secondly, in order to make full use of the CSI features of multiple antennas, a number of DTW-based FKNN classifiers are constructed to jointly judge behaviors at the level of neighboring samples. Experimental results show that the accuracy of the method is 95.33% and 91.33% respectively in the meeting room and the laboratory, and the system training time is greatly reduced compared with the KNN classifier.

Keywords: Behavior recognition · Channel state information · FKNN · Multi-antenna joint decision

1 Introduction

In recent decades, the analytical recognition of human motion and behavior has become an emerging research area in pervasive computing due to advances in computing and sensing technologies and interest in behavioral or gesture recognition applications such as security and surveillance, human-computer interaction, and somatic gaming. However, there are some limitations in the traditional methods of human activity perception. The method based on computer vision will be affected by lighting conditions, obstacles and other factors, and it is also easy to invade privacy. The running distance of a low-cost radar system is limited, usually about 10 cm [1]. Although the solution based on wearable sensors realizes fine-grained behavior perception, its high cost and the need to carry the sensor around limit its practicality. To overcome the above problems and meet people's needs for low cost, high precision and convenient use of human behavior perception technology, WiFi-based behavior recognition technology has emerged.

Channel state information (CSI) is available to common commercial WiFi devices by modifying the Linux driver of the Intel 5300 NIC. In contrast to received signal strength

© Springer Nature Singapore Pte Ltd. 2021
L. Cui and X. Xie (Eds.): CWSN 2021, CCIS 1509, pp. 136–149, 2021.
https://doi.org/10.1007/978-981-16-8174-5_11

(RSS), CSI is a fine-grained value of the physical layer that provides channel estimates for each subcarrier of each transmission link and can reflect multipath effects caused by small-scale fading and micro-motion [2]. The CSI-Speed model proposed by the CARM system in the literature [3] quantifies the relationship between the amplitude variation of CSI and human motion speed and provides a model basis for subsequent studies, but the time complexity of the identification method is high. The literature [4] and [5] used a method based on moving variance for data extraction, but this method is susceptible to environmental and the threshold usually varies from environment to environment. The Wi-Alarm system proposed in the literature [6] ignores the data preprocessing process, extracts the mean and variance as features directly from the original CSI magnitude, and uses the support vector machine (SVM) for human perception. Although the computational overhead is saved, the extracted features are not accurate enough due to the vulnerability of the original CSI data to interference from the external environment. Moreover, only limited time-domain statistical features are used, which fails to make full use of the CSI data information and eventually leads to limited recognition accuracy. Literature [7] proposes an exercise activity recognition system based on CSI, which uses principal component analysis (PCA) to obtain activity features, and uses K nearest neighbor (KNN) classifier to find the nearest neighbor sample of unknown samples in the pre-built standard activity feature library, and takes it as the final activity type. However, this method only uses CSI amplitude information of a single antenna and fails to make full use of the Multiple Input and Multiple Output (MIMO) system.

Given the problems existing in the above documents, an accurate CSI-based human behavior recognition using Gaussian goodness is proposed. Since the phase information is easily affected by clock synchronization error, the original phase distribution received is disorganized and cannot be used directly. Therefore, the amplitude signal, which is relatively stable and easy to extract, is used as the base signal in this paper for human behavior recognition. Firstly, in view of the phenomenon that CSI data obeys the Gaussian distribution and the signal distribution in action stage is different from that in still stage due to the influence of human motion, this paper effectively extracts action behavior data by introducing the Gaussian goodness of fit. Secondly, most human behavior recognition algorithms directly extract the signal features of a single antenna, but these features are often random, which leads to low accuracy of behavior recognition. Therefore, UACHR builds a one-transmitter and three-receiver system, makes full use of the data information of each receiving antenna, and implements joint judgment on action categories at the level of neighboring samples to improve the accuracy of action recognition. At last, aiming at the problem that traditional KNN has a large amount of computation and slow classification speed, and cannot effectively calculate the distance between two similar but misaligned actions, a classification algorithm combining fast K nearest neighbor (FKNN) and dynamic time warping (DTW) is proposed, which greatly reduces the computational overhead of the system.

The main contributions of UACHR are summarized as follows:

- UACHR demonstrates that the amplitude distribution of CSI obeys the Gaussian distribution, and the Gaussian distribution fitted by CSI amplitude in action stage is different from that in still stage. According to this, an action data extraction method is proposed. The method can realize accurate action extraction and reduce the time complexity of the system.

- UACHR analyzes the shortcomings of single-antenna signal for feature modeling and proposes a multi-antenna signal information fusion method to overcome its shortcomings. This method makes full use of the CSI information on all antennas, reduces the direct impact of bad links on the results, and improves the recognition accuracy of the system. FKNN algorithm is used to further reduce the computational overhead of the system.
- We implemented UACHR in a relatively empty meeting room and a laboratory with severe multipath. The experimental results show that the average recognition accuracy reaches 95.33% in the meeting room and 91.33% in the laboratory, which proves that the system proposed in this paper has high recognition accuracy even in different environments.

The rest of this paper is summarized as follows: First, we summarize the related work in Sect. 2, and introduce the system design in Sect. 3. In Sect. 4, we give our experimental design and evaluation results. Finally, we summarize our work in Sect. 5.

2 Related Work

Generally speaking, the methods of action recognition can be divided into invasive action recognition and non-invasive action recognition.

2.1 Invasive Action Recognition

TypingRing [8] designs a ring composed of embedded sensors and a microcontroller, and asks the user to wear the ring on the middle finger to detect the position of the user's hand and typing gesture. This method can detect and report key events in real-time, with an average accuracy rate of 98.67%. Xu et al. [9] recognizes 37 gestures with 98% accuracy by capturing accelerometer and gyroscope data from a smartwatch worn on the wrist. Although the action recognition based on wearable sensors has achieved high recognition accuracy, wearing devices will bring some discomfort, and in addition, it also faces the problem of forgetting to carry them. Literature [10] uses cameras to collect human image data, then extracts the body contour from the background, and uses SVM to identify the falling action, and finally achieves more than 96% accuracy in different databases. Martin et al. [11] achieve the recognition of seven dangerous actions of the driver by capturing the driver's body nodes with a Kinect depth camera. However, they are limited to line-of-sight perception, cannot be identified when the target is blocked by obstacles, and require high illumination conditions. Infrared-based sensing uses infrared to image the human body, which is not limited by light conditions and can realize non-line-of-sight sensing, but the sensing range is limited, and expensive additional equipment is needed. Furthermore, all intrusive perception inevitably involves privacy issues.

2.2 Non-invasive Action Recognition

WiFi-based action recognition not only protects the user's privacy well, but is also unaffected by light. WiSee [12] uses software radio peripherals to receive signals and extracts Doppler frequency shift caused by human motion to detect nine gestures such as push and pull, with an average accuracy of 94%. Adib and Katabi [13] use inverse synthetic aperture radar and USRP software radio system to collect frequency modulated continuous wave (FMCW) signals from the environment and realize through-wall monitoring of human body and through-wall transmission of gesture information. Literature [3] establishes the CARM model by investigating the relationship between WiFi signal and human body speed. The model can cope with the change of environment and achieve 96% recognition accuracy. However, the above methods need special USRP equipment, which limits their large-scale application.

In addition to specialized hardware devices, common commercial WiFi devices can provide RSS and CSI to sense human activities. WiGest [14] recognizes seven gestures by analyzing the changing characteristics of RSS signals. Haseeb et al. [15] propose an RSS-based gesture recognition system, which adopts Long Short-Term Memory (LSTM) and Recurrent Neural Network (RNN). The system achieves a classification accuracy of 94%. However, RSS is the measurement of radio signal power, which is greatly influenced by the environment.

Compared to RSS, CSI is fine-grained physical layer information, which has multipath resolution and can sense subtle changes of signals. Therefore, CSI has natural advantages in action recognition. Unlike traditional recognition methods, the CSI-based approach uses existing WiFi devices in the environment to collect data and does not require the deployment of new devices. Moreover, it has a wide working range and can realize non-line-of-sight perception, even through wall perception. Inspired by this, we design an efficient behavior recognition method based on CSI.

3 System Design

The UACHR system consists of four basic modules: Data Collection, Data Preprocessing, Action Extraction and Action Recognition. The architecture and workflow of the system are shown in Fig. 1.

3.1 Data Processing

The CSI amplitude signal cannot be directly used for activity recognition due to the unstable distribution of indoor environment interference and electromagnetic noise. Since the frequency of human motion is only in the low-frequency band, Butterworth low-pass filter can effectively remove the random fluctuation of CSI amplitude signal caused by high-frequency interference information and retain the fluctuation characteristics of the original signal.

Considering that the amplitude changes of the CSI of all subcarriers are correlated when the human body moves, and each antenna pair receives CSI information from 30 subcarriers, its high dimensionality leads to an increase in computational time

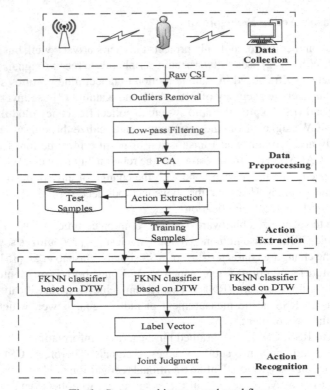

Fig.1. System architecture and workflow

complexity. Therefore, PCA is applied in this paper to keep the information related to motion and effectively reduce the dimension of subcarriers. Because of the irrelevance of environmental noise, PCA can also remove some in-band random noise.

The principal components processed by PCA are arranged in order of decreasing variance. The amplitudes of the top four principal components are shown in Fig. 2.

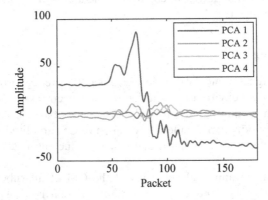

Fig.2. Signal amplitude diagram of main components after PCA

It can be seen from the figure that the first principal component has the largest variance, is superior to other components in the description of motion characteristics, and can provide the highest contribution rate. Since the principal components are irrelevant, the first principal component can be retained independently without losing any information.

3.2 Action Extraction Based on Gaussian Goodness of Fit

As the collected CSI signals are continuously stored, the signals processed by the method described in Sect. 3.1 contain both effective action signals and some invalid signals. If the first principal component of the processed signal is used directly as a feature, the accuracy would be affected due to a large amount of stationary data information. And this also greatly increases the computational overhead. Therefore, it is necessary to extract the signals corresponding to human motion behavior.

It is clear that when the human body is in a still state, the collected CSI data reflects the reflection of static objects in the room. Ideally, the CSI signal amplitude should be constant during this time. However, in the practical environment, the signal is often affected by environmental noise as it propagates through space. And this noise is usually white Gaussian noise. As is known to all, the amplitude distribution of white Gaussian noise follows the Gaussian distribution, that is, the amplitude of CSI in the still state should follow the Gaussian distribution. To verify this analysis, the probability density distribution curve of CSI amplitude data in the still state of human body is obtained by simulation, and then the CSI amplitude data in this still state is fitted by Gauss, and the result is shown in Fig. 3.

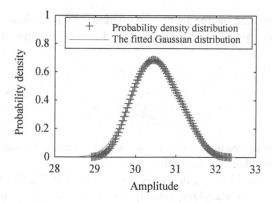

Fig.3. Probability density and fitting Gaussian distribution of raw data

The abscissa represents the amplitude information of CSI, the ordinate represents the probability density, the blue scatter diagram represents the probability density distribution of the human body in the still state. Each point represents the probability density value corresponding to the amplitude, and the red curve is the Gaussian distribution diagram fitted by the raw CSI data. It can be seen from Fig. 3 that although they are not completely coincident, the trends are basically the same, indicating that the CSI amplitude in the still state is basically subject to the Gaussian distribution.

When the human body conducts behavior, CSI data information fluctuates obviously. The fluctuation is not only caused by environmental noise, but also caused by the change of human behavior. Since the action has an effect on the signal fluctuations, the Gaussian distribution fitted by amplitude information must be different from that when the human body is still. The first principal component in Fig. 2 is evenly divided into 8 segments, and the probability density distribution of each segment is shown in Fig. 4. It can be seen from the figure that the trends of the third, fourth, fifth, and sixth segments are obviously different from that of the distribution in the still state. Based on this, we propose an action extraction algorithm based on Gaussian goodness of fit.

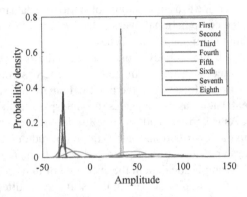

Fig.4. The fitting Gaussian distribution of each segment

To better measure the degree of fit of the values, R^2 is often used in statistics to describe how well the model fits the data, and the formula is shown in Eq. (1) [16]:

$$R^2 = 1 - \frac{\sum\limits_{i=1}^{n} (Y_i - y_i)^2}{\sum\limits_{i=1}^{n} \left(Y_i - \overline{Y}\right)^2} \tag{1}$$

Where y_i and Y_i are the values on the fitting line and the corresponding actual values, and $\overline{Y}$ is the average value of the actual values.

In order to measure the fitting degree of each segment in Fig. 4, the goodness of fit R^2 of each segment is calculated respectively. The results are shown in Fig. 5. It can be seen from the figure that the minimum value of R^2 exists in the action stage. Therefore, the action data can be extracted by taking this as a node and extracting the data on both sides of this node according to the actual needs.

3.3   Action Classification

Construction of FKNN Classifier Based on DTW. The core idea of FKNN is to sort the training samples effectively, and construct the index table by sampling at equal intervals. When the samples to be classified are given, they can be compared with the index

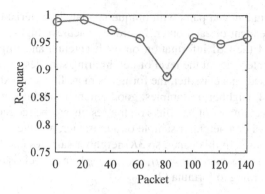

Fig. 5. R-square value distribution of each segment

table, and the K nearest samples can be obtained after calculation [17]. Compared with the traditional KNN, this algorithm can reduce the search range of K nearest neighbors of samples and greatly reduce the computational complexity of the system. When calculating the feature distance between two samples, because of the randomness of human actions, even when the same person does the same action, the execution time and speed will not be completely the same, so the obtained feature vectors are very similar in shape but not completely aligned. DTW algorithm can effectively measure the similarity between two action features by distorting one or both of the two sequences [18]. Therefore, this paper combines the FKNN algorithm with DTW algorithm and makes full use of the advantages of the two algorithms. The specific implementation steps are as follows.

Step1: Randomly select a training sample as the reference point, assuming that the point $P(p_1, p_2, ..., p_n)$, where $p_1, p_2, ..., p_n$ are the extracted feature values.

Step2: Calculate the DTW distance d from each training sample to point P, and form an ordered queue by sorting from small to large. The queue contains the distance d from all samples to P, labels, and feature vectors.

Step3: To search and find quickly and conveniently, the sample information of the ordered queue is sequentially registered in an index table with l as the sampling interval, and the value of l is taken according to the actual needs.

Step4: Given any sample x in the test sample, calculate the DTW distance d_{xP} from x to P, and find the sample Q closest to P in the index table. With Q as the center, determine the previous sample Q_1 and the next sample Q_2 in the index table. Then take these two samples as the boundary, intercept all samples between these two samples in the ordered queue established in Step2, calculate the DTW distance between these samples and sample x, and select the K samples closest to x.

Multi-antenna Joint Decision. In theory, human activity recognition can be realized by using a single link on a single antenna pair. However, due to the different sensitivity of different actions, bad links appear randomly in different antenna pairs, so directly using a specific single WiFi link will lead to inaccurate extracted action information. Because

CSI is collected from antenna pairs with unique spatial characteristics, the changes of each link are independent of each other. In order to achieve higher spatial resolution, we make full use of the CSI information on each antenna and implements the joint decision on action categories at the level of neighboring samples. Compared with joint decision directly based on a classifier, the former is more fine-grained. By adjusting the output parameters of neighboring samples, good antenna link information can be fully utilized, and the direct impact of bad links on the results can be reduced. Specifically, if q_i represents the label of a neighbor sample of a classifier, and there are three antennas at the receiving end used in this paper, so $3K$ neighbor samples can be obtained. Then the label vector of all classifiers is $q = [q_1, q_2, ..., q_{3K}]$, and the class of unknown action can be obtained according to formula (2):

$$M = \max_{j \in [1,2,\cdots,n]} \left[\frac{\sum_{i=1}^{3K} (q_i == j)}{3K} \right] \tag{2}$$

Where n represents the number of predefined actions, and the M value corresponding to j is the final action label.

The final action label M is determined by using the CSI on three antennas, which fully considers the spatial diversity of antennas. CSI information fusion on three antennas overcomes the shortcomings of single antenna judgment and improves the recognition accuracy of the system. Moreover, SIMO system achieves a good balance between judgment accuracy and system efficiency, which ensures that the accuracy is improved without greatly increasing the running time.

4   Implementation and Evaluation

In this section, we conduct experiments to evaluate the performance of UACHR. In Sect. 4.1, we describe the experimental setup. In Sect. 4.2, we give the experimental environment. In Sect. 4.3, we analyze the experimental results.

4.1   Experimental Setup

We use the commercial TP-Link wireless router as the sender, which works in the mode of IEEE 802.11n AP at 2.4 GHz, with a packet rate of 50 pkts/s. We use the desktop computer equipped with Intel 5300 network card as the receiver, analyze the CSI value by using Linux CSI-Tool, and further process it by using MATLAB software.

4.2   Experimental Environment

In this paper, two real experimental environments are selected for performance analysis, including an empty meeting room and a relatively complex laboratory, as shown in Fig. 6. In these two environments, the sender and receiver are deployed. The height of the antenna from the ground is 1m, and the distance between the sender and receiver antennas is 2 m. Volunteers are invited to conduct experiments repeatedly in experimental environments. Four volunteers provided five behavioral activities: bending, sitting down, squatting, standing up, and walking. For each activity in different environments, each person performed 25 times, and finally, 500 sets of data were collected in each experimental environment. Randomly select 70 sets of data for each action as training samples, and use the remaining 30 sets of data for each action as test samples.

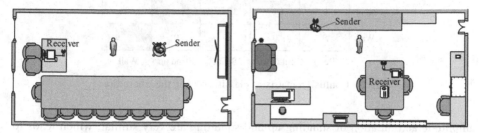

Fig. 6. Experimental environment for behavior activities

4.3 Analysis of Experimental Results

Activity Identification Accuracy. Figure 7 and Fig. 8 are confusion matrices for identifying five actions in the meeting room and laboratory environment respectively, where each row represents the real behavior and each column represents the predicted behaviour.

	Bend	Sit down	Squat	Stand up	Walk
Bend	96.67	0	3.33	0	0
Sit down	0	93.33	6.67	0	0
Squat	6.67	3.33	90	0	0
Stand up	0	0	3.33	96.67	0
Walk	0	0	0	0	100

Fig. 7. Confusion matrix of classification in the meeting room

It can be seen from Fig. 7 that the recognition accuracy of "bend", "sit down", "squat", "stand up" and "walk" in the meeting room environment is 96.67%, 93.33%, 90%, 96.67%, and 100%, respectively, and the average recognition rate of these five actions is 95.33%. The highest misjudgment rate mainly comes from squatting. This action has a top-down process, as does bending down and sitting down. In addition to the similarity of the movement directions, bending down is often included in squatting down and sitting down due to behavioral habits, thus affecting the classification results. It can be seen from Fig. 8 that the recognition accuracy in the laboratory environment is 86.67%, 96.67%, 93.33%, 80%, and 100% respectively, and the average recognition rate is 91.33%. The

	Bend	Sit down	Squat	Stand up	Walk
Bend	86.67	6.67	3.33	3.33	0
Sit down	0	96.67	3.33	0	0
Squat	0	3.33	93.33	3.33	0
Stand up	0	6.67	13.33	80	0
Walk	0	0	0	0	100

Fig. 8. Confusion matrix of classification in the laboratory

amplitude and duration of standing up and squatting are very similar, which leads to a poor recognition effect in a multi-path complex laboratory. The recognition rate of walking can reach 100% in both complex laboratory and empty meeting room due to the fact that it is quite different from the other four actions.

Multi-antenna Combination and a Single Antenna. After many experiments, it is found that when K takes 3, there is an optimal value. At this time, the recognition accuracy of each action under multi-antenna joint decision and the single antenna is shown in Fig. 9.

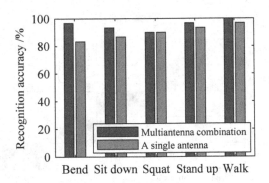

Fig. 9. Comparison of the classification effects of each action under the optimal K value

It can be seen from the figure that the recognition rate of the multi-antenna joint decision adopted in this paper is higher than that of the single antenna except that the recognition rate of squatting action is the same as that of the single antenna. The recognition advantage for bending movements is more prominent. This is because the multi-antenna joint decision can make full use of the rich detailed information of multiple antennas to effectively identify actions. On the whole, the multi-antenna joint decision method adopted in this paper is better than the single-antenna method, which reduces the recognition error and is beneficial to the recognition of activities.

Comparison of FKNN and KNN. In order to verify the performance of the FKNN algorithm, KNN and FKNN are used for recognition in the meeting room and laboratory respectively. The error rate and running time of the two classification algorithms are shown in Table 1. It can be seen from the table that the error rates of FKNN in the two environments are 4.67% and 7.33%, which are slightly higher than those of the KNN algorithm, but the running time of the FKNN algorithm are 5.8793 s and 5.7099 s, which are far lower than that of KNN algorithm in the same environment, greatly reducing the calculation time of the system. Therefore, the FKNN algorithm can effectively improve the system operation efficiency at the expense of certain accuracy.

Table 1. Comparison of error rate and running time of two classification algorithms

Environment	Algorithm	Error rate (%)	Running time (s)
Meeting room	KNN	4.00	40.2914
	FKNN	4.67	5.8793
Laboratory	KNN	6.00	40.5137
	FKNN	7.33	5.7099

Comparison of Methods. To verify the overall performance of the UACHR method proposed in this paper, comparative experiments are carried out with the WIG [19] and the traditional RSSI model system. The recognition accuracy rates of the three methods are shown in Fig. 10. The average recognition accuracy of the WIG method is 89.33%, among which the highest rate of misrecognition is squatting and standing up. The reason is that these two actions are reciprocal processes, and the limited time-domain statistical features extracted by the WIG method are very similar. The method based on the traditional RSSI model uses coarse-grained received signal strength, which fluctuates greatly due to environmental interference, so the average recognition rate is low, which is 84.67%.

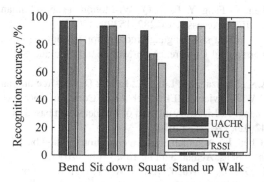

Fig. 10. Comparison of classification effect of three methods

It can be seen from Fig. 10 that the UACHR method used in this article is superior to the other two methods regardless of the single action or the overall recognition accuracy. This advantage is particularly obvious for the recognition of squatting actions, which are easily confused with other actions, demonstrating the effectiveness and robustness of the method in this paper.

5 Conclusion

We propose an accurate CSI-based human behavior recognition using Gaussian goodness. The method uses low-pass filtering and principal component analysis to denoise the original data, and effectively extracts the action behavior data through Gaussian goodness of fit. The first principal component with time-frequency details is used as feature vector. We use the feature vectors of each antenna at the receiving end to construct the FKNN classifier based on DTW and make a joint judgment, thus realizing the recognition of five actions. The algorithm is verified in two typical indoor environments, and the experimental results show that the average recognition rate reaches 95.33% in the empty meeting room and 91.33% in a laboratory with severe multipath, which proves that this method has a better recognition rate in different environments, and compared with the traditional RSSI method, the CSI-based human behavior recognition is more robust. It should be pointed out that in this paper, the single action of a single person is recognized, and the detection and recognition of continuous actions or simultaneous actions of multiple people will be studied in future work to realize human behavior recognition in more complex scenes.

Acknowledgments. This work was supported by the National Key Research and Development Program of China (No. 2018YFB1403303), and Liaoning Provincial Natural Science Foundation of China (No. 2019-ZD-0038).

References

1. Li, H., He, X., Chen, X., Fang, Y., Fang, Q.: Wi-motion: a robust human activity recognition using WiFi signals. IEEE Access **7**, 153287–153299 (2019)
2. Shang, J., Wu, J.: A robust sign language recognition system with multiple Wi-Fi devices. In: IEEE 14th International Conference on Mobile Ad Hoc and Sensor Systems (MASS), pp.19–24 (2017)
3. Wang, W., Liu, A.X., Shahzad, M., Ling, K., Lu, S.: Device-free human activity recognition using commercial WiFi devices. IEEE J. Sel. Areas Commun. **35**(5), 1118–1131 (2017)
4. Ran, Y., Yu, J., Chang, J., Li, X.: A method of fall detection based on CSI. J. Yunnan Univ. (Nat. Sci. Edn.) **42**(02), 220–227 (2020)
5. Guo, A., Xu, Z., Chen, L.: A human action recognition method based on WiFi channel state information. Chin. J. Sens. Actuat. **32**(11), 1688–1693 (2019)
6. Wang, T., Yang, D., Zhang, S., Wu, Y., Xu, S.: Wi-alarm: low-cost passive intrusion detection using Wi-Fi. Sensors **19**(10), 23–35 (2019)

7. Xiao, F., Chen, J., Xie, X., Gui, L., Sun, L., Wang, R.: SEARE: a system for exercise activity recognition and quality evaluation based on green sensing. IEEE Trans. Emerg. Top. Comput. 1–10 (2018)

8. Nirjon, S., Gummeson, J., Gelb, D., Kim, K.H.: TypingRing: a wearable ring platform for text input. In: 13th Annual International Conference on Mobile Systems, Applications, and Services (2015)

9. Xu, C., Pathak, P.H., Mohapatra, P.: Finger-writing with smartwatch: a case for finger and hand gesture recognition using smartwatch. In: 16th International Workshop on Mobile Computing Systems and Applications, pp.9–14 (2015)

10. Harrou, F., Zerrouki, N., Sun, Y., Houacine, A.: Vision-based fall detection system for improving safety of elderly people. IEEE Instrum. Meas. Mag. **20**(6), 49–55 (2017)

11. Martin, M., Popp, J., Anneken, M., Voit, M., Stiefelhagen, R.: Body pose and context information for driver secondary task detection. In: 29th IEEE Intelligent Vehicles Symposium (IV), pp.2015–2021 (2018)

12. Pu, Q., Gupta, S., Gollakota, S., Patel, S.: Whole-home gesture recognition using wireless signals. In: the 19th Annual International Conference on Mobile Computing and Networking, pp.27–38 (2013)

13. Adib, F., Katabi, D.: See through walls with Wi-Fi! In: ACM Conference Special Interest Group Data Communication, pp.75–86 (2013)

14. Abdelnasser, H., Youssef, M., Harras, K.A.: WiGest: a ubiquitous WiFi-based gesture recognition system. In: 2015 IEEE Conference on Computer Communications (INFOCOM), pp.1472–1480 (2015)

15. Haseeb, M.A.A., Parasuraman, R.: Wisture: RNN-based learning of wireless signals for gesture recognition in unmodified smartphones. arXiv:1707.08569 (2017)

16. Xu, J.: Further research on fatigue statistics intelligence. Acta Aeronaut. Astronaut. Sinica 1–12 (2021)

17. Leng, Y., Zhang, H., Zhang, W.: Introduction to Machine Learning to Actual Combat: Practical Application of MATLAB. Tsinghua University Press, Beijing (2019)

18. Melgarejo, P., Zhang, X., Ramanathan, P., Chu, D.: Leveraging directional antenna capabilities for fine-grained gesture recognition. In: 2014 ACM International Joint Conference on Pervasive and Ubiquitous Computing, pp.13–17 (2014)

19. He, W., Wu, K., Zou, Y., Ming, Z.: WiG: WiFi-based gesture recognition system. In: International Conference on Computer Communication & Networks, pp.1–7 (2015)

Security and Privacy Protection on Internet of Things

A Fast General Image Encryption Method Based on Deep Learning Compressed Sensing and Compound Chaotic System

Yuan Guo, Jinlin Jiang[✉], and Wei Chen

College of Computer and Control Engineering, Qiqihar University, Heilongjiang 161006, China

Abstract. Compressed sensing aims to reduce image storage space and transmission costs. It is widely used in image reconstruction and encryption algorithm. Nowadays, an increasing number of researchers are focusing on the combination of these two tasks, but most of the current algorithms have low reconstruction quality, long running time, small key space and poor security. For this reason, this paper proposes a general image compression encryption algorithm based on deep learning compressed sensing and compound chaotic systems. This algorithm has a larger key space and great advantages in terms of time-consuming. By using bilinear interpolation, fully connected layer and convolutional network compress the image. Then the two-dimensional cloud model and Logistic composite chaotic system encrypt the compressed image, and complete the scrambling and XOR in one step. In the reconstruction network, after the decrypted image is amplified by bilinear interpolation, the convolutional neural and the fully connected layer reconstruct the image contour and color information respectively. The experimental results show that the compression encryption algorithm can be applied to both grayscale images and RGB format color images, and the reconstruction quality is greatly improved. The composite chaotic encryption algorithm closely associates the plaintext with the key to achieve the encryption effect of one image and one encryption. Scrambling and XOR are performed at the same time so that the compression encryption algorithm has higher security.

Keywords: Deep Learning · Image encryption · Compressed sensing · Compound chaotic system

1 Introduction

With the rapid development of Internet technology, digital images have become an important carrier of information transmission. The compressed sensing theory proposed by Candes, Tao et al. [1–3] enables the sampling rate to be much lower than the Nyquist sampling rate to compress the signal. The traditional compressed sensing reconstruction

This work was partially supported by National Natural Science Foundation of China (Grant No. 61872204); Natural Science Foundation of Heilongjiang Province (Grant No: LH2021F056); Postgraduate Innovation Research Project (Grant No. YJSCX2020050).

© Springer Nature Singapore Pte Ltd. 2021
L. Cui and X. Xie (Eds.): CWSN 2021, CCIS 1509, pp. 153–169, 2021.
https://doi.org/10.1007/978-981-16-8174-5_12

method is based on the sparse characteristics and finds the optimal solution to an under-determined equation to reconstruct the image. However, the real image does not exactly satisfy the sparsity in some transformations, making the reconstruction quality low and the Iterative solution is time-consuming. The compressed sensing algorithm based on deep learning uses a purely data-driven way for compression and reconstruction, which relaxes the assumption conditions on the sparsity of image signals. The reconstruction network of ReconNet [5] consists of a fully connected layer and two SRCNN models [6], DR^2-Net [7] applying residual blocks to the reconstruction network, and MSRNet [8] proposes a multi-scale residual network structure, which are all compressed sensing algorithms based on deep learning. Compared with traditional compressed sensing algorithms, they time-consuming more short and have high reconstruction quality, but their focus is on reconstructing the network, and the image quality of using random matrix compression is poor, which limits The reconstruction quality of the image. CSNet+ [9] uses a convolutional neural network, which consists of three parts: compressed sampling, initial linear reconstruction and non-linear reconstruction, which consumes less time and has higher reconstruction quality.

Chaotic systems are widely used in image encryption due to their pseudo-random, ergodic and non-periodic characteristics, such as in literature [10–12]. Although they can obtain good encryption results, the sizes of the chaotic sequence and the ciphertext are as large as the original image. And the scrambling and diffusion are performed separately, which the number of cycles is large, so there are problems such as time-consuming and inconvenient transmission. Reference [13–15] combines traditional compressed sensing with image encryption to facilitate the storage and transmission of gray-scale images, and the security is also guaranteed, but the total time is longer than the time for direct encryption on the original image.

Different from traditional image encryption methods that directly perform encryption operations such as scrambling and diffusion on plaintext images, this paper combines the theory of deep learning compressed sensing to design a general image fast encryption algorithm. Convolutional neural network is used to compress the image in blocks, and a compound chaotic system is designed to encrypt the compressed image. Decryption is the reverse operation of encryption, and finally the image is restored by reconstructing the network. Deep learning compression and reconstruction of the network effectively shorten the running time, the proposed compound chaotic system and one-step scrambling XOR improve the security of encryption. The specific innovations are as follows:

(1) Bilinear interpolation is used on the compression network to compress the width and height of the image. The lost information is learned by the fully connected layer. Then the 3 channels are compressed into 1 channel through the convolutional neural network, which makes the compression network can obtain high-quality compressed images. For color images, the fully connected layer is very important, and the image quality reconstructed without the fully connected layer will be very poor.

(2) In the encryption algorithm, the two-dimensional cloud model and the use of Logistic associate the plaintext with the key to realize one-picture encryption and improve the security of the algorithm. At the same time, scrambling and XOR are performed at the same time. Under the premise of ensuring the encryption effect, the number of cycles is reduced and the encryption time is shortened.

(3) Compared with traditional compressed sensing, the application of deep learning compressed sensing can greatly reduce the running time and improve the quality of the algorithm.

2 Basic Theory

2.1 Structure of Compound Chaotic System

In this paper, we use the 6 digital features of the expected value (referred as (Ex_1, Ex_2)), entropy (referred as (En_1, En_2)) and super entropy (referred as (He_1, He_2)) of the two-dimensional cloud model to generate a set of random membership degrees (referred as u_i). The forward generator algorithm of the two-dimensional cloud model can be expressed as:

Generate two sets of normal random numbers, with En_1 and En_2 as expected values, He_1 and He_2 as standard deviations, as shown below:

$$\begin{cases} y_{1i} = R_n(En_1, He_1), \\ y_{2i} = R_n(En_2, He_2), \end{cases} \tag{1}$$

The n is the number of generations. Then generate two sets of normal random numbers, with Ex_1 and Ex_2 as expected values, y_{1i} and y_{2i} as standard deviations, as shown below:

$$\begin{cases} x_{1i} = R_n(Ex_1, y_{1i}), \\ x_{2i} = R_n(Ex_2, y_{2i}), \end{cases} \tag{2}$$

Finally calculate u_i, as shown below:

$$u_i = \exp(-\frac{(x_{1i} - Ex_1)^2}{2 \times y_{1_i}^2} - \frac{(x2i - Ex_2)^2}{2 \times y_{2_i}^2}), 0 < u_i < 1, \tag{3}$$

Logistic sequence expression as:

$$z_i = r \times z_i \times (1 - z_i), 0 < z_i < 1, \tag{4}$$

Concatenate u_i and Logistic to get the C-L chaotic sequence as:

$$c_i = (u_i + z_i) \bmod 1, 0 < c_i < 1. \tag{5}$$

2.2 Encryption Formula

The encryption algorithm in this paper will perform scrambling and XOR synchronously, which can be expressed as:

$$\begin{cases} encry\_img_i = img_{\arg \text{sort}(u_i)} \oplus \text{int}(c_i \times 255) \oplus encry\_img_{i-1}, i! = 0 \\ encry\_img_i = img_{\arg \text{sort}(u_i)} \oplus \text{int}(c_i \times 255) \oplus \text{int}(img\_mean \times 255), i = 0 \end{cases} \quad (6)$$

Among them, the img is the compressed image and $\oplus$ is the XOR operation. The argsort(u_i) is the corresponding subscript after arranging the uisequence from small to large.

3 Image Compression and Reconstruction

The compressed reconstruction network (CCSNet) of this paper, before compression the image needs to be divided into multiple original image blocks with a size of $3 \times 33 \times 33$ without overlapping and then spliced into a large image after reconstruction. The network uses RGB format color images by default. For grayscale images, it can be copied to become 3 channels and then compressed. After reconstruction, the average value of the corresponding positions of computing the 3 channels to become 1 channel, so that the entire network is also suitable for grayscale images, and there is no need to train the network separately. The compression reconstruction network with color image sampling rate MR $= 0.2$ is shown in Fig. 1.

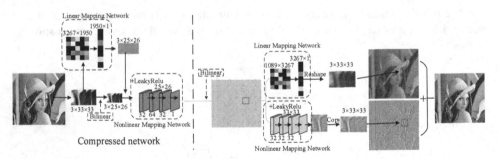

Fig.1. Color image compression and reconstruction network, sampling rate MR $= 0.2$ (Color figure online)

3.1 Compression Network

In the compression network, bilinear interpolation is used to compress the width and height of the image, which miss the part information is learned by the fully connected layer. The convolutional neural network is responsible for merging the 3 channels into 1 channel.

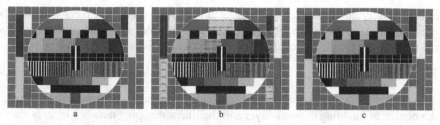

Fig. 2. The impact of the presence or absence of a fully connected layer in the compression network on reconstruction quality (a) Original image; (b) PSNR = 24.25; (c) PSNR = 32.81.

It can be seen from Fig. 2 that after the lack of a fully connected layer, the quality of the reconstructed image is poor, especially the color information. So for color images, a fully connected layer is essential. The input value of the compression network (referred as F^c) is the original image block (referred as x_i). Convolutional layer weights (referred as W^c), fully connected layer weights (referred as W^f) and compressed images (referred as y_i) are obtained through Adam method training, which can be expressed as:

$$y_i = F^c(\text{Bilinear}(x_i), W^f, W^c). \tag{7}$$

3.2 Structure of Compound Chaotic System

In the reconstruction network, bilinear interpolation is used to enlarge the compressed image. The nonlinear mapping network layer and the linear mapping network layer are used to reconstruct the image.

3.2.1 Non-linear Mapping Network Layer

This network layer consists of a convolutional neural network, which is mainly responsible for reconstructing the contour information of the image. The contour information can be displayed using 1 channel, but to merge with the linear mapping network layer, 1 channel needs to be copied as 3 channels. The y_i reconstructs the contour information of x_i (referred as F^b) through a convolutional neural network (referred as x_i^b), which can be expressed as:

$$x_i^b = Copy\left(F^b(y_i, W^b), 3\right). \tag{8}$$

The W^b is the weight parameter, and the Copy means copying 1 channel as 3 channels.

3.2.2 Linear Mapping Network Layer

Compared with contour information, color information is more complex and requires more weight parameters. Although the convolutional neural network can reconstruct the image contour information very well, the weight parameters are limited, and too many network layers will cause the reconstruction time to increase. So the network layer uses a fully connected layer, which is mainly responsible for reconstructing the color information on the image. The y_i reconstructs the color information of x_i (referred as $x_i{}^l$) through the fully connected layer (referred as F^l), which can be expressed as:

$$x_i^l = F^l(y_i, W^l). \tag{9}$$

The W^l is the weight parameter of the fully connected layer. The image reconstructed by the nonlinear mapping network layer and the linear mapping network layer is shown in Fig. 3.

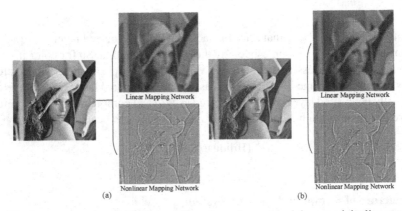

Fig.3. The image reconstructed by the nonlinear mapping network layer and the linear mapping network layer (a) Color image; (b) Gray image (Color figure online)

Figure 3 shows the comparison of the reconstructed image structure of each network layer, and the functions of these two mapping networks can be intuitively compared. The images reconstructed by the nonlinear mapping network layer of Lena (Color) and Lena (Gray) are very similar, with clear outlines but monotonous colors. The image reconstructed by the linear mapping network layer is blurry, but the color is richer.

3.3 Data Set and Configuration

This paper uses the dataset in Reference [5], a total of 91 color images. The image is scaled by the ratio of 0.75, 1, and 1.5, then the image is divided into blocks with a size of $3 \times 33 \times 33$ and a step size of 14, resulting in a total of 87104 small images. By using the Pytorch open-source tool to train the network, and the equipment is mainly configured with Intel Core i5–8500 CPU, 16GB memory, and GTX 2080ti graphics card. The loss function uses the mean square error function, which can be expressed as:

$$L(W^c, W^l, W^b) = \frac{1}{N} \sum_{i=1}^{N} \left\| x_i' - x_i \right\|_2^2. \tag{10}$$

The Adam method is used to train the entire network. The initial learning rate is set to 0.001, and the learning rate is reduced to 0.5 times for every 200,000 times, for a total of 1,000,000 time sare trained.

4 Encryption Algorithm

4.1 Encryption

The detailed process of the general image encryption scheme in this paper is shown in Fig. 4

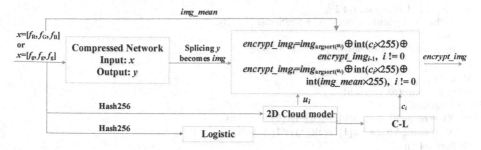

Fig. 4. Encryption algorithm flow chart.

The detailed encryption steps are as follows:

Setp1: Set the color image to RGB format, and the grayscale image can be copied as 3 channels first. After being compressed by the compression network, the compressed image block is 4-dimensional. Before encryption, it needs to be spliced and converted into a 2-dimensional compressed image (referred as *img*).

Step2: The hash value of the original image is first calculated according to the SHA256 algorithm, and the hash value is cut in steps of 2 and converted to decimal to obtain 32 values in the range of 1–256. The hash value is then divided by 256 to obtain a decimal number between 0 and 1 as the key of the original image (referred as k_1).

Step3: According to k_1, the two-dimensional cloud model sequence, Logistic sequence and C-L sequence of the same size as img are generated again. The initial value of the two-dimensional cloud model as $(Ex_1, Ex_2) = (2, 100)$, $(En_1, En_2) = (4, 88)$, $(He_1, He_2) = (6, 50)$. The parameter r = 3.9999 of the Logistic sequence, the initial value is k_1. The specific process of generating two-dimensional cloud model sequence, Logistic sequence and C-L cascade sequence is shown in Algorithm 1.

Algorithm 1 Compound chaotic system	

1: **Function**sequence_generator(k_1, Ex, En, He, n)
2: **Input:**Key k_1 of the original image; Ex=(Ex$_1$, Ex$_2$);En=(En$_1$, En$_2$);He=(He$_1$, He$_2$); Compressed image consists of n pixels;
3: **Output:**y, b;
4: Sha256 = sha256()
5: shaEx, shaEn,shaHe = sha256.update(Ex,En, He)
6: shaSum = shaEx+shaEn+shaHe;
7: **for**i = 1 : len(ShaSum) : 2
8: hashList.append(hex_dec('0x' + ShaSum[i : i + 2]));
9: **end**
10: rand_seed = int(mean(hashList) × k_1 × 256);
11: r = 3.9999;
12: z = k_1;
13: y, b = zeros(n), zeros(n);
14: seed(rand_seed);
15: X0 = normal(loc = En[0], scale = He[0], size = n);
16: X1 = normal(loc = En[1], scale = He[1], size = n);
17: **for**i = 1 : n
18: Enn0 = X0[i];
19: X0[i] = normal(loc = Ex[0], scale = abs(Enn0), size = 1);
20: Enn1 = X1[i];
21: X1[i] = normal(loc = Ex[1], scale = abs(Enn1), size = 1);
22: y[i] = exp(− (X0[i] − Ex[0])2 / (2×Enn0×Enn0) − (X1[i] − Ex[1])2 / (2×Enn1×Enn1));
23: z = r × z × (1 − z);
24: b[i] = mod(y[i] + z, 1);
25: **end**
26: **end function**

Setp4: After calculating the two-dimensional cloud model and the C-L sequence, encrypt the img according to formula 9 to obtain the encrypted image (referred as *encrypt_img*).

4.2 Dencryption

The decryption process is the reverse process of the encryption process. The detailed process is shown in Fig. 5.

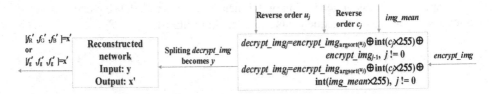

Fig. 5. Dencryption algorithm flow chart.

The detailed decryption steps are as follows:

Step1: After calculating the two-dimensional cloud model and C-L sequence according to the key, as shown in Fig. 5, the ciphertext is decrypted sequentially from back to front to obtain the decrypted image (referred as *decrypt_img*).

Step2: Splice the 2-dimensional *decrypt_img* into a 4-dimensional image block y, and then reconstruct the image x' through the reconstruction network.

5 Experiment and Algorithm Performance Analysis

5.1 Analysis of Reconstruction Quality

Compared with TVAL3 [16], NLR-CS [17], D-AMP [18], ReconNet, DR^2-Net, MSRNet in terms of reconstruction quality, the first three are based on traditional compressed sensing algorithms, and the last three are Compressed sensing algorithm based on deep learning. The comparison of reconstruction results mainly uses peak signal to noise ratio (PSNR) and structural similarity (SSIM) as evaluation indicators.

5.1.1 Reconstruct the Gray Image

Testing the generalization ability of the algorithm on the large data set BSD500, a total of 500 images, and results are shown in Table 1.

Table 1. MeanPSNR and SSIM of different algorithms and different sampling rates on the BSD500 test set

Sampling ratio	Algorithm							
	ReconNet		DR^2-Net		MSRNet		CCSNet	
	PSNR	SSIM	PSNR	SSIM	PSNR	SSIM	PSNR	SSIM
0.25	25.48	0.7241	27.56	0.7961	27.93	0.8121	**29.27**	**0.8578**
0.1	23.28	0.6121	24.26	0.6630	24.73	0.6837	**26.10**	**0.7264**
Avg.	24.38	0.6681	25.91	0.7296	26.33	0.7479	**27.68**	**0.7921**

Table 1 shows the PSNR and SSIM values of each algorithm on the data set BSD500. When the sampling rate MR = 0.25 and 0.10, the PSNR and SSIM values of CCSNet are the highest, and the reconstruction performance is better than ReconNet, DR2-Net and MSRNet based on deep learning. Experiments show that CCSNet has higher reconstruction quality than other algorithms on gray images, and it has good generalization ability.

5.1.2 Reconstructthe Color Image

In this paper, CCSNet is also applicable to color images of RGB format. Table 2 shows the PSNR and SSIM values of CCSNet and the Reference [9] on the dataset Set5. When the sampling rate MR = 0.05, 0.1 and 0.2, the reconstruction quality of CCSNet is higher. Experiments show that CCSNet also has a good performance on color images.

Table 2. PSNR of the reconstructed set5 under different algorithms and different sampling rates

Algorithm	Sampling ratio				
	0.2	0.1	0.05	0.01	Avg
CSNet +	35.19	32.08	29.23	**24.35**	30.21
CCSNet	**35.88**	**32.31**	**29.33**	23.62	**30.29**

Table 3. Lena image effects at various stages, sampling rate MR = 0.6 (Gray), 0.2 (Color)

Original images	Sampling Ratios	Compressed images	Cipher images	Reconstructed images	PSNR	SSIM
	0.6				37.1015	0.9761
	0.2				34.1378	0.9605

The effects of 256 × 256 Lena images at each stage are shown in Table 3.It can be seen from Table 3 that when Lena's sampling rate is MR = 0.6(Gray), 0.2(Color), the original outline can no longer be seen in the ciphertext image, and the reconstructed image is also very close to the original image, has a good visual effect. So the following performance analysis uses these two sampling rates.

5.2 Key Space Analysis

Generally, when the key space is large enough, the image encryption algorithm can effectively resist brute force cracking. The chaotic system in this paper, the keys of the Logistic sequence have r and z, and the keys of the two-dimensional cloud model have random seeds k_1, (Ex_1, Ex_2), (En_1, En_2) and (He_1, He_2), which have 9 keys in total. The accuracy of the simulation device is 15 bits, and the key space is 15 bits, and the key space can meet the security requirements [19]. So the key space of the encryption algorithm in this paper is enough large that brute force cracking cannot effectively decrypt the image.

5.3 Correlation Analysis

Generally, the correlation between adjacent pixel values of the original image will be relatively high, but for an ideal ciphertext image, the correlation between adjacent pixel values should be zero. Therefore, the correlation coefficient of the adjacent pixel values of the ciphertext image is an important indicator of the quality of the encryption algorithm. The correlation coefficient is divided into three directions: horizontal, vertical and diagonal. The correlation coefficients of the algorithm in this paper, [21] and [22] in the three directions are shown in Table 4, and the minimum value has been marked in bold. It can be seen from Table 4 that the algorithm in this paper is closer to 0 in the average value of the correlation coefficient, which is better than other algorithms.

Table 4. Comparison of correlation coefficients of different encryption algorithms

Test images	Direction	Plain images (Gray)	Cipher images			
			Proposed (Gray)	Proposed (Color)	Reference [21]	Reference [22]
Lena	Horizontal	0.9396	−0.0089	**0.0009**	−0.0048	0.0011
	Vertical	0.9639	−0.0031	**−0.0022**	−0.0112	0.0098
	Diagonal	0.9189	**0.0012**	−0.0023	−0.0045	−0.0227
Peppers	Horizontal	0.9769	0.0101	**−0.0018**	−0.0056	0.0071
	Vertical	0.9772	−0.0092	**0.0006**	−0.0162	−0.0065
	Diagonal	0.9625	−0.0040	**0.0003**	−0.0113	−0.0165
Avg	Horizontal	—	0.0006	**−0.0004**	0.0052	0.0041
	Vertical	—	−0.0061	**−0.0008**	−0.0137	0.0017
	Diagonal	—	−0.0014	**−0.0010**	−0.0079	−0.0196

5.4 Information Entropy Analysis

The global information entropy reflects the chaos of the pixel values of the entire image. The larger the information entropy, the more chaotic the information contained in the image. The ideal value of en is 8. In this paper, after the algorithm encrypts the test picture, the grayscale Lena 7.9953, color Lena 7.9957, grayscale Peppers 7.9961 and color Peppers 7.9956.

Reference [20] proposed a new statistical test of image randomness based on local information entropy, which is an extension of global information entropy, which is measured the randomness of the image by calculating the sample mean value of information entropy on multiple non-overlapping and randomly selected image blocks. Using a total of 30 non-overlapping image blocks of the size of 44 × 44, the local information entropy of this algorithm on Lena, Peppers and Cameraman is shown in Table 5.

In Table 5, the values of local information entropy are also within the critical range. Therefore, it can be considered that the distribution of ciphertext pixel values obtained by the algorithm in this paper is very confusing and can better conceal the plaintext image information.

Table 5. Compare local entropy of different encryption algorithms

Test images	Local entropy (Gray/Color)	Critical value		
		$u_{0.05}^{*-} = 7.9019$ $u_{0.05}^{*+} = 7.9030$	$u_{0.01}^{*-} = 7.9017$ $u_{0.01}^{*+} = 7.9032$	$u_{0.001}^{*-} = 7.9015$ $u_{0.001}^{*+} = 7.9034$
Lena	7.9020/7.9021	Pass	Pass	Pass
Peppers	7.9021/7.9025	Pass	Pass	Pass

5.5 Plaintext Sensitivity Analysis

The key used in the encryption algorithm in this paper is related to the plaintext and the plaintext is very sensitive from the ciphertext so that the ciphertext obtained after slight modification of the plaintext is very different from the original ciphertext, and the encryption system cannot be deciphered. The algorithms in this paper and [14] and [21] compares the NPCR and UACI of ciphertext on Lena and Peppers as shown in Table 6, 7.

Table 6. Compare NPCR of different encryption algorithms

Test images	NPCR (Gray/Colo)	NPCR theoretical critical value		
		$N_{0.05}^{*} = 99.5693\%$	$N_{0.01}^{*} = 99.5527\%$	$N_{0.001}^{*} = 99.5341\%$
Lena	0.9961/0.9963	Pass	Pass	Pass
Lena [14]	0.9954/—	Fail	Fail	Pass
Lena [21]	0.9962/—	Pass	Pass	Pass
Peppers	0.9960/0.9957	Pass	Pass	Pass
Pepp. [14]	0.9944/—	Fail	Fail	Fail
Pepp. [21]	0.9963/—	Pass	Pass	Pass

It can be seen from Tables 6 and 7 that the algorithm in this paper is in the critical range on both NPCR and UACI, indicating that the encryption algorithm in this paper can better resist differential attacks.

5.6 Robustness Analysis

The ciphertext may suffer from noise pollution or data loss during network transmission, so a good encryption algorithm should have a certain ability to resist noise and cutting attacks. The robustness of the compression encryption algorithm in this paper is greatly affected by the compression and reconstruction network, so when training the network, adding Gaussian noise with an intensity of 0.10 to the compressed image can improve the robustness of the entire algorithm. As shown in Fig. 6, 7.

Table 7. Compare UACI of different encryption algorithms

Test images	UACI (Gray/Color)	UACI theoretical critical value		
		$u^{*-}_{0.05} = 33.2824\%$ $u^{*+}_{0.05} = 33.6447\%$	$u^{*-}_{0.01} = 33.2255\%$ $u^{*+}_{0.01} = 33.7016\%$	$u^{*-}_{0.001} = 33.1594\%$ $u^{*+}_{0.001} = 33.7677\%$
Lena	0.3353/0.3356	Pass	Pass	Pass
Lena [14]	0.3303/—	Fail	Fail	Fail
Lena [21]	0.3370/—	Fail	Pass	Pass
Peppers	0.3334/0.3335	Pass	Pass	Pass
Pepp. [14]	0.3305/—	Fail	Fail	Fail
Pepp. [21]	0.3369/—	Fail	Pass	Pass

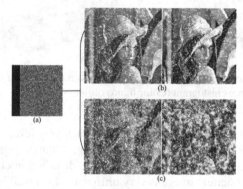

Fig. 6. Add Gaussian noise when training the network to counter the impact of shearing attacks:(a) Ciphertext cut 14%;(b) The network adds Gaussian noise during training;(c) The network did not add Gaussian noise during training

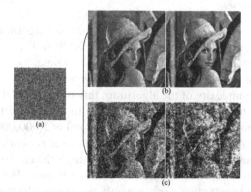

Fig. 7. Add Gaussian noise when training the network to counter the impact of noise attacks:(a) Add Gaussian noise with an intensity of 0.03 to the ciphertext;(b) The network adds Gaussian noise during training;(c) The network did not add Gaussian noise during training

5.7 Histogram Analysis

The histogram reflects the number of pixels of each gray level in the image and the more uniform the encryption effect the better, so this section evaluates the algorithm in this section through histograms of plaintext and ciphertext. Lena's histograms on grayscale and color images are shown in Fig. 8.

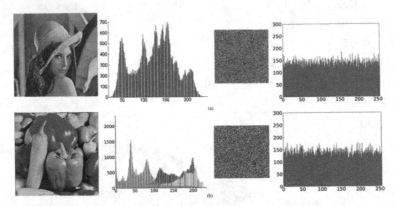

Fig. 8. Histograms of Lena (Gray), Lena (Color) images in plain text and ciphertext: (a) Plain text histogram;(b) ciphertext histogram (Color figure online)

The histogram reflects the number of pixels of each gray level in the image and the more uniform the encryption effect the better. In Fig. 8, the histogram of the plaintext image of Lena and Peppers has obvious pixel value distribution characteristics, while the histogram of the ciphertext image is very uniform, which well hides the pixel value distribution characteristics of the plaintext image. It shows that the algorithm in this paper can resist statistical attacks very well.

5.8 Histogram Analysis

Time complexity is also an important indicator to measure algorithm performance. To verify that one-step completion of scrambling and XOR in the encryption algorithm of this paper can shorten the encryption and decryption time, the comparison with the separate encryption of scrambling and XOR is shown in Table 8.

Considering the complexity of the algorithm, this section explains the training process of the network: the initial learning rate is set to 0.001, and the learning rate is reduced to 0.5 times for every 200,000 times, for a total of 1,000,000 times are trained. At the same time, the Adam method is used to improve the network training efficiency. Since the network training is a separate preparation stage, the encryption operation will not repeat the training after the network weights are trained. Because in the subsequent compression and encryption work, we only need to use the trained weights of the network to perform compression and reconstruction operations, so we ignore the time required for network training in the operation of the algorithm, calculate the time spent on compression, encryption, decryption, and reconstruction.

Table 8. The impact of one-step completion and separate completion on running time(s)

Image size	Encryption type(Gray)	Encryption and decryption time	Programming tools	CPU
256 × 256	Complete in one step	**0.28**	Pycharm	i5–8500
	Complete separately	0.42		
512 × 512	Complete in one step	**1.57**		
	Complete separately	2.07		

To verify that the deep learning-based compressed reconstruction network in this paper can reduce the time consumed by the whole algorithm, a comparison with the time consumed by using this paper's encryption algorithm directly on the original graph is shown in Table 9.

Table 9. The time-consuming(s) comparison that the compression encryption algorithm of this paper and use the encryption algorithm on the original image

Image size		Compression reconstruction (Gray/Color)	Encryption and decryption (Gray/Color)	Total time (Gray/Color)	Programming tools
256 × 256	Ref. [23]	8.89/—	1.08/—	9.98/—	Pycharm + Pytorch + i5–8500
	Ref. [24]	—	—/1.30	—/1.30	
	Ref. [25]	—	—/0.75	—/0.75	
	Ref. [26]	0.21/0.20	0.66/0.65	0.87/0.85	
	Ref. [26]	—	0.93/2.81	0.93/2.81	
	Compression encryption	0.16/0.17	0.58/0.58	**0.74/0.75**	
	Direct encryption	—	1.12/3.36	1.12/3.36	
512 × 512	Ref. [26]	0.91/0.89	2.51/2.51	3.42/3.40	
	Ref. [26]	—	3.89/11.96	3.89/11.96	
	Compressionencryption	0.7/0.69	2.27/2.30	**2.97/2.99**	
	Direct encryption	—	4.56/13.39	4.56/13.39	

It can be seen from Table 9 that the total time consumption of the compression encryption algorithm in this paper is shorter than that of directly using the encryption algorithm in the original image, especially for color images, which shows that the compression encryption algorithm in this paper has a great advantage in time.

6 Conclusion

Image compression and image encryption are two important tasks in image processing. This paper proposes a new compression encryption algorithm through these two technologies. The compression encryption algorithm is quick and secure, and is suitable for grayscale images and RGB color images. Under the premise of ensuring the encryption performance, the size of the encrypted image is reduced by the neural network and the overall running time is reduced. Through experiments and performance analysis, it is verified that the compression encryption algorithm in this paper not only has higher reconstruction quality, but also greatly improves the security of the algorithm. It has great advantages and wide application prospects in image storage and transmission. Finally, the encryption operation in this paper mainly revolves around chaotic systems and deep learning. In the future, we can study the performance of chaotic systems and design more lightweight and high-performance deep learning networks to improve the speed and quality of algorithms, and extend this ideas to more information security directions.

References

1. Donoho, D.L.: Compressed sensing. IEEE Trans. Inf. Theor. **52**(4), 1289–1306 (2016)
2. Candes, E.J., Romberg, J., Tao, T.: Robust uncertainty principles: exact signal reconstruction from highly incomplete frequency information. IEEE Trans. Inf. Theory **52**(2), 489–509 (2006)
3. Candes, E.J., Wakin, M.B.: An introduction to compressive sampling. IEEE Sig. Process. Mag **25**(2), 21–30 (2008)
4. Mousavi, A., Patel, A.B., Baraniuk, R.G.: A deep learning approach to structured signal recovery. In: Proceedings of 53rd Annual Allerton Conference on Communication, Control, and Computing, Monticello, pp.1336–1343 (2015)
5. Kulkarni, K., Lohit, S., Turaga, P., Kerviche, R., Ashok, A.: ReconNet: non-iterative reconstruction of images from compressively sensed measurements. In: IEEE Conference on Computer Vision and Pattern Recognition (CVPR), pp. 449–458 (2016)
6. Dong, C., Loy, C.C., He, K., Tang, X.: Image super-resolution using deep convolutional networks. IEEE Trans. Pattern Anal. Mach. Intell. **38**(2), 295–307 (2016). https://doi.org/10.1109/TPAMI.2015.2439281
7. Yao, H., Dai, F., Zhang, S.: DR^2-Net: deep residual reconstruction network for image compressive sensing. Neurocomputing **359**(24), 483–493 (2019)
8. Lian, Q., Fu, L., Chen, S., Shi, B.: A compressed sensing algorithm based on multi-scale residual reconstruction network. Acta Autom **45**(11), 2082–2091 (2019)
9. Shi, W., Jiang, F., Liu, S., Zhao, D.: Image compressed sensing using convolutional neural network. IEEE Trans. Image Process. **29**, 375–388 (2020). https://doi.org/10.1109/TIP.2019.2928136
10. Sun, S.: A novel Hyperchaotic image encryption scheme based on DNA encoding, pixel-level scrambling and bit-level scrambling. IEEE Photonics **J10**(2), 1–14 (2018)

11. Li, F., Wu, H., Zhou, G., Wei, W.: Robust real-time image encryption with aperiodic chaotic map and random-cycling bit shift. J. Real-Time Image Proc. **16**(3), 775–790 (2018). https://doi.org/10.1007/s11554-018-0801-0

12. Guo, Y., Jing, S., Zhou, Y., Xin, X., Wei, L.: An image encryption algorithm based on logistic-Fibonacci cascade chaos and 3D bit scrambling. IEEE Access **8**, 9896–9912 (2020). https://doi.org/10.1109/ACCESS.2019.2963717

13. Zhang, D., Liao, X., Yang, B., Zhang, Y.: A fast and efficient approach to color-image encryption based on compressive sensing and fractional Fourier transform. Multimedia Tools Appl. **77**(2), 2191–2208 (2017). https://doi.org/10.1007/s11042-017-4370-1

14. Shi, H., Wang, L.-D.: Multi-process image encryption scheme based on compressed sensing and multi-dimensional chaotic system. Acta Physica Sinica **68**(20), 200501 (2019). https://doi.org/10.7498/aps.68.20190553

15. Gong, L., Qiu, K., Deng, C., Zhou, N.: An optical image compression and encryption scheme based on compressive sensing and RSA algorithm. Opt. Lasers Eng **121**, 169–180 (2019)

16. Li, C., Yin, W., Jiang, H., Zhang, Y.: An efficient augmented Lagrangian method with applications to total variation minimization. Comput. Opt. Appl. **56**(3), 507–530 (2013). https://doi.org/10.1007/s10589-013-9576-1

17. Dong, W., Shi, G., Li, X., Ma, Y., Huang, F.: Compressive sensing via nonlocal low-rank regularization. IEEE Trans. Image Process **23**(8), 3618–3632 (2014)

18. Metzler, C.A., Maleki, A., Baraniuk, R.G.: From denoising to compressed sensing. IEEE Trans. Inf. Theory **62**(9), 5117–5144 (2016)

19. Guo, Y., Jing, S.: Lossless compression optical image encryption based on L-L cascade chaos and vector decomposition. Acta Photon. Sin **49**(7), 710002–0710002 (2020)

20. Wu, Y., Zhou, Y., Saveriades, G., Again, S., Noonan, J.P., Natarajan, P.: Local Shannon entropy measure with statistical tests for image randomness. Inf. Sci **222**, 323–342 (2013)

21. Belazi, A., EI-Latif, A.A.A., Belghith, S.: A novel image encryption scheme based on substitution-permutation network and chaos. Sign. Process, **128**, 155–170 (2016)

22. Hua, Z., Zhou, Y., Pun, C., Chen, C.L.P.: 2D sine logistic modulation map for image encryption. Inf. Sci **297**, 80–94 (2015)

23. Liu, X., Cao, Y., Lu, P., Lu, X., Li, Y.: Optical image encryption technique based on compressed sensing and Arnold transformation. Optik-Int. J. Light Electron Opt. **124**(24), 6590–6593 (2013)

24. Gan, Z.-H., Chai, X., Han, D.-J., Chen, Y.-R.: A chaotic image encryption algorithm based on 3-D bitlane permutation. Neural Comput. Appl. **31**(11), 7111–7130 (2018). https://doi.org/10.1007/s00521-018-3541

25. Guo, Y., Jing, S., Zhou, Y., Xu, X., Wei, L.: An image encryption algorithm based on logistic-Fibonacci cascade chaos and 3D bit scrambling. IEEE Access **8**, 9896–9912 (2020)

26. Chen, W., Guo, Y., Jing, S.W.: A generalized image encryption algorithm based on deep learning compressed perception and composite chaotic system. J. Phys. **69**(24), 99–111 (2020)

Cascading Failure Mitigation Strategy for Urban Road Traffic Networks

Xudan Song[1], Jing Wang[2], Sijia Liu[1], Xiaohan Cui[1], and Rong-rong Yin[1(✉)]

[1] Yanshan University, Qinhuangdao 066004, China
yrr@ysu.edu.cn
[2] Northeastern University, Shenyang 110167, China

Abstract. Aiming at the cascading failure problem, this paper proposes a cascading failure mitigation strategy based on edge control, which controls the cascading failure of nodes in a small range. In this paper, we introduce a cascading failure model with the transmission rate as well as the load distribution mechanism. Then, the cascading failure mitigation strategy is developed by controlling the transmission rate coefficient of the edge. The theoretical and experimental results show that this congestion mitigation strategy can control the scale of cascading failure within a certain range. It can reduce the outward congestion propagation of nodes by changing the transmission rate coefficient of the edge. In addition, it can also enhance the robustness of the network, repair the congested nodes in the network and ensure the normal operation of the network.

Keywords: Traffic network · Cascading failure · Mitigation strategy · Edge control

1 Introduction

At present, the problem of traffic congestion has attracted the wide attention of many researchers. Li et al. [1] constructed the geometric topology diagram of the road network and calculated the road network congestion when the cascading failure occurred. Solé-Ribalta et al. [2] proposed a traffic network congestion prediction model. Du et al. [3] came up with an improved whale optimization algorithm (IWOA) which was introduced into the wavelet neural network (WNN) to predict traffic flow. Chen et al. [4] put forward an urban road network model applicable to the opening of gated communities. Chen et al. [5] presented an algorithm to identify congested road segments and congestion propagation map was constructed to simulate congestion propagation in urban road network. The literatures above make a theoretical study on the problem of traffic congestion by using complex network, which is conductive to the alleviation of traffic congestion.

The phenomenon of cascading failure caused by traffic congestion is more destructive and harmful [6]. Various methods have been used to study the propagation mechanism of cascading failure in traffic network. The literatures [7, 8] studied the impact of network topology on traffic congestion, and established a space-time model of urban road

© Springer Nature Singapore Pte Ltd. 2021
L. Cui and X. Xie (Eds.): CWSN 2021, CCIS 1509, pp. 170–180, 2021.
https://doi.org/10.1007/978-981-16-8174-5_13

congestion radiation to eliminate traffic congestion. The literatures [9, 10] proposed a cell transmission model applied to accident congestion and effective control strategy by utilizing the spatial topology structure of traffic congestion propagation. These literatures analyze the cascading failure model of traffic network congestion from multiple perspectives, which provide references for the solution of the congestion problem.

The literatures [11, 12] established the model and algorithm about cascading failure of urban traffic, but their practicability had not been verified. The literatures [13, 14] used complex network theory to study the cascading failure of traffic network. However, the cascading failure models and mitigation methods based on complex network needed to be further improved in robustness.

This paper establishes the cascading failure model and provides strategies for mitigating the damages of cascading failure of complex traffic network under the model of load-capacity, the transmission rate coefficient, the transmission rate and load distribution rule. By changing the transmission rate coefficient of the edge, the outward congestion propagation of nodes can be reduced, thus controlling cascading failure. By example verification, the congestion mitigation strategy can control the scale of cascading failure within a certain range and repair network nodes at the same time, thus enhancing the robustness of the network and ensuring the normal operation of the network.

The rest of this paper is organized as follows. In Sect. 2, we propose CFEC (Cascading failure based on Edge Control) mitigation strategy. In Sect. 3, the network evaluation indicator is given. Section 4 presents experimental evaluation of CFEC. In the end, the conclusion is given in Sect. 5.

2 CFEC Mitigation Strategy

In the traffic network, traffic flow of road (i.e., edge) can be controlled by controlling the cycle of traffic lights and the duration of each phase to alleviate road junction (i.e., node) congestion. On this basis, we present a cascading failure mitigation strategy for urban road traffic network. The traffic congestion of nodes can be alleviated by adjusting the transmission rate coefficient of the controlled edges.

2.1 Node Load-Capacity Model

The traffic flow in the road is considered the load on the two-way edge of the network. Numerous studies have shown that the initial flow on each node is closely related to its degree [15]. Therefore, the initial load of the node is defined as a function related to the degree of node, as shown in Eq. (1):

$$L_i^0(t) = k_i^\tau \tag{1}$$

where i is any node in the network. $L_i^0(t)$ represents the initial load of node i. k_i is the degree of node i. τ is the adjustable parameter that controls the initial load intensity of node, otherwise, $\tau \geq 1$.

Node capacity refers to the maximum load that a node can hold. In general, the capacity of a node is defined as a quantity proportional to the initial load of the node [16], which is expressed as shown in Eq. (2):

$$C_i(t) = (1 + \beta)L_i^0(t) \tag{2}$$

where $C_i(t)$ is the capacity of node i. β represents the ratio of the node capacity to the initial load of the node, otherwise, $\beta \geq 0$.

2.2 Load Distribution Model

The transmission rate of edge is related to the degree of the node. The larger the degree of the node, the more load to be transmitted outward. In addition, the longer the transmission distance between adjacent nodes, the more information is transmitted. Therefore, the transmission rate of edge is related to the degree and transmission distance of the node, so the transmission rate of edge is defined as

$$\rho_{ij} = k_i \cdot D_{ij}/\overline{D} \tag{3}$$

where ρ_{ij} is the transmission rate of the edge between node i and neighbor node j. $\overline{D}$ represents the average distance between adjacent nodes in the network. D_{ij} represents the transmission distance between node i and its neighbor node j.

In this paper, the mitigation of congested node is realized by controlling the flow of the edges. Since the inflow/outflow is determined by the network itself, it is possible to control the transmission rate coefficient λ of edge between the nodes to mitigate congestion. Thus, the definition of transmission rate coefficient λ is shown as

$$\lambda = \begin{cases} 0 & i \in \omega \cap j \in \omega_2 \\ \lambda_{ij} & i \in \omega \cap j \in \omega_1 \\ 1 & i, j \in \omega \end{cases} \tag{4}$$

where ω is the set of congested nodes. ω_1 is the set of critical nodes. ω_2 is the set of normal nodes. λ_{ij} represents the transmission rate coefficient of the edge between congested node i and its neighbor node j, and $\lambda_{ij} = \begin{cases} \delta & \delta \leq 1 \\ 1/\delta & \delta > 1 \end{cases}$, in which δ is the ratio of the inflow and outflow of node j.

Then the load transmitted from node i to node j is

$$\Delta_{ij} = \sum_{t=0}^{T^{ij}} \lambda \rho_{ij} \tag{5}$$

where Δ_{ij} represents the load of node i transmitted to node j. T^{ij} is the time required for node i to transmit the load Δ_{ij} to node j.

Since the transmission rate coefficient from congested node i to node j is variable, the transmission rate coefficient of each stage is different, then the corresponding time of congestion alleviation is also different. Therefore, the time of congestion relief T^{ij} is

$$T^{ij} = T_1^{ij} + T_2^{ij} + T_3^{ij} \tag{6}$$

where T_1^{ij} is the time corresponding to the transmission rate coefficient $\lambda = 1$. T_2^{ij} is the time corresponding to the transmission rate coefficient $\lambda = \lambda_{ij}$. T_3^{ij} is the time corresponding to the transmission rate coefficient $\lambda = 0$.

The update load of node j is represented as

$$L_j(t + T) = L_j(t) + \sum_{\substack{j \in Nei\ i \\ i \in \omega}} \Delta_{ji} - \sum_{k \in Nei\ j} \Delta_{jk} \qquad (7)$$

where $L_j(t + T)$ represents the load of node j at time $t + T$. $L_j(t)$ represents the load of node j at time t. Nei is the set of neighbor nodes. $\sum_{\substack{j \in Nei\ i \\ i \in \omega}} \Delta_{ij}$ represents the load transmitted from multiple congested nodes to node j in the time from t to $t + T$. $\sum_{k \in Nei\ j} \Delta_{jk}$ represents the load transmitted from node j to its neighbor node k in the time from t to $t + T$.

2.3 Cascading Failure Mitigation Strategy

When node i is overloaded, the excess load of node i is distributed to the neighbor nodes. The congestion is alleviated by adjusting the transmission rate coefficient of the two-way edge between the congested node i and its adjacent nodes, and the time taken to alleviate the load in this process is calculated. The mitigation of cascading failure is that the congestion can be controlled within the range of the initial failure nodes and the outward propagation of congestion can be reduced by changing the transmission rate coefficient of the edges. The schematic diagram of the mitigation strategy involved in the whole process is shown in Fig. 1. The flow chart of the specific congestion alleviation strategy is shown in Fig. 2.

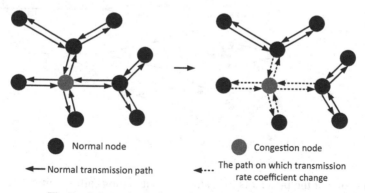

● Normal node   ● Congestion node

◀— Normal transmission path   ◀··· The path on which transmission rate coefficient change

Fig. 1. Schematic diagram of CFEC mitigation strategy

It can be seen from the above steps that the CFEC mitigation strategy in this paper mainly achieves the purpose of alleviating cascading failure by changing the transmission rate coefficient of the edges, resulting in the decrease of the outward congestion propagation and distributing the redundant load of congested nodes to neighboring nodes. According to the flow chart of congestion mitigation strategy, the time of congestion

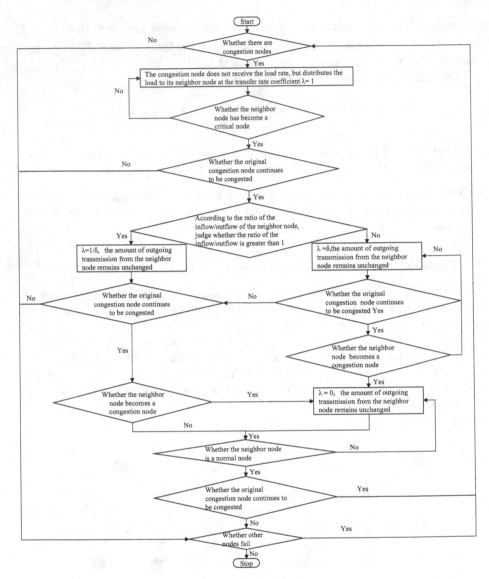

Fig. 2. Flow chart CFEC mitigation strategy

alleviation is one of the indicators to evaluate the cascading failure mitigation strategy. The expected effect is as follows: compared with other mitigation strategies, the scale of cascading failure after using CFEC mitigation strategy is smaller. Under the condition of the same cascading failure scale, the congestion mitigation strategy applied in this paper takes less time to alleviate the congestion.

3   Network Evaluation Indicator

The network state reflects the comprehensive utility of all nodes in the whole network at this moment. When the initial time is $t = t_0$, all nodes in the network remain normal [16], so $SG(t_0) = N$. Therefore, network state can be normalized (network normalization) as follows:

$$Q = \frac{SG(t)}{SG(t_0)} = \frac{SG(t)}{N} \tag{8}$$

where Q represents the value of network normalization. $SG(t)$ represents the number of normal nodes in the network at time t. N is the total number of nodes in the network.

4   Simulation Verification

Taking Tianjin city as an example, the OSM (Open Street Map) file was imported into SUMO for simulation in Fig. 3. There are currently 200 intersections with 756 edges involved. According to the degree distribution diagram of city nodes in Fig. 4, there are most nodes with small degrees in the urban road map of Hongqiao district in Tianjin, and a small number of nodes with large degrees. The overall degree distribution conforms to the power-law distribution and has the characteristics of scale-free network, which can be described by using the BA network model.

According to the CFEC mitigation strategy, the cascading failure scale of the network is related to the load mitigation time of the nodes. Therefore, through simulation verification, the parameters affecting load mitigation time are determined, then determine the load mitigation time of nodes. After that, based on the load mitigation time of the nodes, the cascading failure scale of the network is measured. In the simulation, the influencing factors of node load mitigation time are studied, and the way of deliberately attacking a single node is adopted, that is, setting an initial congested node. To study the effect of mitigation strategy on cascading failure, a random attack on multiple nodes is adopted, that is, a certain number of initial congested nodes are set.

4.1   Initial Condition Setting

The network topology constructed based on the real traffic network data of Tianjin city has 200 nodes, and two methods of intentional attack and random attack are adopted. The number of nodes deliberately attacked is one, and the number of nodes randomly attacked were 5% and 20% of the total nodes, respectively. The results are the average of 50 simulation experiments. We set the load parameter $\tau = 1.0 : 0.5 : 3.5$ and the capacity parameter $\beta = 0.1, \beta = 0.5, \beta = 1.0, \beta = 1.5$.

4.2   The Impact of Parameters on Load Mitigation Time

In order to verify the impact of parameters τ, β on mitigation time, it is necessary to determine the congestion node firstly. In Fig. 3, node 185 in red is deliberately attacked.

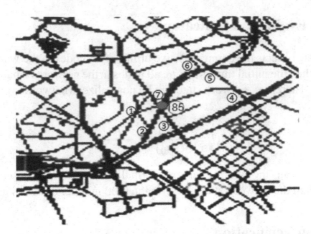

Fig. 3. Urban road map drawn by SUMO

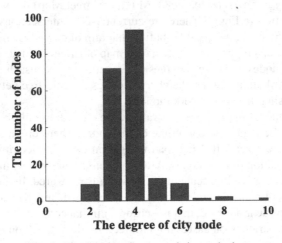

Fig. 4. Distribution diagram of city node degree

The degree of the red node is 7. Nodes 1–7 in the circle are the neighbors of the attacked node. Then, the load and capacity of the congested node are determined.

The variation of load mitigation time T^{ij} with parameters τ, β is shown in Fig. 5 and Fig. 6. In Fig. 5, the x-coordinate is the number of nodes participating in congestion mitigation. The load of the congested node is only transmitted to its neighbors 1–7 when the deliberately attacked node is alleviated, and these nodes don't fail, which verifies the effectiveness of the CFEC mitigation strategy. With the increase of load parameter τ, the load mitigation time T^{ij} of each node increases. Therefore, the mitigation strategy described in this paper can effectively control the congestion within the neighbor nodes of the failure node and prevent the spread of cascading failures.

As can be seen from Fig. 6, with the increase of the capacity parameter β, the load mitigation time T^{ij} of each node also increases with the same trend. Generally, the larger the capacity of a node, the less likely it is to fail. Once a node fails, the more load the node has, the larger the cascading failure scale will be. Therefore, the larger β is, the larger the capacity is. The more load of the congestion node, the longer it takes to alleviate congestion.

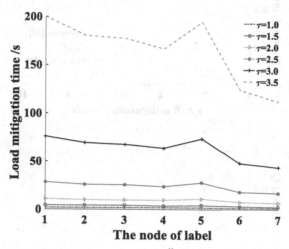

Fig. 5. Node load mitigation time T^{ij} changes with load index τ

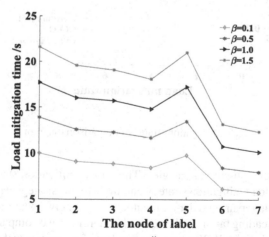

Fig. 6. Node load mitigation time T^{ij} changes with capacity ratio β

4.3 Comparison of Algorithm Results

In order to further verify the effectiveness of the CFEC strategy in this paper, the effective nodes in the network are observed by random attacks on some nodes in the network and

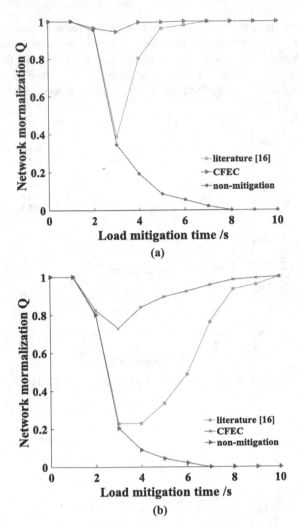

Fig. 7. Mitigation strategy comparison diagram

compared with other mitigation strategies. The CFEC mitigation strategy proposed in this paper includes load mitigation strategy and node repair strategy. However, literature [16] aims at the node repair model after the nodes in the network are overloaded, which can alleviate the cascading failure in the network. Therefore, we compare the two models. The number of total nodes is 200, and the number of random attack nodes is 5% and 20% of the total nodes. The results are the average of 50 simulation experiments. Set load parameter $\tau = 2$ and capacity parameter $\beta = 0.2$.

In Fig. 7, Fig. 7(a) is the comparison graph of 5% nodes attacked, and Fig. 7(b) is the comparison graph of 20% nodes attacked. As shown in Fig. 7, the network cascading failure scale of the two mitigation strategies reaches the maximum at 3s. As shown in the two figures above, the network normalization Q of CFEC mitigation strategy decreases to 0.95, 0.77, respectively. The mitigation strategy in literature [16] decreases to 0.38, 0.22, respectively. There is a gap in the cascading failure scale of the network, which clearly shows that the mitigation strategy proposed in this paper is better. According to the comparison of Fig. 7(a) and 7(b), the larger the scale of initial attack nodes is, the more seriously the network is damaged, and the longer the time of congestion alleviation is. Under the same attack scale, both mitigation strategies take the same time to repair the network.

Through the above simulation verification, the CFEC mitigation strategy proposed in this paper alleviates congestion through the neighbor nodes of congested nodes, and the failure nodes in the network can be controlled within the range of the initial failure nodes without causing large-scale cascading failure. After the load is alleviated for a period, there are no congested nodes in the whole network, so the network nodes are repaired. Compared with the congestion mitigation method in literature [16], the CFEC mitigation strategy proposed in this paper has stronger robustness and can repair network nodes in the same time. Besides, it has the smaller scale of cascading failure.

The simulation results show that: Load parameter τ and capacity parameter β have similar effects on the time of congestion mitigation. With the increase of load parameter τ and capacity parameter β, the mitigation time T^{ij} of each node also increases. Within the same mitigation time, the CFEC mitigation strategy proposed in this paper can control the cascading failure scale within a smaller range and enhance the robustness of the network. In Fig. 7(a) shows that the congestion mitigation time in this paper is better than other methods when 5% nodes are attacked. From Fig. 7(b), when 20% nodes are attacked, the CFEC mitigation strategy can control the cascading failure within the initial range.

5 Conclusion

Considering the cascading failure of traffic network, a cascading failure mitigation strategy based on edge control is proposed in this paper. By changing the transmission rate coefficient of the edge, the scale of congestion can be controlled within the initial failure nodes and the outward congestion propagation is reduced. Besides, the excess load of the congested nodes can be transmitted out. By simulating verification, the CFEC congestion mitigation strategy in this paper can control the scale of cascading failure within a certain range, enhance the robustness of the network, and repair the network nodes to ensure the normal operation of the network.

References

1. Li, Y., Luo, X., Wang, Y.: A cascading failure simulation of urban road network considering multi-node congestion. Ind. Eng. J. **21**(4), 1–7 (2018). https://doi.org/10.3969/j.issn.1007-7375.2018.04.001
2. Soleribalta, A., Sergio, G., Alex, A.: A model to identify urban traffic congestion hotspots in complex networks. R. Soc. Open Sci. **3**(10), 160098 (2016). https://doi.org/10.1098/rsos.160098

3. Du, W., Zhang, Q., Chen, Y., et al.: An urban short-term traffic flow prediction model based on wavelet neural network with improved whale optimization algorithm. Sustain. Cities Soc. **69**(3), 102858 (2021). https://doi.org/10.1016/j.scs.2021.102858
4. Wei-Zhe, C., Xiang-Ru, L.: Research on traffic opening strategy of closed communities by complex network. Acta Automatica Sinica **44**(11), 2068–2082 (2018). https://doi.org/10.16383/j.aas.2017.c160819
5. Li, C., Yue, W., Mao, G., et al.: Congestion propagation based bottleneck identification in urban road networks. IEEE Trans. Veh. Technol. **69**(5), 4827–4841 (2020). https://doi.org/10.1109/TVT.2020.2973404
6. Zhang, X., Hu, S., Zhang, H., Hu, X.: A real-time multiple vehicle tracking method for traffic congestion identification. KSII Trans. Internet Inf. Syst. **10**(6), 2483–2503 (2016). https://doi.org/10.3837/tiis.2016.06.003
7. Li, S., Wu, J., Gao, Z., Lin, Y., Fu, B.: The analysis of traffic congestion and dynamic propagation properties based on complex network. Acta Physica Sinica, **60**(5), 050701 (2011). CNKI: SUN: WLXB.0.2011-05-022
8. Hu, L., Yang, J., He, Y., Meng, L., Luo, Z., Hu, C.: Urban traffic congestion radiation model and demage caused to service capacity of road network. China J. Highw. Transp. **32**(3), 145–154 (2019)
9. Long, J., Gao, Z., Zhao, X., Lian, A., Orenstein, P.: Urban traffic jam simulation based on the cell transmission model. Netw. Spat. Econ. **11**(1), 43–64 (2011). https://doi.org/10.1007/s11067-008-9080-9
10. Long, J., Gao, Z., Orenstein, P., Ren, H.: Control strategies for dispersing incident-based traffic jams in two-way grid networks. IEEE Trans. Intell. Transp. Syst. **13**(2), 469–481 (2012). https://doi.org/10.1109/TITS.2011.2171035
11. Sun, L., Huang, Y., Chen, Y., Li, Y.: Vulnerability assessment of urban rail transit based on multi-static weighted method in Beijing. China. Transp. Res. Part A **108**, 12–24 (2018). https://doi.org/10.1016/j.tra.2017.12.008
12. Wang, S., Zhao, J., Zheng, J.: Urban traffic congestion load redistribution control based on complex network. J. Highw. Transp. Res. Denelopment **13**(3), 98–103 (2019). https://doi.org/10.1061/JHTRCQ.0000694
13. Wang, B., Dai, J., Deng, X.: Failure analysis of urban complex metro network cascading failure. J. Univ. South China **33**(6), 91–96 (2019)
14. Zhang, L., Lu, J., Fu, B., Li, S.: A cascading failures model of weighted bus transit route Network under route failure perspective considering link Prediction effect. Physica A **523**, 1315–1330 (2019). https://doi.org/10.1016/j.physa.2019.04.122
15. Tian, H., Guo, R.: Study of urban road network cascading failure based on network load capacity model. J. Dalian Jiaotong Univ. **40**(6), 15–20 (2019). https://doi.org/10.13291/j.cnki.djdxac.2019.06.003
16. Cui, Q., Li, J., Wang, H., Nan, M.: Resilience analysis model of networked command information system based on node repairability. Comput. Sci. **45**(4), 117–136 (2018). https://doi.org/10.11896/j.issn.1002-137X.2018.04.018

Analysis and Countermeasure Design on Adversarial Patch Attacks

Yinan Fu[✉], Xiaolong Zheng, Peilun Du, and Liang Liu

Beijing University of Posts and Telecommunications, Beijing, China
fyn@bupt.edu.cn

Abstract. Adversarial patch is an image-independent patch that misleads deep neural networks to output a targeted class. Existing defense strategies mainly rely on patch detection based on the frequency or semantic gaps between the patch and clean image. But we found that they are effective because the gap is huge. This is because existing patch attacks only look for an effective patch instead of the optimized patch that minimizes the gap. We then propose two improved patches, enhanced and smoothed patches, to reduce the gap. Consequently, the decision boundary for adversarial examples of the existing defense means is successfully obscured. To cope with the improved patches, we propose a defense method based on image preprocessing. We leverage multi-scale Gaussian blur to amplify the reduced gap between the patch and clean image. Due to the dense information of patches, for a patch, the dissimilarities of Gaussian blurs with different scales are higher than that of clean images. By enhancing the local multi-scale details and weakening them in another scale set, we maximize its effect on patch with high-frequency information. In this way, our defense method can efficiently distort adversarial patches and cause only a negligible impact on clean images.

Keywords: Adversarial patch · Defense

1 Introduction

The past decade has witnessed the prosperity of Deep Learning. Deep neural networks (DNNs) are widely used in computer vision [9], pattern recognition [10], natural language processing [11], and autonomous driving [15]. However, recent studies have revealed that DNNs are vulnerable to adversarial examples that fool the classifier with subtle modifications. Since adversarial examples modify pixels in the whole image, it is not easy to launch physical attacks. Different from the imperceptible changes of adversarial examples, the adversarial patch is an image-independent patch that misleads the classifier to output a targeted class for any image (Fig. 1). Since it is image-independent, adversarial patches can be printed or placed in the scene to launch physical attacks without any prior knowledge of the scene [12].

© Springer Nature Singapore Pte Ltd. 2021
L. Cui and X. Xie (Eds.): CWSN 2021, CCIS 1509, pp. 181–195, 2021.
https://doi.org/10.1007/978-981-16-8174-5_14

Dog (91.0%)   **Toaster (94.8%)**

Fig. 1. Adversarial patches for ResNet-50.

As a targeted attack method, the adversarial patch imitates images of the targeted class to mislead the classifier focusing on the patch and making wrong recognition. Nevertheless, a gap between the patch and clean images is inevitable, leaving room for defense methods to differentiate the patch from clean images. Since a successful patch will be the salient activation source, the defense method can locate the patch and compare its feature with the expected features of the predicted class to detect the inconsistency [6]. Besides, as a universal attack method [13], adversarial patches contain more high-frequency information in a concentrated area than normal images to achieve their versatility. Hence, defense methods can also detect and distort the patch based on this high-frequency information which means the higher gradient of an image.

However, we analyze those defense methods and found that they are effective because the gap between the patch and the clean image is huge. This is because the goal of generation is only finding the patch successfully fool the threat model instead of the patch that is more robust to the defense. Based on this observation, we propose the enhanced and smoothed adversarial patches to respectively obscure the decision boundary of the feature inconsistency detection- and high-frequency information-based defense methods. To enhance the patch with more similar features of the targeted class, we leverage an antagonistic training strategy at the early stage of the patch generation training. To cope with the high-frequency information-based defense method, we propose generating the patch with proactive smoothing. Experimental results demonstrate our improved adversarial patches can significantly decrease the defending ability of existing methods.

To cope with the improved patches, we propose EGP, a new defense method based on image preprocessing that enlarges the reduced gaps of improved patches by amplifying the frequency difference between patches and the original image.

Different from the conventional image preprocessing based defense methods such as blur or JPEG that process the whole image, EGP only processes the key regions of the input image. We leverage multi-scale Gaussian blur [8] to obtain the multi-scale details of the image which will amplify the frequency properties of the original image. We magnify the details and add them to the original image to further enlarge the effect of subtle frequency differences on image processing. With this preprocessing, the clean images will be enhanced with details, while patches will be distorted due to the much higher frequency. To reduce the impact of preprocessing on the clean images, we further propose weakening the local multi-scale details by another Gaussian kernel set. Experimental results show that EGP can significantly improve the classification accuracy of adversarial examples, and cause little impact on clean images.

The main contributions of this paper are as follows: 1) We analyze the effectiveness of existing defense methods against adversarial patches and find that defense methods are effective because the generated adversarial patches are just effective to successfully fool the classifier rather than optimal with the minimized gap to the characteristic of a clean image. 2) Based on the observation, we propose two patch generation methods to obtain the enhanced and smoothed patches that can effectively obscure the decision boundary for adversarial patches and further reduce the effectiveness of current defense methods. 3) As for the countermeasure design, we propose a new defense method based on image preprocessing. The key idea is enlarging the reduced gap between the patch and the clean image by multi-scale Gaussian blur.

2   Related Work

2.1   Adversarial Patch Attacks

Adversarial patch [1], a localized patch, which enjoys strong robustness to position and angle alternation. To further optimize the generation of adversarial patch, Karmon [2] created adversarial patch using optimized loss function and they concentrated on the selection of categorys for targeted attack. Duan [4] adopted style loss and content loss to generate imperceptible patches. Recently, Liu [3] proposed a universal adversarial patch generation framework based on model bias, which can effectively attack the invisible categories in the model training process.

Defenses Against Adversarial Patch Attacks. Naseer [5] proposed a local gradient smoothing scheme to resist adversarial patch attacks. To eliminate the influence of noises, the local high gradient region of the image is detected and smoothed. Hayes [7] put forward a defense strategy based on image inpainting. They discover the location of patches and further leverage image inpainting technology to remove them. To address the lack of versatility and computation of previous methods, Xu [6] was concerned about the feature dissimilarity between input and image of the corresponding category. If the degree of dissimilarity exceeds a threshold, the input is considered to be an adversarial example.

3 Analysis and Improvement on Adversarial Patch

In this section, we mainly analyze the defense mechanism of the existing defense methods. Based on the analysis results, we improve the universal adversarial patch generation method.

3.1 Existing Adversarial Patch

Adversarial Patch [1] generates a universal patch, which can be applied to any image x in the dataset X to mislead the image into the target category regardless of the scale, orientation, or location of the patch.

Given an adversarial patch p, an image x in dataset X, a target class t, a random location in the location space of images $l \in L$, and a random angle transformation over a set of angle transformations $t \in T$, the patch p is then placed in a location l of image x. The algorithm renovates the patch iteratively by optimizing the loss function:

$$\hat{p} = \arg\max_{p} E_{x \in X, t \in T, l \in L}[logPr(\hat{y}|A(p, x, l, t))] \tag{1}$$

3.2 Enhanced Adversarial Patch

Although adversarial patches are effective for digital or physical world attacks, it should be noted that they tend to be abrupt and unreal. The feature similarity between the patch and the image of the predicted class is not high. Therefore, both artificial means and the existing defense method [6] can distinguish them without difficulty. Consequently, we consider proposing an enhanced adversarial patch, which is an improvement based on the original method [1]. Aiming at mining deeper semantic information about the target category, the enhanced adversarial patches can be more realistic and closer to the target category.

Our improvement focus on the early input images in the train set (a pre-training process). For the early inputs, based on the optimization of the objective function, a strategy of antagonistic training is leveraged. The brief ideology of antagonistic training is shown in Fig. 2.

Early generated patches always contain insufficient features. It is due to the over-fitting of the white-box model that an image with an early patch is misclassified successfully. The purpose of patch training is to find an effective patch by fitting the white-box model, rather than to generate a more realistic adversarial patch with details, which leads to premature convergence on the white box. For solving this problem, We feed the adversarial patches generated in the intermediate process to retrain the target model for fooling and generating patch. Specifically, we consider retraining the adversarial image that has been successfully misclassified with the original tag, and then updating the target model for fooling and generating a patch constantly. By constantly feeding the adversarial images with early generated patches to retrain the target model, the target model will be more robust and more difficult to be fooled. While the target model is

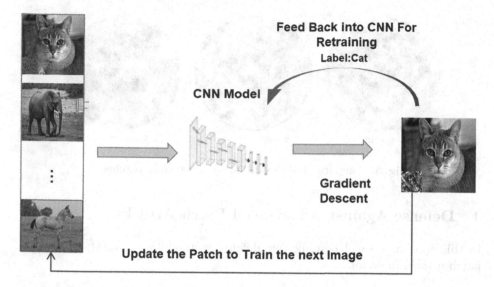

Fig. 2. Antagonistic pretraining of adversarial patch.

more robust, the generated patch is stronger. In short, we strengthen the update of the patch through the continuous update of the target model used for generating patch. In this way, we force the patch training process to continue learning enhanced adversarial features, which reduce the gap between adversarial patch and target image.

3.3   Smoothed Adversarial Patch

Adversarial patches always contain more high-frequency information, which can be the motivation of diverse defense methods. Therefore, by adding smooth processing intermittently during the updating of adversarial patches, we propose generating smoothed patches (Fig. 3).

In Adv Cam [4], adversarial patch for a specific image can generate imperceptible patches by adding style and content loss to the optimization objective function. However, as a targeted universal adversarial patch, we can not add the smoothing loss to the objective loss function to achieve the smoothed patch, because it will cause the direction of smoothing unable to focus on the target category. Therefore, we consider periodically smoothing the patch slightly in the training process to guide the update. Specifically, regarding to slight smoothing, we can get the intermediate smoothed patch p_{sm} as follow:

$$p_{sm} = k * (p_g - p) + p \tag{2}$$

p is the original patch, p_g is a Gaussian blur of p, k is a fuzzy coefficient ($k < 1$) which is used to get images with different blur levels.

(a) Adv Patch   (b) Enhanced Patch   (c) Smoothed Patch

Fig. 3. Comparison of three different adversarial patches.

4   Defense Against Adversarial Patch Attacks

In this section, we will describe our defense methodology against adversarial patch attacks in detail.

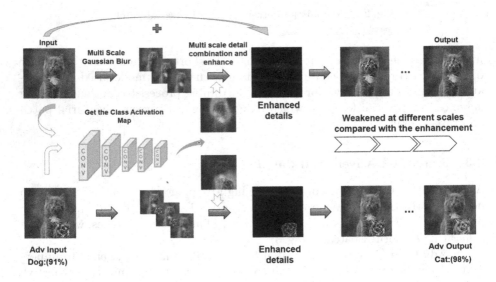

Fig. 4. EGP defense architecture.

4.1   Obtain the Attention Heatmap Matrix

The representative classification models based on convolutional neural networks pay more attention to the local features of images. The adversarial patch will be the salient activation source if the attack successes. Therefore, compared with the global image processing, we aim to process the local areas with strong attention of the models, which causes less impact on the clean image. Consequently, we need to derive the importance of diverse features in different regions to model decisions, namely, the model's attention heatmap matrix [14]. Specifically, we regard α_k^t as the sensitivity to the $k-th$ channel of the output feature map of the last layer A^k about category t. Then we take α_k^t as weights and combine them linearly. Furthermore, the intermediate result of the weighted combination is fed into the activation function to output the required heatmap matrix M_t.

$$\alpha_k^t = \frac{1}{Z} \sum_i \sum_j \frac{\partial y^t}{\partial A_{ij}^k} \tag{3}$$

$$M_t = RELU \left\{ \sum_k \alpha_k^t A^k \right\} \tag{4}$$

Here Z is a normalizing constant such that $\alpha_k^t \in [-1, 1]$. k is the sequence number of the channel dimension of the feature map, i and j are the sequence number of the width and height dimension respectively, and t is the target category.

4.2   Enhance the Local Multi-scale Details

As an indiscriminate processing method, our method aims to make the distortion of clean image I_c small, but the distortion of adversarial example I_{adv} large.

$$max \left\{ D\left(I_c, I\right) - D\left(I_{adv}, I\right) \right\} \tag{5}$$

D is the measurement of image distance.

Compared with clean images, the feature distribution of patches is demonstrated to be dense and irregular with higher local frequency. Therefore, the dissimilarities of Gaussian blurs with different scales are higher than that of clean images. Specifically, our enhanced image can be obtained by Equation (6). For the original image I, by fusing the Gaussian blur decrease values between different scales, we can obtain the contour details of the target category for the clean image I_c. However, for the adversarial example I_{adv}, details tend to be dense and intensive after the same treatment as clean image I_c.

$$I_{en} = norm \left\{ I + \lambda \cdot \sum_{g_i, g_j \in G} w_{ij}\left(g_i - g_j\right) * M \right\} \tag{6}$$

G is the Gaussian fuzzy set with different Gaussian kernels. λ is the magnification factor $(\lambda > 1)$ to enlarge the detailed information. w is the proportional coefficient. M is the mask matrix from the heatmap matrix that limits the processing to the local key region. $norm$ is the normalization process. Then, we multiply the multi-scale details by a magnification factor λ to enhance the details of input image. Furthermore, we add the enlarged local details to the original image I and normalize to obtain the enhanced image I_{en}. As shown in Fig. 4, the clean image appears as a regional detail enhancement, while the adversarial example shows high distortion at the location of the patch.

4.3   Weaken the Local Multi-scale Details

To minimize the influence of preprocessing on the clean images and cause further distortion on the adversarial examples, we consider weakening the local multi-scale details in another Gaussian kernel set based on the local multi-scale details enhancement. The enhanced image I_{en} is regarded as the input, we weaken the local multi-scale details in another Gaussian kernel set $G_{de} = \{g_1, g_2, \ldots, g_n\}$. It should be emphasized that although the patch after details enhancement has been distorted and it is difficult to recover after details weakening. To avoid the reduction of distortion on pixel value caused by processing in the same scale set, we think that it is better to weaken the details in another scale set. For a clean image, the details obtained in another scale set are contour details, which are similar to the details obtained during the enhancement process. However, as for a patch, the weakened details in another scale set are not similar to the enhanced details, because the patch is already distorted and more sensitive to different scales.

The output images can be obtained by Eq. (7). We can still obtain the multi-scale details of the enhanced clean image, which is similar to the multi-scale detail information obtained during enhancement. Consequently, the distance between the clean image and the original image is reduced after weakening. On the contrary, for the adversarial example, since the enhanced image I_{en} has been distorted, further detail weakening under the Gaussian blur of another scale set will only aggravate the distortion of the adversarial example. As shown in Fig. 4, both the clean image and the adversarial example are correctly classified as a cat.

$$I_{out} = norm \left\{ I_{en} - \sum_{g_i, g_j \in G_{de}} w_{ij} \left(g_i - g_j \right) * M \right\} \tag{7}$$

I_{en} is the enhanced image, G_{de} is a Gaussian fuzzy set without intersection with G, I_{out} is the output image.

5   Experiments

5.1   Feasibility of Attack Reinforcement

Experimental Setup for Attack. We consider the validation set available with the ImageNet-2012 dataset in our experiments. We choose images of 10 categories comprised of 10000 images to generate our adversarial patches. The pre-training models are used for patch training with a learning rate of 0.0005. The size of patch is 70×70 covering 10% of the image. During the training of adversarial patches, the number of iterations is set to 8, 100 images of each category are randomly selected in each iteration. Furthermore, to generate the enhanced adversarial patch, we leverage our antagonistic pretraining strategy for the top 100 input images of the first iteration (early inputs) and the learning rate is set to 0.001 to retrain the model to be attacked. Besides, to generate smoothed adversarial patches, we implement a slight Gaussian blur on the updated adversarial patch every 50 inputs during the generation of the ordinary universal adversarial patch. The Gauss kernel is 5 and the fuzzy coefficient is set to 0.2.

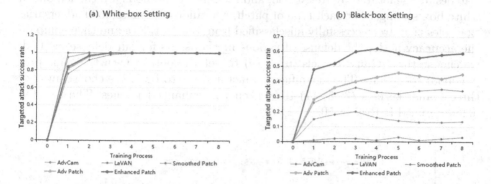

Fig. 5. A comparison of existing methods and our methods for creating adversarial patches. Note that these patches are generated by single model ResNet-50 and the targeted attack success rate refers to the average attack success rate tested in black boxes for the black-box setting.

Attack Performance. We evaluate the performance of our enhanced and smoothed adversarial patches in both white-box and black-box settings. As for the black-box attack, we generate adversarial patches based on ResNet-50, then use them to attack other models with different architectures and unknown parameters (i.e., VGG-16, Inception-V3, and ResNet-152) and record the average target attack success rate.

As indicated in Fig. 5, our generated enhanced adversarial patch enjoys stronger transferability. The enhanced patch avoids the overfitting of the white-box model through the antagonistic pre-training process of the adversarial patch. This process enables the patch to mine the deeper semantic information of the target category rather than to meet the judgment bias of the white-box model, so that it can have better migration ability under the black-box setting. However, regarding our generated smoothed adversarial patch, the attack performance will decline in the black-box setting, but the targeted attack success rate can also reach 100% in the white-box setting. In the process of obtaining the smoothed adversarial patch, some details are discarded. However, our goal is to make the patch smoother on the premise of ensuring the success of the white-box setting attack. Therefore, our smoothed universal adversarial patch may enjoy a better effect in some white-box scenarios with a defense mechanism.

5.2   Evaluation of EGP

Experimental Setup for Defense. Our defense method is evaluated for adversarial patches, enhanced adversarial patches, and smoothed adversarial patches. Patches are generated by ResNet-50, and all defense methods are carried out in white-box settings. For each type of patch, we randomly select 3000 adversarial examples that are successfully misclassified from our test data and then compare the accuracy under the defense of various methods. As for our defense method, we choose three Gauss kernels (5, 9, 19) to get the details with the same proportional coefficient. The magnification factor is set to be 5. We choose another three Gauss kernels (3, 5, 11) to weaken the enhanced images. The selected defense model is ResNet-50.

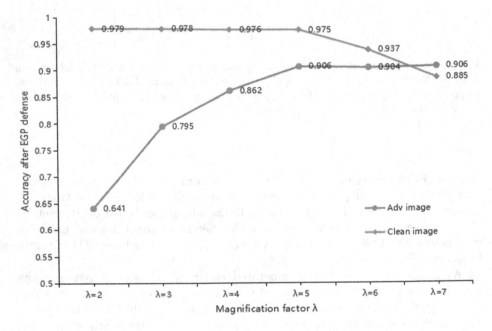

Fig. 6. The effect of amplification factor λ on the experimental results. Note that the accuracy refers to the classification precision after defense on clean images and adversarial images.

The intensity of multi-scale details obtained from the patch is greater than that of a clean image. Therefore, we multiply the multi-scale details by a magnification factor λ to enhance the details of a clean image and limit them to $[-1, 1]$. It should be noted that the values of multi-scale details of adversarial patch are multiple than that of a clean image. Therefore, an appropriate magnification factor λ can be choose to make enhanced details of the patch out of range $[-1, 1]$. As shown in Fig. 6, with the increase of λ, the adversarial images will be distorted due to the excessive enhancement of details, thus increasing the accuracy of adversarial images. However, the classification accuracy of clean images also decreases due to the processing of our method, but when λ is small, the enhancement does not make the pixel value out of range $[-1, 1]$, and the enhanced images can still be restored through the weakening process. But when λ is too large and exceeds a certain threshold, the clean images will be irreversibly enhanced like the adversarial images which cause a significant decrease. Through the experiment, we found that the experimental result is better when λ is set to 5.

Defense Performance. It should be noted that Table 1 shows the comparison of the efficiency of various defense methods against Adv Patch, enhanced patch, and smoothed patch. Accuracy refers to the accuracy of adversarial examples under the defense. The accuracy of original clean images is 98%. The size of the patch is 70*70 covering 10% of the image (Fig. 7).

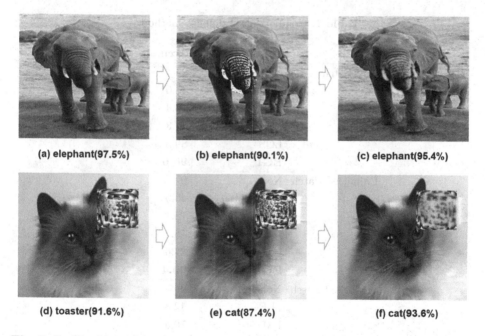

(a) elephant(97.5%)   (b) elephant(90.1%)   (c) elephant(95.4%)

(d) toaster(91.6%)   (e) cat(87.4%)   (f) cat(93.6%)

Fig. 7. ResNet-50 confidence scores are shown for example images. (a), (b) and (c) represent the processing of a clean image. (d), (e) and (f) represent the processing of an adversarial example. (b) and (e) represent the enhanced images after local multi-scale details enhancement. (c) and (f) are the output images. As illustrated, EGP restores correct class confidence and causes a negligible impact on clean images.

We directly use the JPEG method to globally compress the images to implement defense. PM constructs a saliency map of the image to detect localized and visible adversarial perturbations. Once a saliency map for the input has been found, PM uses a combination of erosion and dilation to remove the adversarial perturbations. Lance locates the significant activation sources with CAM [14] and calculates the local input semantic inconsistency with the expected semantic patterns according to the prediction label. Once the inconsistency exceeds a predefined threshold which can be set between 0.1 and 0.18, Lance conducts a recovery process to recover the input image. About LGS, it first estimates the region of interest in an image with the highest probability of adversarial patch and then performs gradient smoothing in only those local regions. Specifically, LGS divides the image into several regions, and then performs gradient smoothing in the region where the image gradient exceeds the threshold value. LGS is used with $\gamma = 2.3$, γ is the smoothing factor for LGS. Note that the accuracy of the detection-based method (i.e., PM, LGS, Lance) is obtained by multiplying the success rate of detection and inpainting.

Table 1 shows the overall defensive performance. Our method EGP outperforms state-of-the-art defense methods for Adv Patch. As for the enhanced adver-

Table 1. Comparison of defense method.

	Defense method	Accuracy (%)
Adv Patch	None	0
	JPEG	45.0
	PM	76.4
	Lance	81.3
	LGS	89.5
	EGP	**90.6**
Enhanced Patch	None	0
	JPEG	45.0
	PM	73.1
	Lance	55.4
	LGS	87.6
	EGP	**90.4**
Smoothed Patch	None	0
	JPEG	42.8
	PM	70.5
	Lance	75.2
	LGS	79.8
	EGP	**89.2**

Table 2. Effect of defense method on clean images.

Method	None	EGP	JPEG	PM	LGS
Accuracy (%)	98.1	97.5	90.5	98.1	98.1

sarial patch, the defense efficiency of the method based on inconsistent features (Lance) [6] will be significantly reduced. Regarding the smoothed patch, our indiscriminate defense method is also excellent. Although other defense methods based on detection also enjoy considerable defensive effect on smoothed patches, it should be emphasized that the defense performance of them decreases more compared with dealing with Adv Patch. Furthermore, as shown in Table 2, the effect of our method on clean images can be ignored compared with other indiscriminate defense methods such as JPEG.

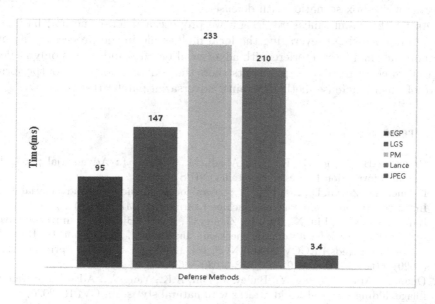

Fig. 8. Average processing time cost comparison of different defense methods. For better display, the average processing time of each image is shown at the top of the histogram.

Moreover, we compare the computational cost of EGP and existing defense methods. The compared methods include both preprocessing based and detection based. Note that our method processes image locally and skip the detection process of adversarial patches. Therefore, our defense strategy costs less computation. As shown in Fig. 8, our defense method only takes 95ms to process per image, which is better than most of the existing defense methods. Although our method is not as good as JPEG in computational cost, our defense efficiency is much better than JPEG.

6 Conclusions

In this paper, we analyze the effectiveness of existing defense methods against adversarial patches. Based on the analysis, we propose two improved patch generation methods to obtain the enhanced and smoothed patches that can effectively obscure the decision boundary for adversarial patches and reduce the effectiveness of existing defense methods. To generate the enhanced patch, we strengthen the generation of the patch through the continuous update of the target model used for generating patch. Taking ImageNet as the data set, extensive experiments are conducted which demonstrate that our proposed enhanced patch enjoys stronger transferability and be robust to some defense mechanisms. Besides, to generate the smoothed patch, we add smooth processing intermittently during the updating of adversarial patch [1] to guide the update. Experimental results show that our smoothed patches enjoy better attack performance in some white-box scenarios with defense.

As for the countermeasure design, we propose a defense method based on image preprocessing. Leveraging the local multi-scale image processing [8], our method can efficiently interfere with adversarial patches and causes only neglect impact on clean images. Experiments show that our methodology outperforms state-of-the-art defense methods against adversarial patch attacks.

References

1. Brown, T.B., Mane, D., Roy, A., Abadi, M., Gilmer, J.: Adversarial patch. In: Neural Information Processing Systems (NIPS) (2017)
2. Karmon, D., Zoran, D., Goldberg, Y.: Lavan: localized and visible adversarial noise. In: International Conference on Machine Learning (ICML) (2018)
3. Liu, A., Wang, J., Liu, X., Cao, B., Zhang, C., Yu, H.: Bias-based universal adversarial patch attack for automatic check-out. In: Vedaldi, A., Bischof, H., Brox, T., Frahm, J.-M. (eds.) ECCV 2020. LNCS, vol. 12358, pp. 395–410. Springer, Cham (2020). https://doi.org/10.1007/978-3-030-58601-0_24
4. Duan, R., Ma, X., Wang, Y., Bailey, J., Qin, A.K., Yang, Y.: Adversarial Camouflflage: hiding physical-world attacks with natural styles. In: CVPR (2020)
5. Naseer, M., Khan, S., Porikli, F.: Local gradients smoothing: defense against localized adversarial attacks. In: Proceedings Of WACV, pp. 1300–1307 (2019)
6. Xu, Z., Yu, F., Chen, X., LanCe: a comprehensive and lightweight CNN defense methodology against physical adversarial attacks on embedded multimedia applications. In: Asia and South Pacific Design Automation Conference (ASP-DAC) (2020)
7. Hayes, J.: On visible adversarial perturbations and digital watermarking. In: Proceedings of CVPR Workshops, pp. 1597–1604 (2018)
8. Kim, Y., Koh, Y.J., Lee, C., Kim, S., Kim, C.S.: Dark image enhancement based on pairwise target contrast and multi-scale detail boosting. In: IEEE International Conference on Image Processing, pp. 1404–1408 (2015)
9. Krizhevsky, A., Sutskever, I., Hinton, G.E.: ImageNet classification with deep convolutional neural networks. In: Neural Information Processing Systems (NIPS) (2012)
10. Mohamed, A.R., Dahl, G.E., Hinton, G.: Acoustic modeling using deep belief networks. In: IEEE T Audio Speech (2011)
11. Sutskever, I., Vinyals, O., Le, Q.: Sequence to sequence learning with neural networks. In: Neural Information Processing Systems (NIPS) (2014)
12. Kurakin, A., Goodfellow, I., Bengio, S.: Adversarial examples in the physical world. arXiv preprint arXiv: 1607.02533 (2016)

13. Moosavi-Dezfooli, S.M., Fawzi, A., Fawzi, O., Frossard, P.: Universal adversarial perturbations. In: CVPR (2017)
14. Zhou, B., Khosla, A., Lapedriza, A., Oliva, A., Torralba, A.: Learning deep features for discriminative localization. In: CVPR (2016)
15. Chen, C., Seff, A., Kornhauser, A., Xiao, J.: Deepdriving: learning affordance for direct perception in autonomous driving. In: ICCV (2015)

Fog Computing and Wireless Computing

Online Offloading of Delay-Sensitive Tasks in Fog Computing

Yu-Jie Sun, Hui Wang[✉], Yu-Chen Shan, and Chen-bin Huang

Zhejiang Normal University, Jinghua 321000, China
hwang@zjnu.cn

Abstract. Fog computing, which provides low-latency computing services at the network edge, is an enabler for the emerging Internet of Things (IoT) systems. Task offloading is one of the main technologies of fog computing. The IoT devices with insufficient computing power will offload tasks to other devices with surplus resources to process. Those devices include IoT devices and fog devices. It exists a problem with how to find suitable devices to offload effectively. For this problem, this paper proposes a Short-Sighted-UCB (SS_UCB) algorithm based on the Upper Confidence Bound (UCB1) algorithm to perform one-to-many predictive offload, predicting which device can be offloaded to reduce task latency and improve quality of service (QoS). Furthermore, this paper proposes an Online-Learning-GS algorithm to solve many-to-many offload to minimize overall task latency. The experiments show that the effectiveness of the SS_UCB and Online-Learning-GS algorithm in a dynamic environment.

Keywords: Fog computing · Cloud computing · Offloading · UCB1 · GS

1 Introduction

Due to the rapid growth of the Internet of Things (IoT), a large number of IoT devices are connected to the wireless network. As the increasing number of computation-intensive applications (e.g., augmented reality and face recognition) appears, higher requirements of computing power are placed on IoT devices. The IoT devices with limited memory and computing power cannot handle computation-intensive applications effectively. To solve this problem, cloud computing is proposed. The IoT devices can send tasks to cloud devices to process. However, if all the IoT devices send tasks to the cloud devices for computing, it will inevitably cause network congestion and high latency. Therefore, the CISCO proposed fog computing, sending tasks on the IoT devices to fog devices that are closer to IoT devices for processing. Not only can fog computing handle low-latency tasks but also effectively reduce network congestion. Nevertheless, fog computing also faces many challenges which are introduced [1]. One of the challenges is to find suitable devices to offload in a dynamic environment. With the widespread distribution of IoT devices, the task can be offloaded to a nearby device through device to device (D2D) to reduce latency and save energy [2]. This paper will use the assumption in [2], which

© Springer Nature Singapore Pte Ltd. 2021
L. Cui and X. Xie (Eds.): CWSN 2021, CCIS 1509, pp. 199–209, 2021.
https://doi.org/10.1007/978-981-16-8174-5_15

means that the IoT devices with insufficient computing power can offload tasks to fog devices or nearby devices to process.

To solve the challenge proposed in [1], the Short-Sighted-UCB (SS_UCB) algorithm is proposed based on the Upper Confidence Bound (UCB1) algorithm to predict which device the task should offload to in this paper. The UCB1 algorithm was originally applied to the Multi-Armed Bandits (MAB) problem to select a suitable bandit to maximize the rewards. The rewards represent the money got from bandits. The traditional MAB problem has a constant action space. In this paper, with the movement of IoT devices and fog devices, the constant changes of channel state, the situation we need to consider is difficult. The action space of this paper is dynamic. The SS_UCB is different from the UCB1 algorithm. The algorithm pays more attention to the recent rewards. So, we introduce a discount factor about rewards in SS_UCB. It is still a question after using SS_UCB that more than one IoT device will select the same device to offload which will cause extra latency. For this problem, we propose an Online-Learning-GS algorithm to minimize the overall delay and improve QoS. The simulation results show the effectiveness of the SS_UCB and Online-Learning-GS algorithm. The main contributions of this paper are summarized as follows:

1) The SS_UCB algorithm is proposed to predict which device the tasks should be offloaded to according to offloading history without knowing other device information in a dynamic environment.
2) The goal of this paper is to minimize the overall latency and improve the quality of service (QoS). However, the SS_UCB only solve one-to-many offload question and it cannot improve the overall latency. Therefore, the Online-Learning-GS algorithm was first proposed to solve many-to-many offloads for improving the overall offload by combining SS_UCB with the GS algorithm. The Online-Learning-GS algorithm is different from offline algorithms. Every time a new record is generated, it will affect the selection result of the fog device. Therefore, online algorithms are more suitable for dynamic environments.

2   Related Works

Offloading is not a trivial issue in fog computing. A large body of recent research worked on addressing the challenges in offloading. The four offload methods 1) Local Mobile Execution, 2) D2D Offloaded Execution, 3) Direct Fog Offloaded Execution, 4) D2D-Assisted Fog Offloaded Execution were proposed in [1]. In [3, 4], a new offload method of fog-to-fog offloading was proposed. Offloading the overloaded tasks in the fog node to other fogs for processing, and using Lyapunov to prove the stability. The second and third offload methods are used in this article. In [5], the tasks are divided into three categories: 1) hard-deadline-based tasks 2) soft-deadline-based tasks and 3) no-deadline-based tasks. In this paper, we mainly focus on hard-deadline-based tasks. Hard-deadline-based tasks mean that if the processing time of tasks exceeds the deadline, it is failed. Multilevel Feedback Queuing is used for task processing and computation offloading in [6]. The integrated edge-fog computing systems indicate that tasks can be offloaded to edge nodes to minimize latency [2]. The IoT devices in this paper are similar to edge devices. The Gale-Shapley (GS) algorithm is applied to reach a stable matching to achieve many-to-many offload in [7]. But the tasks are offloaded based on knowing all the information of other devices in [2, 6, 7]. However, this is unrealistic. Due to the privacy of the device and the instability of the channel and the network, the device information cannot be available in many cases. Therefore, Artificial Neural Networks (ANN) were used to predict the offloading time and find the optimal device to offload in [8]. ANN did not need the information about others devices including IoT devices and fog devices. However, the feasibility of ANN in a dynamic network is not considered. In [9], the Nash equilibrium is used to perform the offloading game between multiple IoT devices and multiple fog nodes in a dynamic environment. Nash equilibrium needs frequent information exchange between IoT devices. However, frequent information exchange between device and device will increase channel traffic.

Considering the problem mentioned above, the Short-Sighted-UCB (SS_UCB) algorithm is proposed to perform one-to-many predictive offload and Online-Learning-GS algorithm was proposed to solve many-to-many offload. The algorithms perform well in a dynamic environment and do not need information about other devices in advance.

3 System Model

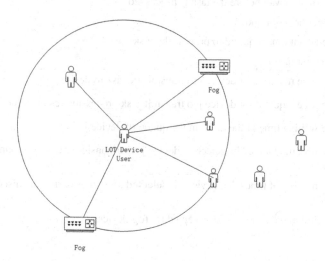

Fig. 1. System model

As shown in Fig. 1, the IoT devices can offload their tasks to other IoT devices or offload tasks to fog devices for processing. Assume that the set of IoT devices are $D = \{D_1, D_2, \dots D_m\}$ and the set of fog devices are $F = \{F_1, F_2, \dots F_n\}$. The m stands for the subscript of IoT devices and n stands for the subscript of fog devices. Here, we consider a time-slotted system, $t = \{1, 2, 3, \dots\}$. We assume the state of channel and fog remain constant in one slot and change in different time slots. The task $T_i = \{l_i, c_i, d_i\}$ where l_i is the size of the task in bits. The c_i is the processing density in cycles per bit, which is the number of cycles required to process a unit bit of data. Furthermore, d_i indicates the deadline of the task and the unit is millisecond. The D2D is used for communicating between IoT devices. The cellular network connections are used between IoT devices and fog devices. The time required for local processing in D_i is related to the processing rate f_i. The τ^{wait} represents the time to wait before the task is processed. Table 1 summarizes important notations used in the paper.

Table 1. Notations

Notation	Meaning
D	The collection of IoT devices
F	The fog collection of IoT devices
T_i	Task i
l_i	The size of task i
c_i	The number of CPU cycles required to process a bit task i
τ^{lcoal}	Time to process task i locally
τ_{ij}^{off}	Time to offload task i to device j
τ^{wait}	The time to wait before the task is processed
β^i	Helper node for node i
τ_i	The actual time required to process the task
λ	Discount factor
τ_{ij}^{up}	The time required for device i to transfer the task to device j
τ_{ij}^{down}	The time required for device j to transmit task processing results to device i
τ_{ij}^{wait}	The waiting time of the task i in the queue of device j
$I_j(t)$	The reward obtained by selecting device j after considering the discount factor at time t
$N_j(t)$	The number of times that device j is selected after considering the discount factor at time t
T^{max}	Maximum number of tasks accepted by fog devices

The time to process the data locally is expressed as follows:

$$\tau^{lcoal} = l_i c_i / f_i + \tau^{wait} \tag{1}$$

The time for offloading tasks to IoT devices or fog nodes includes four parts: 1) time for transmission task τ_{ij}^{up}, 2) time for processing task, 3) time for getting the result from helper node τ_{ij}^{down}, 4) the waiting time of request at the helper node τ_{ij}^{wait}. The helper nodes are devices that the tasks can be offloaded. We call the set of helper nodes of D_i as β^i, $\beta^i = \{\beta_1, \beta_2, \ldots \beta_k\}$. The K stands for the subscript of helper nodes. The needed time τ_{ij}^{off} that D_i offload T_i to β_j is expressed as follows:

$$\tau_{ij}^{off} = l_i c_i / f_j + \tau_{ij}^{up} + \tau_{ij}^{down} + \tau_{ij}^{wait} \tag{2}$$

The real time τ_i for processing T_i is expressed as follows:

$$\tau_i = \min\left(\tau^{lcoal}, \tau_{ij}^{off}\right) \tag{3}$$

4 Problem Statement

With the privacy and security of the device, the information of other devices is not available. The channel status and device busyness are constantly changing. In such a dynamic environment, how to find a suitable device to offload. The following formula is used to express above the question.

$$\min_j \tau_i \, j \in (0, 1, 2 \ldots, K). \tag{4}$$

When $j = 0$, it means that the task is processed locally. To minimize the time required, the SS_UCB algorithm based on UCB1 is proposed. The UCB1 algorithm originally proposed to solve MAB question in [10]. The MAB question is which arm is chosen to maximize revenue. The UCB1 algorithm selects an arm with the greatest possible reward based on the history of selection. In this paper, the helper node β^i is same as the arm that can be selected. The goal is to predict which helper node is chosen to minimize delay and improve QoS. But UCB1 cannot be adapted to dynamic environment well. Due to the mobility of device, dynamic about channel and device state, we should pay more attention to the recent reward. A discount factor λ of reinforcement learning is proposed in this paper. This discount factor λ is usually not very small. If λ is too small, the predictions are not very accurate. The $I_j(t)$ represents total rewards after selecting equipment β_j until time slot t. The $\tau^{real}(t)$ represents the actual delay in selecting equipment β_j in time slot t. The $\tau^{lcoal}(t)$ indicates the delay of the task being processed locally in time slot t. The $N_j(t)$ indicates the number of times that β_j is selected after considering the discount factor until time slot t. In time slot t, if β_j is selected $I_j(t)$ and $N_j(t)$ will be updated according to the following formula.

$$I_j(t) = \lambda I_j(t - 1) + \tau^{lcoal}(t) - \tau^{real}(t) \tag{5}$$

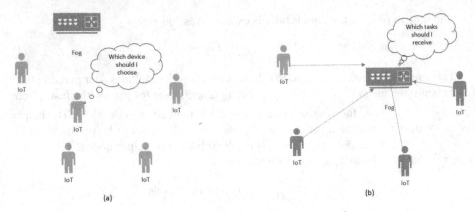

Fig. 2. One to many and many to many questions

$$N_j(t) = 1 + \lambda N_j(t - 1) \qquad (6)$$

The $\tau^{lcoal}(t) - \tau^{real}(t)$ in formula (5) represents the reward in slot t. The SS_UCB algorithm is summarized in algorithm 1. The t represents time slot in first line and the $|\beta^i|$ indicates the number of helper nodes. The k in line 14 of algorithm 1 represents the total selection times after considering the discount factor. Algorithm 1 can only solve the problem of one-to-many predictive offload (see Fig. 2(a)). Another question is how to perform many-to-many offload. As shown in Fig. 2(b), IoT devices can offload tasks to nearby IoT or fog devices. If all IoT devices choose to be offloaded to fog, what tasks will the fog device receive. The question is expressed as follows:

$$\min \sum_{i=1}^{n} \sum_{j=1}^{|\beta^i|} \tau_i a_{ij} \qquad (7)$$

$$St: a_{ij} \in [0, 1] \qquad (8)$$

$$\sum_{j=1}^{|\beta^i|} a_{ij} = 1 \qquad (9)$$

Algorithm 1. SS_UCB Algorithm

Input: offloading history

Output: the helper node that should be selected for each time slot t

1: $t = 1$

2: Initialize the total reward and the number of selected times $I_j(t) = 0$,
    $N_j(t) = 0$

3: WHILE $t \leq |\beta^i|$:

4:      Offload task to β_t and get $\tau^{real}(t)$

5:      $N_t(t) = 1$

6:      $I_t(t) = \tau^{local}(t) - \tau^{real}(t)$

7:      $k = 1 + \lambda + \lambda^2 + \ldots\ldots + \lambda^{t-1}, t = t + 1, R_t(t) = I_t(t) + \sqrt{2\ln K}$

8: WHILE $t \geq |\beta^i|$:

9:      $j = \max_j R_j(t)$

10:     Offload task to β_j and get $\tau^{real}(t)$

11:     $I_j(t) = \lambda I_j(t-1) + \tau^{local}(t) - \tau^{real}(t)$

12:     $N_j(t) = 1 + \lambda N_j(t-1)$

13:     $k = 1 + \lambda + \lambda^2 + \ldots\ldots + \lambda^{t-1}$

14:     $R_j(t) = I_j(t) / N_j(t) + \sqrt{\dfrac{2\ln K}{N_j(t)}}$

15:     $t = t + 1$

The constraint in (8), if a_{ij} equals 1, it represents T_i is offloaded to β_j. If a_{ij} equals 0, it represents T_i is not offloaded to β_j. The constraint in (9) represents that a task can only be offloaded to one device. For this question, the GS algorithm combined with the previous SS_UCB algorithm is used to generate a task offloading plan to minimize the overall task completion time. The GS algorithm is used for matching proposed in game theory in [2]. It allows many-to-one matching between IoT device and fog devices, and one-to-one matching between IoT devices. If SS_UCB running in all IoT devices, a question will occur. More than one device will select the same device to offload which causes a delay. The Online-Learning-GS algorithm is proposed to solve the offloading conflict. The difference between online and offline is that each record of the online model will change the model, while the offline model is unchanged. Every new offloading history will change the existing model, so Online-Learning-GS algorithm is online algorithm. The step of Online-Learning-GS algorithm is as follows:

1. The SS_UCB algorithm is used in all IoT devices and the $R_j(t)$ is calculated by the SS_UCB algorithm. Generate a preference list in IoT device by sorting by $R_j(t)$, $j \in (0, 1, 2 \ldots, K)$.

2. The IOT devices send the generated preference list to specified fog device.

3. In specified fog device, IoT devices first choose the highest position helper node in its preference list for processing. If more than one device selects the same helper

node and the helper node is IoT device, it will only receive task with higher $R_j(t)$. Others will be rejected. Otherwise, it will receive all task ordering by reward.

4. The rejected IoT devices will select the helper node of next position in preference list.
5. Repeat 3–4 until no rejection happen.
6. Send the matching result to IoT devices.
7. In following slot, repeat 1–6.

In the third step, if the fog device accepts all requests, it may cause congestion in the queue, so we propose to set a maximum number of accepted tasks T^{max} for the fog devices. Only the queue length of the fog device does not exceed this length to receive. Every device can be rejected at most K times. The time complexity of Online-Learning-GS algorithm is relevant to the number of task and helper nodes in every time slot. The task number is limited within a time slot, so we define it as a constant α. The worst time complexity is $O(\alpha k)$.

5 Simulation

For the simulations, we consider that the calculation rate of fog nodes is uniformly distributed between $[5 \times 10^9, 9 \times 10^9]$ cycle/s and the calculation rate of IoT devices is uniformly distributed between $[1 \times 10^8, 7 \times 10^8]$ cycle/s. We consider the task size is uniformly distributed between [7000, 9000] bit. Assuming the number of CPU cycles required to process a bit of task is located in [100, 200] and the deadline of the task is located in [1, 3] millisecond. In Fig. 3, we assume that there are 10 IoT devices and 2 fog devices. The SS_UCB, ε-greedy algorithm and local processed algorithm is run in IoT device. When the discount factor equals 1, the SS_UCB algorithm will degenerate to the UCB1 algorithm. It can be seen from Fig. 3, as the number of tasks increases, the average processing time of tasks continues to decrease. It shows that SS_UCB algorithm is better than the ε-greedy, UCB1 algorithm and local-process algorithm in a dynamic environment. The SS_UCB algorithm works well in predicting one-to-many offloading question. It can always find the fog node with the shortest processing time. The ε-greedy algorithm is the e-greedy curve in the figure. The discount factor is not the smaller the better the effect. We can see from Fig. 3 when the discount factor is equal to 0.55, the average processing time is greater than the discount factor is equal to 0.6. In actual applications, the discount factor should be determined according to the specific situation.

We assume that there are 15 IoT nodes, 2 fog node, and 5 IoT nodes generate tasks in each time slot, and other nodes are idle in Fig. 4, Fig. 5 and Fig. 6. As shown in Fig. 4, the x-axis represents the number of time slots. The y-axis represents the average processing delay. As the t increase, the overall average process time continues to decrease. The Online-Learning-GS algorithm effectively solves the problem in Eq. (7). It shows the effectiveness of the Online-Learning-GS algorithm in a dynamic environment.

We propose to set a maximum number of accepted tasks T^{max} for the fog devices in Online-Learning-GS algorithm. We can see the impact of the different maximum number of accepted tasks on the offloading success ratio from Fig. 5. Considering that the max accepted num is equal to 4, 6, 8 respectively. As T^{max} increases, the offloading

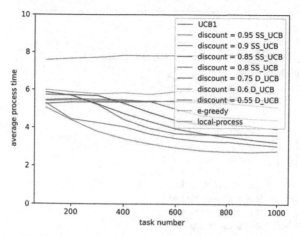

Fig. 3. Average process time of different algorithms

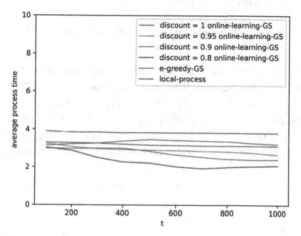

Fig. 4. Overall average process time of different algorithms

success ratio increases. However, when it reaches 10, the offloading success ratio will decrease. This is because the queue length is too long, causing the task to exceed the deadline. Then the offloading success ratio begins to decreases. When T^{max} continues to rise, the IoT device will select other devices for offloading. The offloading success rate will slowly rise instead of continuing to fall. The T^{max} should not be too small or too large. Too small will cause many tasks to be unable to process, and too large will cause the task processing deadline to be exceeded. Choose a suitable number according to the actual situation.

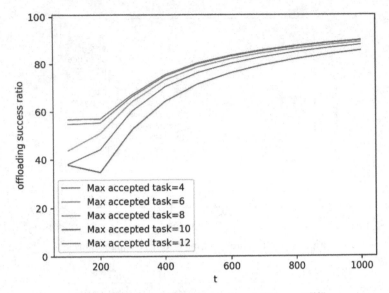

Fig. 5. The offloading success ratio of different T^{max}

It shows in Fig. 6, as the t increase, the success ratio increases. If $\tau^{real}(t)$ is greater than $d_i(t)$, it indicates that the task was processed successfully. The $d_i(t)$ is the task deadline of T_i in t slot. If $\tau^{real}(t)$ is less than $d_i(t)$, the task fails to process. The QoS is represented by the success rate in this paper. The larger the QOS, the higher the user satisfaction. The increasing of the success rate indicates that Online-Learning-GS effectively improve the task success ratio and minimize overall latency.

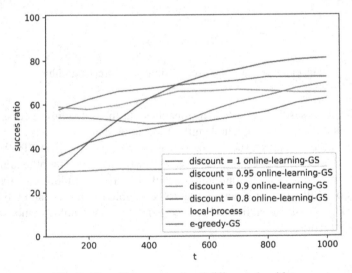

Fig. 6. Overall success ratio of different algorithms

6 Conclusion

In this paper, we propose the SS_UCB algorithm to solve the one-to-many offload question and the Online-Learning-GS algorithm to solve the many-to-many offload question. From the simulation results, the SS_UCB and Online-Learning-GS algorithm is efficient in a dynamic environment. The SS_UCB algorithm introduces a discount factor based on the UCB1 algorithm, thereby improving the applicability of UCB1 in a dynamic environment. The Online-Learning-GS is obtained by combining the SS_UCB algorithm and GS algorithm. The Online-Learning-GS algorithm can minimize the overall latency and improve the success ratio. The question of fog rental prices was proposed in [11]. The fog price is not considered in this paper. This question can be used in the following direction.

References

1. Mouradian, C.: A comprehensive survey on fog computing: state-of-the-art and research challenges. IEEE Commun. Surv. Tutor. **20**(1), 416–464 (2018)
2. Chiti, F.: A matching theory framework for tasks offloading in fog computing for IoT systems. IEEE Internet Things **5**(6), 5089–5096 (2018)
3. Xiao, Y.: Distributed optimization for energy-efficient fog computing in the tactile internet. IEEE J. Sel. Areas Commun. **36**(11), 2390–2400 (2018)
4. Lyu, X.: Distributed online optimization of fog computing for selfish devices with out-of-date information. IEEE Trans. Wirel. Commun. **17**(11), 7704–7717 (2018)
5. Zhang, G.: FEMTO: fair and energy-minimized task offloading for fog-enabled IoT networks. IEEE Internet Things J. **6**(3), 4388–4400 (2019)
6. Adhikari, M.: DPTO: a deadline and priority-aware task offloading in fog computing framework leveraging multilevel feedback queueing. IEEE Internet Things J. **7**(7), 5773–5782 (2020)
7. Darak, S.J.: Multi-player multi-armed bandits for stable allocation in heterogeneous ad-hoc networks. IEEE J. Sel. Areas Commun. **37**(10), 2350–2363 (2019)
8. Abedi, M., Pourkiani, M.: Resource allocation in combined fog-cloud scenarios by using artificial intelligence. In: 2020 Fifth International Conference on Fog and Mobile Edge Computing (FMEC), Piscataway, NJ, pp. 218–222. IEEE (2020)
9. Shah-Mansouri, H.: Hierarchical fog-cloud computing for IoT systems: a computation offloading game. IEEE Internet Things J. **5**(4), 3246–3257 (2018)
10. Bouneffouf, D.: Finite-time analysis of the multi-armed bandit problem with known trend. In: 2016 IEEE Congress on Evolutionary Computation (CEC), Piscataway, NJ, pp. 2543–2549. IEEE (2016)
11. Mukherjee, M.: Revenue maximization in delay-aware computation offloading among service providers with fog federation. IEEE Commun. Lett. **24**(8), 1799–1803 (2020)

A Data Download Scheme Based on Vehicle Mobile Information in Internet of Vehicles

Yabo Sun[1,2(✉)], Lei Shi[1,2(✉)], Xiang Bi[1,2(✉)], Xu Ding[1,2(✉)], and Zhenchun Wei[1,2(✉)]

[1] School of Computer Science and Information Engineering, Intelligent Interconnected Systems Laboratory of Anhui Province, Hefei University of Technology, Hefei 230009, China
{bixiang,dingxu,weizc}@hfut.edu.cn
[2] Engineering Research Center of Safety Critical Industrial Measurement and Control Technology, Ministry of Education, Hefei 230009, China

Abstract. Due to the high mobility and limited transmission range of vehicles, the data download capacity of single vehicle is greatly limited, which brings poor performance to users. In this paper, we divide the data into blocks. We want to design a data block broadcasting scheme so that all vehicles can receive data blocks as many as possible in a base station(BS) range. We first give the mathematical model and find it is difficult to be solved directly. Then we design a heuristic algorithm for solving the problem. The main idea of our algorithm is to give each data block a weight. The data block with the largest weight is broadcast by BS, and several vehicles are selected to broadcast the remaining data blocks. We call our algorithm as the Iterative Strategy for Data Allocation(ISDA) algorithm. Then considering the actual situation, we subsequently propose the online algorithm. Through experiments and simulations, we prove that our scheme can effectively improve the data download rate and reduce the download delay.

Keywords: Data downloading · Cooperative communication · Edge computing · Internet of vehicles

1 Introduction

With the increasing number of vehicles and the rising popularity of on-board applications, the Internet of vehicles (IoV) has attracted great attention in recent years [4,12]. IoV is a new generation of wireless network technology and has many applications [9,14], such as preventing traffic accidents, providing traffic information services, and making driving environment safer and more comfortable. However, as people's pursuit of comfort and safety continues to improve, there

Supported by the Major Science and Technology Projects in Anhui Province under Grant No. 202003a05020009, the Fundamental Research Funds for the Central Universities of China under Grant No. PA2021GDGP0061.

are still many areas worthy of attention and research in vehicle network [21]. Especially in recent years, with the development of artificial intelligence technology, people pay more and more attention to automatic driving technology [11,20]. Automatic driving technology must rely on the full development of vehicle's perception and communication ability to the surrounding environment [13]. Edge computing [15,16] is a hot research field in recent years, which sinks a large number of complex calculations into the edge server environment, thus making automatic driving technology possible [8,19].

Data downloading is a promising and practical application in vehicle network [3]. Further researches on automatic driving have revealed that the demands for data downloading have been on a rise [2]. The two most common communications in IoV are vehicle-to-vehicle(V2V) and vehicle-to-infrastructure(V2I) communications [7]. Cellular network is the most common type of communication in V2I communication. Vehicles can obtain traffic-related and entertainment-related content directly from the service providers by using a cellular network. However, due to the high speed of vehicles, it can be expensive to download large amounts of data (such as videos or high-quality images) over the cellular network [5]. In addition, when mobile data demands are larger than usual, the cellular network will face the problem of network congestion.

To address the limitations of cellular network, a cooperative downloading method can be used. For large size data, there is a high probability that vehicles would not be able to download the data completely. Besides, vehicles on the edge of the communication coverage of BS have a weak communication link, which means that it is difficult for these vehicles to directly download data from the BS. Using cooperative downloading method, vehicles with good communication links with the BS can help the nearby vehicles to download data. In addition, this technology can reduce the conflict of media access control (MAC) layer, and improve the network reliability and transmission throughput of IoV.

In this paper, we study the problem of data allocation in the vehicle network environment. In order to improve the data download rate, we divide the data into blocks, and vehicles can randomly download their missing data blocks from BS or nearby vehicles. We hope that all vehicles can receive complete data in the shortest possible time. We first build a mathematical model for this problem and propose a heuristic algorithm called Iterative Strategy for Data Allocation(ISDA) to solve the problem. Our algorithm gives each data block a weight and arranges the order of their broadcast according to the size of the weight. Then we propose an online algorithm, which adjusts the weight according to the actual situation. Finally, we compare our scheme with other schemes, and the results show that our scheme can improve the data download rate and reduce the download delay. Both offline algorithm and online algorithm can achieve good performance.

The rest of this paper is organized as follows. In Sect. 2, we introduce the related work. In Sect. 3, we propose our system model and define our problem. In Sect. 4, we design the data allocation algorithm according to the model. In Sect. 5, we give the simulation results and analyze them. In Sect. 6, we conclude the whole paper.

2   Related Work

Cooperative communication as an effective approach to improve the performance(e.g., throughput, delay, etc.) of data transmission in vehicle network, has drawn increasing attention.

For V2V cooperative communications, the authors in [22] analyzed the achievable throughput of cooperative mobile content distribution from road side units (RSU), where packet-level network coding and symbol-level network coding are both exploited. In [17], authors proposed a novel approach for the vehicles to download a common content in a cost-efficient way. The basic idea is to stimulate the vehicles to download the content cooperatively in mutually disjoint coalitions. In [6], authors proposed a V2V collaboration scenario to distribute different types of service messages, and applied a cooperative relay selection algorithm to improve the packet delivery ratio and reduce delay. Nevertheless, these schemes only consider vehicular cooperation for cooperative content download but do not take V2I communications into account.

Recent researches pay more attention to both V2V and V2I cooperations. In [23], authors proposed a multiple-vehicle protocol for collaborative data downloading by using network coding (NC). When multiple vehicles that are approaching each other have a common interest in certain data, they can collaboratively download the data from an RSU to significantly reduce their download time. In [18], authors proposed a novel cooperative store-carry-forward(CSCF) scheme to reduce the transmission outage time of vehicles in the dark areas. In [10], authors proposed a secure incentive scheme to achieve fair and reliable cooperative downloading for IoV. In their paper, the virtual check method was used to achieve incentive mechanism, which can motivate vehicles to help each other download large files. In [1], authors proposed an adaptive multiple-relay selection scheme, which allows RSU to select relay vehicles while considering the most relevant multiple criteria.

Previous works have made some contributions in the field of cooperative downloading. However, most of them tend to download the entire data from BS, without considering the download delay caused by the large amount of data that the vehicle cannot download in a BS range. Different from the previous schemes, our scheme divides the whole data into several data blocks. Vehicles can randomly download their own missing data blocks from BS or nearby vehicles. As each vehicle downloads the complete data in the shortest possible time, the download delay can be greatly reduced.

3   System Model and Problem Definition

3.1   Network Model

Consider a highway scenario where vehicles are moving in the same direction and BSs are deployed along the road, as shown in Fig. 1. Consider each BS can cover the road with a length L. Suppose at a time all vehicles need to download a data from BSs and suppose the data has a large size with the value D. In order to ensure all vehicles can receive the data, we divide it into n blocks equally for downloading. During the whole schedule time T, vehicles can download these blocks with no order. Suppose there are two wireless communication channels. During the download process, vehicles can download data blocks directly from the BS, or download them from other nearby vehicles. As we know all wireless channels are broadcast channels, that means when a transmitter is transmitting, all receivers will receive and only will receive this transmitter's data block. Suppose the communication radius of the vehicle is $R(R < L)$. We want to design a data block broadcast algorithm, so that in the range of one BS, all vehicles can get data blocks as many as possible.

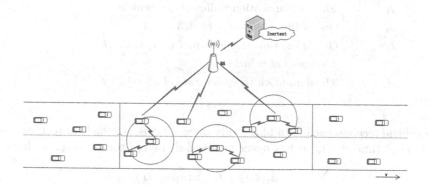

Fig. 1. System model.

3.2 Problem Formulation

Denote $s_i(s_i \in S, i = 1 \dots u)$ as one of the vehicles. Denote $d_i(d_i \in D, i = 1 \dots n)$ as one of the data blocks. We have $d_1 = \cdots = d_n = d$. Suppose the whole scheduling time T is divided into h time slots equally, and denote $t_i(t_i \in T, i = 1 \dots h)$ as one of the time slots (Table 1). We have $t_1 = \cdots = t_h = t$.

Denote $x(s_i, d_j, t_k)$ as the data block receiving cases of vehicle s_i at time slot t_k, we have

$$x(s_i, d_j, t_k) = \begin{cases} 1 : s_i \text{ receives data block } d_j \text{ at time slot } t_k; \\ 0 : \text{otherwise.} \end{cases}$$

Consider that the vehicle has two wireless interfaces, it can receive at most two data blocks at the same time in a time slot, we have

$$\sum_{j=1}^{n} x(s_i, d_j, t_k) \leq 2 \quad (\forall \ s_i \in S, \ t_k \in T), \tag{1}$$

$$\sum_{k=1}^{h} \sum_{j=1}^{n} x(s_i, d_j, t_k) \leq n \quad (\forall \ s_i \in S). \tag{2}$$

Table 1. Notations.

Variables	Meaning
C	The number of data blocks received by all vehicles
d_i	One of the data blocks $i \in \{1, 2, 3, ..., n\}$
L	The length of road covered by BS
$l_{s_i s_0}(t_k)$	The distance between vehicle s_i and BS at time slot t_k
$l_{s_i s_{i'}}(t_k)$	The distance between vehicles at time slot t_k
m_{s_0}	The location of BS
m_{s_i}	The initial location of vehicle s_i
R	The communication radius of the vehicle
s_i	One of the vehicles $i \in \{1, 2, 3, ..., u\}$
t_i	One of the time slot lengths $i \in \{1, 2, 3, ..., h\}$
v_{s_i}	The speed of vehicle s_i
η	The data block reception rate of all vehicles

The vehicle receives each data block only once, that is, if vehicle s_i receives data block d_j at time slot t_k, it has never received d_j before time slot t_k, we have

$$\sum_{k'<k} x(s_i, d_j, t_{k'}) = 0 \quad (x(s_i, d_j, t_k) = 1). \tag{3}$$

Denote $y(s_i, d_j, t_k)$ as the data block broadcasting cases of vehicle s_i at time slot t_k, where $i = 0$ represents the data block broadcasting cases of BS at time slot t_k, we have

$$y(s_i, d_j, t_k) = \begin{cases} 1 : s_i \text{ broadcasts data block } d_j \text{ at time slot } t_k; \\ 0 : \text{otherwise.} \end{cases}$$

For BS or a vehicle, it can only broadcast one data block in a time slot, we have

$$\sum_{j=1}^{n} y(s_i, d_j, t_k) = 1 \quad (\forall \ t_k \in T). \tag{4}$$

For vehicle s_i, it can only receive or broadcast data block at time slot t_k, we have

$$x(s_i, d_{j'}, t_k) + y(s_i, d_j, t_k) \le 1. \tag{5}$$

Denote m_{s_i} as the initial location of vehicle s_i, and m_{s_0} as the location of BS. Consider that all vehicles are moving at a constant speed, we use v_{s_i} to indicate the speed of vehicle s_i. Then the distance between vehicles can be expressed as

$$l_{s_i s_{i'}}(t_k) = |(m_{s_i} - m_{s_{i'}}) + (v_{s_i} - v_{s_{i'}}) \cdot (k-1) \cdot t|, \tag{6}$$

the distance between vehicle s_i and BS can be expressed as

$$l_{s_i s_0}(t_k) = |(m_{s_i} - m_{s_0}) + v_{s_i} \cdot (k-1) \cdot t|. \tag{7}$$

When BS broadcasts data block at time slot t_k, there are vehicles in the BS range that need this data block, we have

$$\exists \, s_i \in S, x(s_i, d_j, t_k) + y(s_0, d_j, t_k) = 2 \quad (l_{s_i s_0}(t_k) \le \frac{L}{2}). \tag{8}$$

Similarly, if vehicle s_i broadcasts data block at time slot t_k, there are vehicles that need this data block in the vehicle s_i range, we have

$$\exists \, s_{i'} \in S, x(s_{i'}, d_j, t_k) + y(s_i, d_j, t_k) = 2 \quad (l_{s_i s_{i'}}(t_k) \le R). \tag{9}$$

From the above discussion, we can get the number of data blocks received by all vehicles through a BS, that is

$$C = \sum_{i=1}^{u} \sum_{j=1}^{n} \sum_{k=1}^{h} x(s_i, d_j, t_k). \tag{10}$$

Then our problems can be formulated as,

$$\max \eta$$
$$\text{s.t.} \quad \eta = \frac{C}{u \cdot n} \tag{11}$$
$$(1)(2)(3)(4)(5)(8)(9)(10)$$

Notice that in (11), $x(s_i, d_j, t_k)$ and $y(s_i, d_j, t_k)$ are binary variables, and their values are determined by the specific network environment. We do not know their values in each time slot. These make the original problem model complex and hard to be solved directly. Therefore, in order to solve the problem, we need to give further analysis and find some way to reduce the complexity of the original problem.

4 Algorithms

Since the original problem is complex and difficult to solve directly, we will try to find some feasible solutions to solve it in this section. Firstly, in order to get the best possible experimental result, we design an offline algorithm. In the offline algorithm, all vehicles information is known in advance, that is, we know the number of missing data blocks for all vehicles at present and the situation of these vehicles at the later time. However, in the real network environment, we only know the number of missing data blocks for all vehicles at present, but we do not know the situation of these vehicles at the later time, which means we need to design an online algorithm. In the following, we first design the offline algorithm in Subsect. 4.1. Then in Subsect. 4.2, we design the online algorithm.

4.1 Offline Algorithm

Now we discuss the offline algorithm. In order to solve Eq. (11), we need to consider the following problems. (i), How to determine the broadcast order of data blocks? (ii), How to select a broadcasting vehicle? (iii), When selecting a broadcast vehicle, how to eliminate the interference caused by overlapping coverage of vehicles? Once these problems are solved, the original problem can be solved.

Therefore, we will try to propose a heuristic algorithm to solve these problems. The main idea of our algorithm is to give a weight to each missing data block, and the data block with the largest weight is broadcast first. We call the designed algorithm based on this idea as the Iterative Strategy for Data Allocation(ISDA) algorithm. In the following we give the main four steps of the algorithm.

First, initialize the original variables, including D, h, and so on. Calculate the weight of all data blocks, and insert the data block into queue Q according to the size of weight. Notice that the data block with the largest weight is first inserted into Q, and the data block with the smallest weight is finally inserted into Q.

Second, take out a data block from the queue Q. Since it is the first data block, it will be allocated to BS for broadcasting. The data block is received by the vehicle missing the data block in the BS range. For other data blocks in the queue Q, select appropriate vehicles with the data block in the BS range for broadcasting.

Third, take out another data block from queue Q and calculate the number of vehicles with this data block in the BS range. If the number of vehicles is 0, continue to judge the next data block in the queue, otherwise add these vehicles into an array. For each vehicle in the array, we count the number f of vehicles that need this data block in its range. Insert these vehicles into queue P according to the size of f. Notice that the vehicle with the largest f is first inserted into the queue. Take out a vehicle from P, we judge whether its communication range overlaps with all the broadcasting vehicles in B. If not, the vehicle is a broadcasting vehicle and add it into B, otherwise continue to judge the next vehicle in queue P.

Fourth, after all broadcasting vehicles are determined, the vehicles with missing data blocks in the range of broadcasting vehicles will receive these data blocks.

The third step will be repeated until the queue Q is empty. The details of ISDA algorithm can be found in Algorithm 1. Line 2–17 are the process of a single time slot. Repeat this process, we can get the number of data blocks received by all vehicles through a BS.

Algorithm 1: The ISDA Algorithm

Input: D:the data block set; S:the vehicle set; B:the broadcast vehicle set; h:the number of time slots; Q:the weight queue of data blocks; P:the vehicle queue with current data block.

Output: the number of data blocks received by all vehicles through a BS.

1 **for** $i = 1$ *to* h **do**
2   calculate the weight of data block and insert it into Q;
3   **while** Q *is not empty* **do**
4          $m \leftarrow Q.pop()$;
5   **if** m *is the first data block* **then**
6   BS broadcast data block m;
7   **else**
8   add the vehicle with m in the BS range into P;
9   **while** P *is not empty* **do**
10                 $e \leftarrow P.pop()$;
11   **if** *the range of e and broadcast vehicles does not overlap* **then**
12   add e into B;
13   **end**
14   **end**
15   **end**
16   **end**
17   vehicles in B broadcast data blocks.
18 **end**

4.2 Online Algorithm

For the online algorithm, most steps are the same as the offline algorithm. But unlike the offline algorithm, we only consider the missing number of current data blocks when calculating the weight of data blocks. The details of the online algorithm refer to Algorithm 1.

5 Simulation

In this section, we give simulation results. We consider the location of the BS is 1000 m, and its coverage radius is 250 m. The whole time T is divided into 30 time slots. All vehicles move at a constant speed in the same direction. We set the communication radius of the vehicle is 40 m. The location of the vehicle ranges from 500 to 1250 m, and the speed of the vehicle ranges from 8 to 11 m/s. In the following we compare our proposed scheme with only-BS and only-vehicle scheme in the same environment. We first give the experimental results in different number of vehicles, and then give the experimental results in different number of data blocks.

5.1   Case of Different Vehicles

In this section, we give the experimental results in different number of vehicles. We set the number of data blocks as 40, and the number of vehicles as 40, 50, 60, 70, 80, 90 and 100 respectively. Then we can get the experimental results as shown in Fig. 2.

In Fig. 2(a), we compare the data download rate. We find that there is no obvious relationship between the data download rate and the number of vehicles. However, the data download rate of our proposed scheme is much higher than that of other schemes, and the gap between them is obvious. The result of our offline algorithm ISDA is always the best because it optimizes the weight of data blocks. The online-algorithm we proposed also performs well. In Fig. 2(b), we compare the average download delay. Similarly, we can see that there is no obvious relationship between the average download delay and the number of vehicles. The average download delay of our proposed scheme is much lower than that of other schemes. Since the online algorithm only considers the missing times when calculating the weight of data block, it has the lowest average download delay.

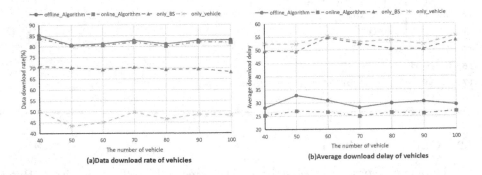

Fig. 2. Different number of vehicles.

5.2   Case of Different Data Blocks

In this section, we give the experimental results in different number of data blocks. We set the number of vehicles as 40, and the number of data blocks as 30, 35, 40, 45 and 50 respectively. Then we can get the experimental results as shown in Fig. 3.

In Fig. 3(a), we compare the data download rate. We find that as the number of data blocks increases, the data download rate gradually begins to decline. The data download rate of our proposed scheme is much higher than that of other schemes, and the result of offline algorithm is always the best. In Fig. 3(b), we compare the average download delay. As the number of data blocks increases, the average download delay also increases. However, the average download delay of our proposed scheme is much lower than that of other schemes, and the online algorithm is the lowest.

In conclusion, the data download rate of our proposed scheme is much higher than that of other schemes, and the average download delay is also lower than that of other schemes. As the number of data blocks increases, the gap between them becomes more and more obvious.

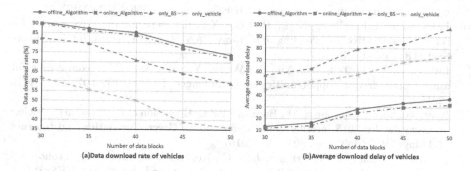

Fig. 3. Different number of data blocks.

6 Conclusion

In this paper, a cooperative data downloading scheme is designed to improve the data download rate in vehicle network. We build a mathematical model for this problem. Since the designed model is complex and can not be solved directly, we propose a heuristic algorithm named ISDA, which sets a weight for each data block, and the data block with the largest weight is first broadcast. Then considering the actual situation, we also propose corresponding online algorithm. Simulation results show that our scheme can effectively improve the data download rate and reduce the download delay compared with other schemes.

References

1. Ahmed, S.H., Mu, D., Kim, D.: Improving bivious relay selection in vehicular delay tolerant networks. IEEE Trans. Intell. Transp. Syst. **19**, 987–995 (2018)
2. Cai, Z., Shi, T.: Distributed query processing in the edge assisted IoT data monitoring system. IEEE Internet of Things J. **PP**(99), 1 (2020)
3. Cai, Z., Zheng, X.: A private and efficient mechanism for data uploading in smart cyber-physical systems. IEEE Trans. Netw. Sci. Eng. 1 (2018)
4. Cai, Z., Zheng, X., Yu, J.: A differential-private framework for urban traffic flows estimation via taxi companies. IEEE Trans. Ind. Inform. 1 (2019)
5. Cui, J., Wei, L., Zhong, H., Zhang, J., Xu, Y., Liu, L.: Edge computing in VANETs-an efficient and privacy-preserving cooperative downloading scheme. IEEE J. Sel. Areas Commun. **38**, 1191–1204 (2020)

6. Das, B., Misra, S., Roy, U.: Coalition formation for cooperative service-based message sharing in vehicular ad hoc networks. IEEE Trans. Parallel Distrib. Syst. **27**, 144–156 (2016)

7. Guo, T., Li, C., Miao, Z., Dong, W., Su, X.: Prefetching-based content download for highway vehicular ad hoc networks. In: 2017 IEEE/CIC International Conference on Communications in China (ICCC), pp. 1–6 (2017)

8. Hou, X., et al.: Reliable computation offloading for edge-computing-enabled software-defined IoV. IEEE Internet Things J. **7**, 7097–7111 (2020)

9. Kaiwartya, O., et al.: Internet of vehicles: motivation, layered architecture, network model, challenges, and future aspects. IEEE Access **4**, 5356–5373 (2016)

10. Lai, C., Zhang, K., Cheng, N., Li, H., Shen, X.: SIRC: a secure incentive scheme for reliable cooperative downloading in highway VANETs. IEEE Trans. Intell. Transp. Syst. **18**, 1559–1574 (2017)

11. Liu, S., Liu, L., Tang, J., Yu, B., Wang, Y., Shi, W.: Edge computing for autonomous driving: opportunities and challenges. Proc. IEEE **107**, 1697–1716 (2019)

12. Keertikumar, M., Shubham, M., Banakar, R.M.: Evolution of IoT in smart vehicles: an overview. In: 2015 International Conference on Green Computing and Internet of Things (ICGCIoT), pp. 804–809 (2015)

13. Nanda, A., Puthal, D., Rodrigues, J.J.P.C., Kozlov, S.A.: Internet of autonomous vehicles communications security: overview, issues, and directions. IEEE Wirel. Commun. **26**, 60–65 (2019)

14. Noussaiba, M., Rahal, R.: State of the art: VANETs applications and their RFID-based systems. In: 2017 4th International Conference on Control, Decision and Information Technologies (CoDIT), pp. 0516–0520 (2017)

15. Panchali, B.: Edge computing- background and overview. In: 2018 International Conference on Smart Systems and Inventive Technology (ICSSIT), pp. 580–582 (2018)

16. Shi, W., Cao, J., Zhang, Q., Li, Y., Xu, L.: Edge computing: vision and challenges. IEEE Internet Things J. **3**, 637–646 (2016)

17. Tong, L., Ma, L., Li, L., Li, M.: A coalitional game theoretical model for content downloading in multihop VANETs. In: 2013 IEEE 11th International Conference on Dependable, Autonomic and Secure Computing, pp. 627–632 (2013)

18. Wang, Y., Liu, Y., Zhang, J., Ye, H., Tan, Z.: Cooperative store-carry-forward scheme for intermittently connected vehicular networks. IEEE Trans. Veh. Technol. **66**, 777–784 (2017)

19. Xie, R., Tang, Q., Wang, Q., Liu, X., Yu, F.R., Huang, T.: Collaborative vehicular edge computing networks: architecture design and research challenges. IEEE Access **7**, 178942–178952 (2019)

20. Xiong, Z., Li, W., Han, Q., Cai, Z.: Privacy-preserving auto-driving: a GAN-based approach to protect vehicular camera data. IEEE

21. Xiong, Z., Xu, H., Li, W., Cai, Z.: Multi-source adversarial sample attack on autonomous vehicles. IEEE Trans. Veh. Technol. **PP**(99), 1 (2021)

22. Yan, Q., Li, M., Yang, Z., Lou, W., Zhai, H.: Throughput analysis of cooperative mobile content distribution in vehicular network using symbol level network coding. IEEE J. Sel. Areas Commun. **30**, 484–492 (2012)

23. Zhu, W., Li, D., Saad, W.: Multiple vehicles collaborative data download protocol via network coding. IEEE Trans. Veh. Technol. **64**, 1607–1619 (2015)

MISC

A Novel Method Based on Random Matrix Theory and Mean Shift Clustering for Spectrum Sensing

Qiyuan Chen[1], Yonghua Wang[1(✉)], Jiawei Zhuang[1], Yi Lyu[2], and Zhixiong Li[1]

[1] School of Automation, Guangdong University of Technology, Guangzhou, China
[2] School of Computer, University of Electronic Science and Technology of China, Zhongshan Institute, Zhongshan, China

Abstract. A novel cooperative spectrum sensing approach based on random matrix theory and mean shift clustering is proposed to detect whether the primary user signal is active or not. First of all, the sensing signals observed by secondary users are transmitted to fusion center. Moreover, with the help of random matrix theory, the covariance matrix is obtained. The maximum eigenvalue and minimum eigenvalue of that matrix can be given, which are used to construct a two-dimensional signal feature vector. Furthermore, by training mean shift clustering algorithm, a new decision classifier can be obtained. Finally, results are clearly shown to illustrate the reliability and validity of the proposed algorithm in simulation section.

Keywords: Spectrum sensing · Covariance matrix · Mean shift clustering · Decision classifier

1 Introduction

Cognitive radio technique is considered as an effective method to solve the current problem of spectrum shortages and the low utilization of spectrum resources [1,2]. Spectrum sensing is one of the key techniques for cognitive radio systems [3,4]. The traditional spectrum sensing methods include energy detection [5], cyclic feature detection [6] and matched filter detection [7]. It is well known that these sensing methods have some shortcomings, such as inaccurate estimation of threshold, poor performance of sensing performance in low signal-to-noise ratios (SNR), requiring prior information for primary user (PU) and so on.

To resolve these shortcomings, some cooperative spectrum sensing schemes based on random matrix theory have been proposed, and it is receiving abundant attention from researchers. For instance, [8] proposed a spectrum sensing method

This work was supported in part by the national natural science foundation of China (Grant No. 61971147), Guangdong Provincial Key Laboratory of Cyber-Physical Systems (Grant No. 008), and Guangdong Province Graduate Education Innovation Project (Grant No. 2020JGXM040).

© Springer Nature Singapore Pte Ltd. 2021
L. Cui and X. Xie (Eds.): CWSN 2021, CCIS 1509, pp. 223–234, 2021.
https://doi.org/10.1007/978-981-16-8174-5_17

based on maximum-minimum eigenvalue, which had better sensing performance at low SNR. [9] proposed a sensing scheme that used the ratio of maximum eigenvalue to average eigenvalue as the received signal features to detect whether the PU signal was active or not. [10] proposed a sensing approach based on the limiting distribution of minimum eigenvalue and the energy quality of the mean eigenvalue. [11] proposed a sensing method based on the ratio of maximum eigenvalue to the matrix trace which had better sensing performance in some cases. The aforementioned eigenvalue-based spectrum sensing methods overcame the noise uncertainty problem well, which did not require the prior information from the PU signal and the noise. Thus, those algorithms had better sensing performance than the traditional methods when the PU signal had a high auto-correlation [12,13]. However, there are some disadvantages for those eigenvalue-based spectrum sensing. For instance, it is difficult and complicated to determine the detection threshold.

Recently, to avoid threshold derivation, spectrum sensing methods based on machine learning have received extensive attention [14–16]. For instance, [17] studied a spectrum sensing method based on clustering algorithm, which classified the signal energy features by using K-means clustering algorithm. [18] studied a sensing scheme based on clustering algorithm and signal feature. [19] proposed a sensing approach based on Empirical Mode Decomposition algorithm and K-means clustering algorithm. [20] studied a sensing method based on signal decomposition and K-medoids algorithm. [21] proposed a multiple-antenna cooperative spectrum scheme based on the wavelet transform and Gaussian mixture model. [22] investigated a sensing approach based on the sample covariance matrix and K-median clustering algorithm. [23] proposed a spectrum sensing scheme based on covariance matrix decomposition and particle swarm clustering. Obviously, the above improved spectrum sensing approaches based on clustering algorithms avoid calculating the detection thresholds, which greatly improve the performance for spectrum sensing. Notice that the mean shift clustering (MSC) method have some advantages: 1) it does not require to make any model assumption as like in K-means or Gaussian mixture; 2) it can model the complex clusters which have nonconvex shape; 3) it has better robustness than K-means scheme. Additionally, to the best of out our knowledge, spectrum sensing scheme based on the MSC method has not yet been fully investigated.

Motivated by the above investigations, a novel cooperative spectrum sensing approach based on random matrix theory and mean shift clustering is proposed in this paper. The overall block diagram of the proposed scheme is displayed in Fig. 1. As can be clearly seen in it, secondary users (SUs) send the sensing signal to the fusion center (FC). Then, the signal features are obtained by calculating the maximum and minimum eigenvalues of covariance matrix. Finally, by training the mean shift clustering (MSC) algorithm, the decision classifier is obtained, which can detect whether the PU signal is active or not. The main contributions of this paper are as follows:

1. A novel scheme for constructing signal feature vector is proposed. Different from [18–22,24], the proposed two-dimensional signal feature vector fails

to require IQ decomposition method or decomposition and reorganization (DAR) scheme. Interestingly, the proposed feature vector is obtained by the maximum and minimum eigenvalues of covariance matrix.

2. Different from [18–22, 24], a novel decision classifier based on the MSC algorithm is proposed. The MSC algorithm is trained by the set of signal feature vector. After training, the decision classifier is constructed by two different class centroids.

3. In simulation section, two different application scenarios are considered. Intriguingly, simulation results are reported to illustrate that the proposed method has better sensing performance than the existing popular sensing schemes investigated in [18–22, 24].

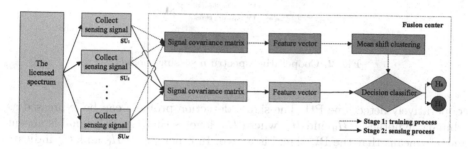

Fig. 1. The overall block diagram of the proposed scheme.

The rest of this paper is reported as follows. The model of cooperative spectrum sensing and the signal model are described in Sect. 2. In Sect. 3, the novel signal feature vector is presented and the new decision classifier based on the MSC algorithm is introduced. Simulation results are displayed and analyzed in Sect. 4 and conclusions are given in Sect. 5.

2 System Model

2.1 Cooperative Spectrum Sensing Model

In this paper, a simple cooperative spectrum sensing model is considered, as drawn in Fig. 2. As shown in Fig. 2, there are $M(i = 1, 2, \ldots, M)$ SUs and one primary user (PU) in the cognitive radio network. The basic steps of cooperative spectrum sensing can be reported as follow: the FC chooses a specific licensed spectrum and allows all SUs to collect the sensing signal. Furthermore, all the sensing signals are delivered to the FC via the reporting channel. Moreover, the FC utilizes the received signals to detect whether the PU signal is active or not.

2.2 Signal Model

Suppose that there are M SUs in the cognitive radio network (CRN), the number of sampling points is N during a certain sensing period for each SU and these SUs

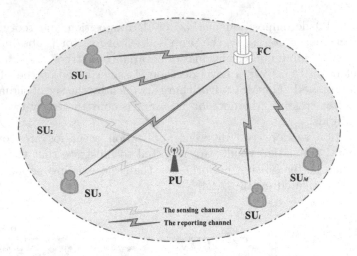

Fig. 2. Cooperative spectrum sensing model.

cooperatively detect one PU. The signal detection problem can be expressed as a binary hypothesis, H_0 and H_1, where H_0 denotes that the PU signal is absent and H_1 means that the PU signal is active. In other word, H_0 and H_1 indicate that the spectrum hole is present and absent, respectively. Based on the binary hypothesis, the mathematical model of the sensing signal can be formulated as

$$\begin{cases} H_0 : x_i(n) = w_i(n), \\ H_1 : x_i(n) = s_i(n) + w_i(n), \end{cases} \tag{1}$$

where $i(i = 1, 2, \ldots, M)$ and $n(n = 1, 2, \ldots, N)$ denote the number of SU and sampling points, respectively. $x_i(n)$ means the sampling signal of ith SU. $s_i(n)$ indicates the PU signal. $w_i(n)$ denotes the Gaussian white noise signal with a mean of 0 and a variance of σ^2. Assume that $s_i(n)$ and $w_i(n)$ are independent of each other, in which $s_i(n)$ is the random signal.

3   The Proposed Spectrum Sensing Scheme

3.1   The Novel Signal Feature Vector

Let $x_i = [x_i(1), x_i(2), \ldots, x_i(N)]$ be the sampling vector of the ith SU, and the number of sampling points is N. The received signal matrix $\mathbf{X}$ during a certain sensing period can be given by

$$\mathbf{X} = \begin{bmatrix} x_1 \\ x_2 \\ \vdots \\ x_M \end{bmatrix} = \begin{bmatrix} x_1(1) & x_1(2) & \ldots & x_1(N) \\ x_2(1) & x_2(2) & \ldots & x_2(N) \\ \vdots & \vdots & \ddots & \vdots \\ x_M(1) & x_M(2) & \ldots & x_M(N) \end{bmatrix}. \tag{2}$$

Thus, from (2), the covariance matrix of the received signal can be obtained by

$$\mathbf{R} = \frac{1}{N}\mathbf{XX}^T. \tag{3}$$

From (3), the eigenvalues of $\mathbf{R}$ can be obtain, which are given by

$$\lambda_1 \geq \lambda_2 \geq \cdots \geq \lambda_i \geq \cdots \geq \lambda_M, \tag{4}$$

which λ_1 and λ_M are the maximum and minimum eigenvalue of $\mathbf{R}$, respectively. Intriguingly, based on (4) and the above binary hypothesis, we can obtain

$$\begin{cases} \lambda_1 = \lambda_2 = \cdots = \lambda_i = \cdots = \lambda_M = \sigma^2, & H_0 \\ \lambda_1 \geq \lambda_2 \geq \cdots \geq \lambda_i \geq \cdots \geq \lambda_M > \sigma^2, & H_1 \end{cases} \tag{5}$$

Thus, the maximum and minimum eigenvalue of $\mathbf{R}$ are used to construct a two-dimensional signal feature vector, which is given by

$$\mathbf{T} = [\lambda_1, \lambda_M]. \tag{6}$$

Next, the complexities of the proposed scheme and other eigenvalue-based sensing approaches will be reported. The complexity of the proposed approach mainly comes from the computation of the covariance matrix and the eigenvalue decomposition of that matrix. The computation of that matrix requires $M(M+1)N/2$ multiplications and $M(M+1)(N-1)/2$ additions. Moreover, based on QR decomposition [23], the eigenvalue decomposition of that matrix requires $o(M^3)$ multiplications and additions. Given what has been discussed above, the computational complexity of the proposed scheme and other methods are reported in Table 1.

Table 1. Computational complexity

Scheme name	Complexity
DMM method	$M(M+1)(2N-1)/2 + o(M^3)$
MENT method	$M(M+1)(2N-1)/2 + (M-1) + o(M^3)$
CAV method	$M(M+1)(2N-1)/2 + (M+2)(M-1) + M^2$
The proposed scheme	$M(M+1)(2N-1)/2 + o(M^3)$

3.2 The Novel Decision Classifier Based on MSC Method

The novel decision classifier based on the MSC method is proposed in this section. From [18–22], the similarity between $A = (x_a, y_a)$ and $B = (x_b, y_b)$ can be evaluated by the Euclidean distance, which is given by

$$d(A, B) = \sqrt{(x_a - x_b)^2 + (y_a - y_b)^2}. \tag{7}$$

Let $\mathbb{T} = [\mathbf{T}_1, \mathbf{T}_2, \ldots, \mathbf{T}_G]$ denote the set of the signal feature vectors. Based on the binary hypothesis, let $\mathbb{C}_{k(k=1,2)}$ indicate two different classes and the corresponding centroid is given by

$$\Lambda_k = \frac{1}{\text{num}(\mathbb{C}_k)} \sum_{\mathbf{T}_g \in \mathbb{C}_k} \mathbf{T}_g, \quad g = 1, 2, \ldots, G \tag{8}$$

where $\text{num}(\mathbb{C}_k)$ means the number of $\mathbf{T}_g$ belong to the class $\mathbb{C}_k$.

Denote a area Θ with the center Λ_k and the bandwidth h. Let N_Θ mean the signal feature vectors in Θ, such that

$$N_\Theta = \{\mathbf{T}_g | d(\mathbf{T}_g, \Lambda_k) < h, \mathbf{T}_g \in \mathbb{T}\}. \tag{9}$$

The Euclidean distance between Λ_k and $\mathbf{T}_g$ among N_Θ can be obtained by (7). Thus, the mean-shift vector $\mathscr{M}$ can be given by

$$\mathscr{M} = \frac{1}{\text{num}(N_\Theta)} \sum_{\mathbf{T}_g \in N_\Theta} d(\mathbf{T}_g, \Lambda_k), \tag{10}$$

where $\text{num}(N_\Theta)$ mean the total number of the signal feature vectors in N_Θ.

And then, the new centroid Λ_k is updated by

$$\Lambda_k = \Lambda_k + \mathscr{M}. \tag{11}$$

Given what has been introduced above, the training steps for the MSC method is reported in Algorithm 1.

Algorithm 1. The training steps for the MSC method

Step 1. Input the training set $\mathbb{T} = [\mathbf{T}_1, \mathbf{T}_2, \ldots, \mathbf{T}_G]$, and set the bandwidth h.

Step 2. Randomly initialize Λ_1 and Λ_2.

Step 3. Identify areas Θ_k with the center Λ_k and the bandwidth h, $k = 1, 2$.

Step 4. Calculate the number of the signal feature in areas Θ_k.

Step 5. Calculate the mean-shift vector $\mathscr{M}$ by (10).

Step 6. Update Λ_k by (10).

Step 7. Repeat steps 3 to 6 until this algorithm converges.

Step 8. Output Λ_k, $k = 1, 2$.

After training, the centroid Λ_1 and Λ_2 are obtained, which can be used to establish the decision classifier that is formulated as

$$\Gamma(\mathbf{T}) = \frac{d(\mathbf{T}, \Lambda_1)}{d(\mathbf{T}, \Lambda_2)} > \varphi, \tag{12}$$

where φ means a parameter, which is utilized to control the probability of false alarm P_f. Assume that Λ_1 belongs to the hypothesis H_0. Thus, it means that the PU signal is active when (12) holds; otherwise, it denotes that that the PU signal is absent.

Remark 1. φ is a key parameter that can be determined in simulation, which is utilized to control P_f. Actually, φ is selected by "trial and error" with repeated simulations. Hence, the choice of parameter φ directly affects the sensing performance. Moreover, in different simulations, φ probably be different.

4   Simulations

In this section, simulations are reported to illustrate the validity of the proposed scheme. The simulations are performed in the platform of the MathWorks MATLAB R2017b.

Two different simulation scenarios are considered, in which one is that all SUs suffer from the same SNRs, while another is that SUs suffer from different SNRs. In simulations, the training set $\tilde{\mathbb{T}} = [\mathbb{T}_1, \mathbb{T}_2, \ldots, \mathbb{T}_J]$, $j = 1, 2, \ldots, J$, is used to train the MSC algorithm, and the test set $\bar{\mathbb{T}} = [\mathbb{T}_1, \mathbb{T}_2, \ldots, \mathbb{T}_S]$, $s = 1, 2, \ldots, S$, is used to evaluate the performance of the proposed method. Assume that the PU signal is AM signal. Similar to [18–22, 24], the probability of false alarm P_f and the probability of detection P_d are used to evaluate the performance of spectrum sensing schemes.

4.1   SUs Suffer from the Same SNRs

First of all, a simulation is demonstrated to explain why the novel decision classifier can be used to detect whether the PU signal is active or not. From Figs. 3 and 4, they show the training set $\tilde{\mathbb{T}}$ and the clustering drawing for $\tilde{\mathbb{T}}$ via the MSC method, respectively, when the number of SUs $M = 7$, the number of sampling point $N = 5000$, and SNR $= -18$ dB. As can be observed in Fig. 4, the training set $\tilde{\mathbb{T}}$ can be divided into two different classes after training, where Λ_1 and Λ_2 indicate the PU signal is active and absent, respectively. Thus, the novel decision classifier constructed by the MSC scheme can be used to detect the state of PU for spectrum sensing.

Moreover, in application scenario that all SUs suffer from the same SNR, the proposed scheme is compared with other popular sensing methods based on clustering algorithm, such as the method based on MENT and K-means algorithm [18], the approach based on DMM and K-medoids algorithm [18], the sensing scheme based on CAV and K-means algorithm [22], and the method based on information geometry (IG) and Fuzzy-c-means (FCM) clustering algorithm [25]. From Figs. 5 and 6, they display the performance of different spectrum sensing methods. As can be seen in Fig. 5, the proposed approach has the best sensing performance than others when simulation parameters are set to $M = 6$, $N = 5000$, and SNR $= -16$ dB. Similarly, in Fig. 6, the proposed approach also

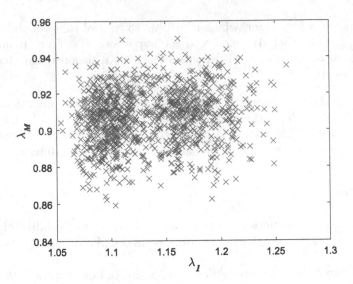

Fig. 3. The training set $\tilde{\mathbb{T}} = [\mathbb{T}_1, \mathbb{T}_2, \ldots, \mathbb{T}_J]$, $J = 1000$.

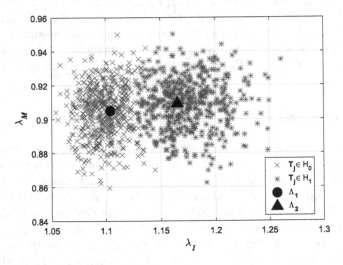

Fig. 4. The clustering drawing for $\tilde{\mathbb{T}}$ via the MSC method.

has the best sensing performance than others when simulation parameters are chosen as $M = 10$, $N = 2000$, and SNR $= -17\,\text{dB}$. Thus, the proposed method is effective and reliable to detect whether the PU signal is active or not.

4.2   SUs Suffer from Different SNRs

In this section, another application scenario that all SUs suffer from different SNRs is considered. Similar to the first scenario, the proposed method

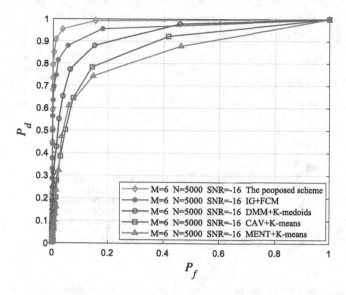

Fig. 5. Performance of different sensing methods when $M = 6$, $N = 5000$, and SNR = -16 dB.

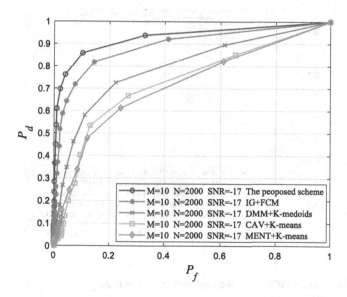

Fig. 6. Performance of different sensing schemes when $M = 10$, $N = 2000$, and SNR = -17 dB.

is compared with other popular sensing methods that are investigated in [18,22] and [25]. Specifically, Fig. 7 displays the performance of different sensing approaches when simulation parameters are chosen as $M = 5$, $N = 3000$, and SNR $= -15.5$ dB, -15 dB, -14.5 dB, -14 dB, -13.5 dB. Addition-

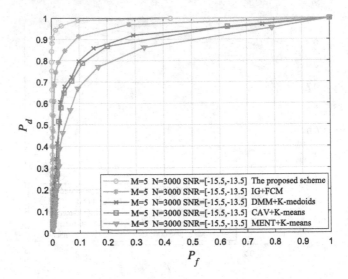

Fig. 7. Performance of different sensing approaches when $M = 5$, $N = 3000$, and SNR $= [-15.5\,\text{dB}, -13.5\,\text{dB}]$.

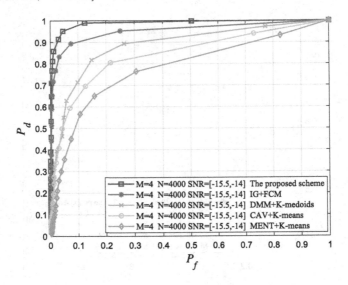

Fig. 8. Performance of different sensing methods when $M = 4$, $N = 4000$, and SNR $= [-15.5\,\text{dB}, -14\,\text{dB}]$.

ally, in Fig. 8, the performance of different sensing approaches is drawn when simulation parameters are chosen as $M = 4$, $N = 4000$, and SNR $= -15.5\,\text{dB}, -15\,\text{dB}, -14.5\,\text{dB}, -14\,\text{dB}$. From Figs. 7 and 8, it is easily concluded that the proposed scheme has the best sensing performance than the mentioned popular methods in the application scenario that all SUs suffer from different SNRs.

Given what has been simulated and reported above, it is no difficult for us to conclude that the proposed approach can considerably improve the sensing performance in two different application scenarios. Apparently, the effectiveness and reliability of the proposed scheme are verified by all of the above simulation results.

5 Conclusion

In this paper, aim to improve the sensing performance, a novel cooperative spectrum sensing method based on random matrix theory and mean shift clustering is developed. Different from the existing sensing method, a novel two-dimensional signal feature vector is extracted by covariance matrix. Additionally, to avoid calculating decision threshold, a new decision classifier is established by training mean shift clustering algorithm. Finally, under two different simulation scenarios, simulation results are clearly displayed to demonstrate the effectiveness of the proposed method.

References

1. Hattab, G., Ibnkahla, M.: Multiband spectrum access: great promises for future cognitive radio networks. Proc. IEEE **102**(3), 282–306 (2014)
2. Tajer, A., Prasad, N., Wang, X.: Beamforming and rate allocation in MISO cognitive radio networks. IEEE Trans. Signal Process. **58**(1), 362–377 (2010)
3. Xiong, T., Yao, Y.-D., Ren, Y., Li, Z.: Multiband spectrum sensing in cognitive radio networks with secondary user hardware limitation: random and adaptive spectrum sensing strategies. IEEE Trans. Wirel. Commun. **17**(5), 3018–3029 (2018)
4. Chen, H., Zhou, M., Xie, L., Wang, K., Li, J.: Joint spectrum sensing and resource allocation scheme in cognitive radio networks with spectrum sensing data falsifification attack. IEEE Trans. Veh. Technol. **65**(11), 9181–9191 (2016)
5. Chatziantoniou, E., Allen, B., Velisavljevic, V., Karadimas, P., Coon, J.: Energy detection based spectrum sensing over two-wave with diffuse power fading channels. IEEE Trans. Veh. Technol. **66**(1), 868–874 (2017)
6. Kozlowski, S.: Implementation and verification of cyclostationary feature detector for DVB-T signals. IET Signal Process **10**(2), 162–167 (2016)
7. Zhang, X., Gao, F., Chai, R., Jiang, T.: Matched filter based spectrum sensing when primary user has multiple power levels. China Commun. **22**(2), 21–31 (2015)
8. Bin Ali Wael, C., Armi, N., Rohman, B.P.: Spectrum sensing for low SNR environment using maximum-minimum eigenvalue (MME) detection. In: 2016 International Seminar on Intelligent Technology and Its Applications (ISITIA), pp. 435–438 (2016)
9. Zhang, S., Yang, J., Guo, L.: Eigenvalue-based cooperative spectrum sensing algorithm. In: 2012 Second International Conference on Instrumentation, Measurement, Computer, Communication and Control, pp. 375–378 (2012)
10. Gao, W., Ma, F., Cheng, G., Liu, W.: A dam spectrum sensing algorithm of cognitive radio network based random matrix. In: 2018 IEEE 2nd International Conference on Circuits, System and Simulation (ICCSS), pp. 95–100 (2018)

11. Ahmed, A., Hu, Y.F., Noras, J.M., Pillai, P., Abd-Alhameed, R.A., Smith, A.: Random matrix theory based spectrum sensing for cognitive radio networks. In: 2015 Internet Technologies and Applications (ITA), pp. 479–483 (2015)
12. Zeng, Y., Liang, Y.-C.: Eigenvalue-based spectrum sensing algorithms for cognitive radio. IEEE Trans. Commun. **57**(6), 1784–1793 (2019)
13. Shakir, M.Z., Rao, A., Alouini, M.-S.: Generalized mean detector for collaborative spectrum sensing. IEEE Trans. Commun. **61**(4), 1242–1253 (2013)
14. Tian, J., et al.: A machine learning-enabled spectrum sensing method for OFDM systems. IEEE Trans. Veh. Technol. **68**(11), 11374–11378 (2019)
15. Shi, Z., Gao, W., Zhang, S., Liu, J., Kato, N.: Machine learning-enabled cooperative spectrum sensing for non-orthogonal multiple access. IEEE Trans. Wirel. Commun. **19**(9), 5692–5702 (2020)
16. Zhuang, J., Wang, Y., Zhang, S., Wan, P., Sun, C.: A multi-antenna spectrum sensing scheme based on main information extraction and genetic algorithm clustering. IEEE Access **7**, 119620–119630 (2019)
17. Kumar, V., Kandpal, D.C., Jain, M., Gangopadhyay, R., Debnath, S.: K-mean clustering based cooperative spectrum sensing in generalized $\kappa - \mu$ fading channels. In: 2016 Twenty Second National Conference on Communication (NCC), pp. 1–5 (2016)
18. Zhang, Y., Wan, P., Zhang, S., Wang, Y., Li, N.: A spectrum sensing method based on signal feature and clustering algorithm in cognitive wireless multimedia sensor networks. Adv. Multim **2017**(2017), 1–10 (2017)
19. Wang, Y., Zhang, Y., Wan, P., Zhang, S., Yang, J.: A spectrum sensing method based on empirical mode decomposition and k-means clustering algorithm. Wirel. Commun. Mob. Comput. **2018**(2018), 1–10 (2018)
20. Wang, Y., Zhang, S., Zhang, Y., Wan, P., Wang, S.: A cooperative spectrum sensing method based on signal decomposition and k-medoids algorithm. Int. J. Sens. Netw. **29**(3), 171–180 (2019)
21. Zhang, S., Wang, Y., Yuan, H., Wan, P., Zhang, Y.: Multiple-antenna cooperative spectrum sensing based on the wavelet transform and gaussian mixture model. Sensors **19**(8), 3863 (2019)
22. Zhuang, J., Wang, Y., Wan, P., Zhang, S., Zhang, Y., Li, Y.: Blind spectrum sensing based on the statistical covariance matrix and k-median clustering algorithm. In: Sun, X., Wang, J., Bertino, E. (eds.) ICAIS 2020. LNCS, vol. 12239, pp. 467–478. Springer, Cham (2020). https://doi.org/10.1007/978-3-030-57884-8_41
23. Zhuang, J., Wang, Y., Wan, P., Zhang, S., Zhang, Y.: Centralized spectrum sensing based on covariance matrix decomposition and particle swarm clustering. Phys. Commun. **46**, 101322 (2021)
24. Golub, G.H., Van Loan, C.F.: Matrix Computations, 4th edn. The Johns Hopkins University Press, London (2013)
25. Zhang, Y., Ma, C., Wang, Y., Zhang, S., Wan, P.: Information geometry-based fuzzy-c means algorithm for cooperative spectrum sensing. IEEE Access **8**, 155742–155752 (2020)

A Consensus Algorithm with Leadership Transfer-LTRaft

Pengliu Tan[✉], Wenshi Zou, and Weiqiang Tang

Nanchang Hangkong University, Nanchang 330063, China
pltan@nchu.edu.cn

Abstract. In the Raft consensus algorithm, some nodes cannot communicate with other nodes due to network malfunction, which will greatly increase the consensus time. Moreover, the leader node in the Raft algorithm has strong leadership. Once something goes wrong with the leader, the consensus time of the entire distributed system will be greatly increased. LTRaft (Raft with Leadership Transfer) consensus algorithm with a state monitoring mechanism and alternative leaders is proposed. In the LTRaft algorithm, outdated node is introduced. Outdated nodes can not participate in the leader election, because they have just resumed communication and do not update logs in time. If they participate in the leader election, the consensus efficiency of the system will be seriously affected. Therefore, outdated nodes are prevented from participating in the leader election. In addition, when the leader node fails, the alternative leader node will take over its leadership and start a new consensus process until the next leader is elected. The experimental results show that LTRaft has significantly improved consensus efficiency and the fault tolerance of the system when the leader node fails and outdated nodes appear.

Keywords: Distributed system · Raft · State monitoring · Alternative leader · Outdated node

1 Introduction

In 2008, Satoshi Nakamoto proposed the concept of bitcoin [1] which was an electronic cash currency implemented entirely through peer-to-peer technology. Since then, blockchain as its core technology has become a research hotspot. Blockchain has the characteristics of decentralization, non-tamperability, traceability, and so on. With the rapid development of blockchain, various consensus algorithms have also been proposed [2], such as Proof of Work (PoW) and Proof of Stake (PoS), etc.

In a distributed system, the consensus algorithm is an extremely important part. It means that multiple nodes can reach an agreement on the state. However, in a distributed system, the server may crash or become unreliable due to various factors. Therefore, it is important to design a consensus protocol to ensure fault tolerance. Even if one or two servers in the system are down, it will not affect the processing process.

The Raft algorithm [4] was proposed in 2014, and it has only one leader at the same time. Therefore, the detailed design of the leader election by Raft algorithm guarantees

© Springer Nature Singapore Pte Ltd. 2021
L. Cui and X. Xie (Eds.): CWSN 2021, CCIS 1509, pp. 235–249, 2021.
https://doi.org/10.1007/978-981-16-8174-5_18

its absolute leadership. In this algorithm, some nodes may not be able to communicate with other nodes due to network problems, resulting in isolation. After the isolation is removed, those nodes will increase the leader election time. After the successful leader election, if the leader node fails to work due to breakdown, the leader election must be re-conducted, which will increase the time consumption of consensus.

To address the above problems, this paper proposes an improved Raft algorithm with leadership transfer. The main contributions of this paper are summarized as follows:

1) Add a state monitoring mechanism to the Raft algorithm to prevent outdated nodes from participating in the election.
2) Add an alternative leader and modify AppendEntry RPC. After the leader node fails, the alternative leader can directly replace the leader to carry out consensus work.
3) The simulation test experiment is designed based on the distributed system. This article reports the experimental process and results in detail. The results show that this method has better performance when the leader node fails and outdated nodes appear.

2   Related Work

Paxos [3] algorithm was proposed by Leslie Lamport in 1990, which can effectively solve the distributed consensus problem. Paxos can achieve consistency according to a certain protocol with message delivery. Later Lamport modified Paxos and proposed algorithms such as Multi Paxos, Fast Paxos [5], Cheap Paxos [6], and so on. In addition, relevant algorithms of Paxos are widely used, such as distributed lock service Chubby [7, 8], the core of Google's Spanner [9] database, etc.

Literature [10] divides Paxos-like algorithms into strong leader consensus algorithms and weak leader consensus algorithms. Among them, strong leader consensus algorithms include Multi-Paxos, Raft, VR [11] (Viewstamped Replication), ZAB [12] (ZooKeeper's Atomic Broadcast), and so on. The characteristic of this type of algorithm is that the main work is completed by selected leaders, while the real-time performance and stability of the system are guaranteed by constantly changing leaders.

The weak leader consensus algorithms weaken and decentralize the leaders' authority and allow each replica to act as a weak leader to jointly handle requests from other nodes. Through other constraints to ensure the security of the system, these weakened leaders work together to complete the consensus work to ensure the consistency of the system. Representative algorithms include Mencius [15] and EPaxos [16], etc. The specific leadership comparison is shown in Table 1.

Aiming at the shortcomings of Paxos, the Raft algorithm is proposed. Compared with Paxos, Raft is easier to understand and implement. The Raft algorithm divides the consensus process into three parts: leader election, log replication, and safety. In a distributed system, the leader is generated by voting among nodes, and then the leader node is responsible for managing the distributed logs. In the case that all nodes in the system can be trusted, the leader node sends the logs to other servers in order after receiving them from the client.

Table 1. Leadership details for different algorithms

Algorithm	New leader	Configuration management	The vote gatherer
Paxos [3]	All servers	$\checkmark$	New leader
VR [11]	A server with the latest logs	$\times$	View manager
Zab [12]	A server with the latest logs	$\times$	New leader
Raft [4]	A server with the latest logs	$\times$	New leader
LTRaft	A server with the latest logs	$\checkmark$	New leader
VBBFT-Raft [13]	A server with the latest logs	$\times$	New leader
...	...	...	...

To verify the correctness of the Raft algorithm, the literature [16, 17] introduced Verdi, a framework for the consistency verification of distributed systems, and implemented successfully it in Coq, a theorem proving auxiliary tool. In literature [18], a model of the Raft algorithm was written using the process-oriented formal language LNT, and the CADP tool was used for verification. However, neither of these two validation methods includes the part of handing over the leadership after the leader node is down. The literature [14] adds cryptography to achieve leader supervision, log matching, and commit confirmation to ensure the system's Byzantine fault tolerance rate, but it does not consider downtime.

3 LTRaft Algorithm

In the traditional Raft consensus algorithm, before the election, if the follower nodes cannot communicate with other nodes due to network reasons, an isolation phenomenon will occur. But these nodes will continue to trigger timeout elections, causing a continuous increase in the Term value. After the isolation is removed, the node can continue to participate in the election. However, because the node does not communicate with other nodes, the log queue is too old and the Term value is greater than other nodes in the cluster. This type of node is an outdated node. If outdated nodes win the election, the consensus time of the entire system will increase. If the leader node fails because of a breakdown, the system triggers a heartbeat detection to rerun the election, which wastes a lot of time. The LTRaft algorithm can prevent outdated nodes from participating in the election through the pre-election state monitoring mechanism, and elect the leader and the alternative leader at the election time. If a timeout occurs during the consensus, the leadership will be transferred to the alternative leader, thus saving the election time of one round.

3.1 The Basis of the Election

In the LTRaft algorithm, there are 4 states: *follower, candidate, secleader, and leader*. During the election, if a node wants to be a leader, its term number and commit index of the commit logs must both be large. Only if the condition is satisfied, it can accept votes from other nodes. Term ensures the consistency of the logs throughout the system, while the index guarantees the uniqueness of the logs.

Term

Raft divides time into consecutive cycles, which are called terms. The term starts with one leader election and ends with the next leader election. Only one leader can be successfully elected for a term and can manage the system during the term, or no leader can be successfully elected. All term numbers are marked with consecutive integers, as shown in Fig. 1.

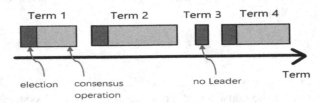

Fig. 1. Terms in the Raft.

The term is responsible for controlling the uniqueness of the leader, which is important when electing and abolishing the leader. The operation is very simple. When the election begins, the candidate node with the largest term number will get votes, and the node with more than half of the votes will be chosen as the leader. Then the leader node sends the term number along with the log. When the follower nodes receive the logs, they compare their term number with the leader's term number. If the leaders' term number is equal to or greater than their terms, they will accept the consensus, store the log in the queue and send the leader node a successful reply that it has accepted successfully. If the acceptance fails, a failed reply message with its term number will be sent to the leader. If the leader node finds that the term number obtained in the reply message is greater than its term number, it will demote itself to the follower node. Thus, the current term ends and the next round of the election begins.

Index of the Commit Log

In the log queue, the log is divided into two parts by the index of the committed log. One part is the committed log, which means that the data has been copied to more than half of the nodes and can be sent to the client for operation; the other part is the uncommitted log, which indicates that more than half of the data has not been copied, as shown in Fig. 2.

The follower nodes receive the logs and store them in the queue in order, but the Commit Index will not update the value at this time, indicating that these logs are uncommitted and cannot be sent to the client. When the leader receives responses from

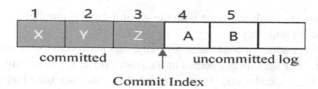

Fig. 2. Schematic diagram of Commit Index in the log storage queue.

more than half of the followers, it will update its index and broadcast it to other follower nodes. At this time, the follower node will update the committed log index, and change the uncommitted log into the committed log according to the index.

In the leader election process, the term number must be compared first, and then compare the index of the committed log. Only when both of these values are large, the node can become the leader.

3.2 States Transition of LTRaft Algorithm

There are four nodes with different states in the LTRaft algorithm, namely *follower, candidate, secleader and leader*. Each of these four types of nodes is essential and has its own division of labor and works together to maintain the stability of the system.

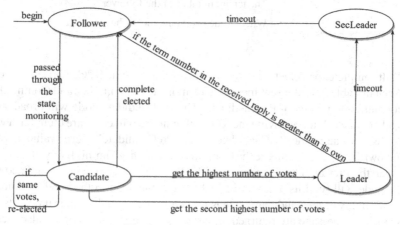

Fig. 3. State transition diagram.

The follower node is the most common node that just passively receives logs, gives feedback to the leader node, and conducts voting operations. candidate nodes that passed the state monitoring mechanism first cast a vote for themselves and then seek votes from other nodes. If more than half of the nodes vote for a candidate node, the node will be upgraded to a leader node. After becoming the leader node, the node will carry out consensus to handle the data exchange of the entire system. If the leader receives a reply with a term number greater than its own, it means that the network where the leader node is located is not good at this time, so it must be converted to the follower node. The secleader node is the candidate node with the second-highest number of votes, but this node has no special authority.

If the system conducts a consensus normally, this node is the same as the follower node. However, after the timeout occurs in the leader node, the node will take over the leader's task if the secleader node exists, and reach consistency based on the log of the node until the next leader node is elected. The specific member state transition is shown in Fig. 3.

3.3 PreState RPC

Table 2. Format and description of the PreState RPC parameters.

PreState RPC	
Initiated by candidate, perform pre-election state monitoring	
Parameters	
Term	The tenure number of the candidate
Commit Index	The committed log index of candidate
Reply	
Term	The tenure number of the follower
Success	Whether the candidate meets the standard

LTRaft completes pre-election state monitoring via PreState RPC, whose RPC format can be seen in Table 2. In the sent message, Term is the term number and Commit Index is the committed log index of PreCandidate. The PreCandidate node will broadcast the RPC to other nodes. After receiving the RPC, other nodes will compare their Term values with the Term value of the PreCandidate. If the PreCandidate's Term value is greater than their own Term, then compare the Commit Index. If the Commit Index of the node is greater than the PreCandidate's Index, then the PreCandidate node is an outdated node. Then the node will send its Term value and a False message to the candidate node. If the Commit Index of the candidate node is greater than or equal to their index, its Term value and a True message are returned; otherwise, the Term value and a False message are returned.

After the candidate node receives the result returned by the follower node, it first compares the Term value. If the Term value of the candidate is smaller than the returned Term value, the node will degrade to the follower node. If the Term value is greater than the returned Term, then compare the Commit Index. If it is greater than the returned index, add 1 to its own Pre. If the Pre is greater than the number of nodes in the cluster, it means that the candidate node meets the requirements, then send RequestVote RPC; if it is smaller than the returned index, then the node will degrade to the follower node, and the Term value of the candidate will be changed to Term-1 that is returned to avoid affecting the next round of elections.

3.4 Roles Transformation of LTRaft Algorithm

When a node timeout occurs and then re-election is triggered, the Campaign() function is first mobilized. This function will take different strategies depending on the parameters called. If the parameter is CampaignPreElection, it indicates that the state is monitored at this time, and the term of the node is kept unchanged. But the node identity temporarily changes to the PreCandidate, calling the PreElection module.

Upon entering the PreElection module, the PreState RPC will be sent first. As described above, this RPC is responsible for comparing the log entries of other nodes in the system with those of the PreCandiDate node. If the PreCandidate node's log entry is similar to the logs of most nodes, other nodes will approve it as a candidate and vote for that node. If more than half of the votes are received, the node is a normal node and the identity of the node will become a candidate. Then the Campaign() will be called again. If the number of votes received is not enough, then the node is an outdated node and is not eligible to become a candidate node. Therefore, the state of the node must be changed to follower. Moreover, since the Term of the outdated node does not follow the system changes, the Term is not legitimate, so it needs to be adjusted. Specifically, the node will randomly select the received Term from follower nodes and change its own Term to the selected Term-1 to avoid the node from participating in the election for leader after the next timeout election is triggered.

If the parameter of the Campaign() is CampaignElection, then this is the election phase. Then the node's Term number will be plus 1 first, and the node's state will be changed to candidate, and then continue the process of normal election voting. First, the node will initiate a vote, and the remaining followers will vote according to the RequestVote requirements. If the number of votes is enough, they will vote for the node. If more than half of the votes are received, the node will become the leader node, send heartbeat detection, reset the timers of other nodes, and then replicate the log. Otherwise, the node will become a follower node, waiting for a new round of voting or accepting the leader node's log. The description of the algorithm is shown below:

Step 1: Trigger a timeout election when the node occurs timeout;
Step 2: Compare the CampaignType, if CampaignType is equal to CampaignPreElection, *node r* will become the PreCandidate;
Step 3: Send PreState RPC to *other nodes f* and compare term and index. When $r.Term >= f.Term$ and $r.CommitIndex >= f.CommitIndex$, the CampaignType will be equal to CampaignElection; otherwise, *node r* will become the follower and $r.Term$ will be equal to f.Term-1;
Step 4: Otherwise *node r* will become the candidate and $r.Term$ will be equal to $r.Term+1$; then *node r* will send RequestVote RPC to *other nodes f*;
Step 5: Count the number of votes of *node r*. If *node r* receives more than half of the votes, it will become the leader; otherwise, *node r* will become the follower.

3.5 Improved AppendEntry RPC

In the Raft algorithm, only two RPCs are used to achieve all the required functions. They are RequestVote and AppendEntry. The RequestVote is sent by the candidate node, and the follower node votes according to the term and the value of the Commit Index in the RequestVote. If the candidate node receives more than half of the votes, the candidate will become the leader. The AppendEntry is sent by the leader node to other nodes and has two functions. The first function is when its Entries are empty, the RPC is a heartbeat signal to reset the timers of other nodes, which indicating the leader node is working normally and does not need to trigger timeout elections. The second is when Entries are not empty, it is log replication RPC, requesting other nodes to copy the logs in Entries into their own log queue. Both of them will carry the Commit Index information, and update the Commit Index in other nodes at any time to ensure that the Commit Index of the nodes in the system is the same and avoid massive rollback in the subsequent consensus.

The LTRaft algorithm modifies the sent information and the reply information in AppendEntry so that it can complete the election of alternative leaders and broadcast after completing the basic functions. Thus, other nodes cannot be triggered by the heartbeat mechanism immediately after the timeout of the leader node during the election. The modified RPC is shown in Table 3.

Table 3. AppendEntry() parameter format and description

AppendEntry ()	
Initiated by the leader node for log replication, or heartbeat detection	
Parameters	
Term	The tenure number for a candidate node
LeaderId	The identifier of the leader node and the follower can be used to redirect the customer request
LeaderCommit	The Commit Index of the leader node
PrevLogIndex	The number of the previous log for the new log entry
PreLogTerm	The tenure number of the previous log for the new log entry
Entries[]	Log entry (as heartbeat if empty)
SecLeaderId	The identifier of the alternative leader node
Returned result	
Term	The currentTerm of the node
Success	If the follower's log entries are the same with the PrevLogIndex and the PrevLogTerm, return True
NextIndex	To speed up the search, return the next log index to be passed
ConflictTerm	Inconsistent terms
ConflictIndex	The last Index of inconsistent terms
VoteCount	The number of votes received by the node

LTRaft adds a parameter called the SecLeaderId to the sent RPC, which can be used to broadcast the unique identifier of the secleader after sorting the votes so that other nodes can get the ID and store it. When the leader node times out, other nodes first determine whether the SecLeaderId is stored. If the parameter is stored in the structure, the re-election will not be triggered. If this parameter is null, the re-election will be triggered, and all nodes will re-elect a new leader for consensus. The secleader will be deleted after the leader node is elected or the current leader node's term expires. This ensures that the alternative leader is real-time and can be selected based on the election results of each leader so that the log can be replicated accurately.

In the returned information, compared with the Raft algorithm, LTRaft adds 4 parameters: NextIndex, ConflictTerm, ConflictIndex, and VoteCount. The NextIndex returns the index of the next log to be passed to the leader node, enabling it to quickly find the next log that needs to deliver. The ConflictTerm and the ConflictIndex transmit the inconsistent terms and log indexes of the node back to the leader node, so that these data can be adjusted in the subsequent consensus process. This guarantees the data consistency between the node and other nodes in the system and avoids affecting subsequent log replication due to the missing logs that need to be replicated in the previous term. The VoteCount is the number of votes received by each follower node after electing the leader. Each node needs to send VoteCount back to the leader node. The leader node in turn sorts the votes among all the replies it receives and stores the ID of the first place in the ranking in a structure. Then it adds the alternative leader's ID to the AppendEntry sent in the next round. After receiving the RPC, other nodes will store the ID of the alternative leader node. In this way, all nodes in the system can get the ID of the alternative leader and prepare for the potential leader timeout. On the other hand, other follower nodes will no longer send their votes after getting the SecleLeaderID to ensure that meaningless information will not be transmitted in the entire system and occupy network resources.

Each member in the LTRaft algorithm transforms the node state according to calling to the two RPCs of RequestVote and AppendEntry the algorithm.

3.6 The Description of LTRaft Algorithm

The LTRaft algorithm process is as follows:

Step 1: Become a candidate. If the system has no leader, the follower node determines whether to upgrade to a candidate according to its Term and Commit Index.

Step 2: Elect. The upgraded candidate will canvass votes from other follower nodes based on its Term and Commit Index, and strive to be elected as the leader node.

Step 3: Select the leader and secleader nodes. The leader node is selected based on the votes, and then the alternative leader node is selected by the leader node according to the number of votes.

Step 4: Judge the state of the leader node. If the leader works normally, it will replicate the log to other nodes until the end of the term. If the leader occurs a timeout before the term expires, first judge whether the SecLeaderID field is empty. If it is not empty then change the alternative leader to the leader; otherwise, initialize the stored leader and secleader information and re-election.

4 Performance Analysis

The LTRaft algorithm introduces a state monitoring mechanism and an alternative leader mechanism based on the Raft algorithm. LTRaft can prevent outdated nodes from participating in the election before the election, and make the alternative leader node act as the leader after the failure of the leader node to continue to carry out the consensus work, which can improve the stability of the system. The experiment in this article is to use Golang for concurrency while ignoring network delay by default and use goroutine and channel to simulate multiple servers. This section will run on a Windows 10 system configured with an i5-8400 processor, 8 GB of RAM, and 128 GB SSD. The experiment code uses the Golang, and through the GoLand 2018 platform, compares LTRaft and other algorithms in terms of time and TPS.

4.1 Election Time

The LTRaft algorithm enhances the robustness of the system by adding the node role of the alternative leader and a state monitoring mechanism. Although the alternative leader has no special privileges under normal circumstances, it still needs to occupy some system resources when it is elected. For example, when the state monitoring mechanism triggers the broadcast of the new RPC, it will increase the processing time of the system. Figure 4 describes the comparison of the time required for the four algorithms of Raft, LTRaft, VBBFT-Raft, and Paxos in the election phase.

It can be clearly seen in Fig. 4 that the election time of these algorithms increases linearly with the increase of the number of nodes. Among them, the Raft algorithm takes about 5ms to select the leader in the case of 10 nodes, and about 33ms to select the leader in the case of 100 nodes. The time of the LTRaft algorithm is slightly higher than that of the Raft. Each additional node increases the election time by 0.072ms. The Paxos algorithm increases by 9ms at least and 115ms at most. As the number of nodes increases, its growth trend will become faster and faster. When the number of nodes is small, the VBBFT-Raft algorithm requires more election time than LTRaft and Raft slightly. However, when the number of nodes increases to 80, the growth rate will become faster and faster.

Each node of Paxos is allowed to take on multiple roles, so its election is extremely complicated. Each node of Raft is only allowed to play one role, and the leader node has strong leadership, so the election time is much less than that of Paxos. Thus, this article will no longer compare with the Paxos algorithm. Relatively speaking, VBBFT-Raft also needs to verify one more digital signature, so it takes longer. Comparing with Raft and VBBFT-Raft, LTRaft has an alternative leader role and state monitoring mechanisms, but the election of alternative leaders does not send RPCs separately and selecting alternative leaders can be completed in the Raft election. The state monitoring mechanism is an important factor that affects election time. However, the node only needs one round of broadcast and reply under normal circumstances in theory. Because the RPC is simple in design and the transmission time is much less than other RPCs, it will not affect the election time too much.

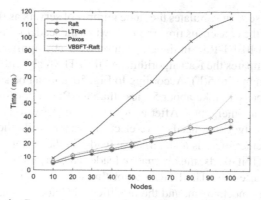

Fig. 4. Comparison of four algorithms in the election phase.

4.2 Consensus Time

This experiment in this section will simulate the time required for three algorithms to carry out a round of consensus in a system with different numbers of servers. The experiment took 10 results and averaged the results. The experimental results are shown in Fig. 5.

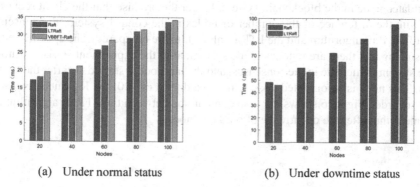

(a)   Under normal status   (b)   Under downtime status

Fig. 5. Comparison of consensus time

According to Fig. 5(a), it can be easily seen that the three algorithms spend almost the same time in the next round of consensus under normal circumstances. The LTRaft algorithm will take a little longer in most cases, but the difference between the three algorithms is not big. The reason is this article has modified the storage structure and RPC in Raft, which makes the message a little more complicated in comparison. It can be seen from the figure that the modified storage structure and RPC have almost no impact on the consensus time and the consensus time of the Raft algorithm is mainly spent on log replication between nodes. However, the VBBFT-Raft algorithm takes more time than the other two algorithms because of the complicated leader election process and the need to verify the digital signature.

In addition, this section simulates the same number of servers as the previous experiment and compares the consensus time required when the leader node goes down. Since the comparison of VBBFT-Raft in the election phase is not significant, this part of the experiment only compares the Raft algorithm and the LTRaft algorithm. The experimental results are shown in Fig. 5(b). According to Fig. 5(b), it can be seen that the LTRaft proposed in this paper will take about 5 s less than the Raft algorithm in the consensus time when there is an emergency. After analysis, that is because after the leader node goes down, the Raft algorithm needs to re-elect the leader, while the LTRaft algorithm determines that whether there is an alternative leader in the system after triggering the heartbeat detection. If it exists, the alternative leader takes over the work of the original leader to reach a consensus. The LTRaft algorithm can omit an election vote through the alternative leader mechanism, and the modified RPC does not increase the original workload. Therefore, in this case, LTRaft has certain advantages.

Comparison Between Raft and LTRaft in the Presence of Outdated Nodes
After the emergence of an outdated node in the system, it is bound to destabilize the system since the node appears after the isolation phenomenon. The state monitoring mechanism proposed in this paper is to deprive the outdated node of its election right during the election process and modify the term of the outdated node. Therefore, it can modify its log queue to become a normal node before participating in the leader's election. The background of the experimental simulation in this section is that there is an outdated node in the blockchain system. Under the premise that the client request is 300, with the difference of the number of nodes in the control system, the consensus time of the Raft algorithm and the LTRaft algorithm are compared. The specific setting is, assuming that there are n nodes in the system, after the experiment starts, n-1 nodes in the system participate in the consensus, and the last node is started 1 s after the system starts. This node is an outdated node with a fixed term of 100; the log queue is also in a pre-set order. Figure 6 shows the time comparison between the LTRaft algorithm and Raft algorithm after the occurrence of outdated nodes.

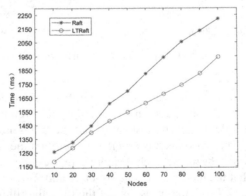

Fig. 6. Comparison of consensus time after the presence of outdated nodes

After the occurrence of outdated nodes, Raft requires 1258 ms and 2222 ms in the case of 10 nodes and 100 nodes, respectively, while LTRaft requires 1187 ms and 1944 ms in the same situation. It can be seen that the emergence of outdated nodes in the system has a significant impact on the entire consensus algorithm. As the number of nodes increases, its impact becomes greater. The LTRaft algorithm is affected by this, but compared to the Raft algorithm, the impact of outdated nodes is much smaller.

According to the analysis, the state monitoring mechanism in LTRaft prevents outdated nodes from continuing to vote in elections by comparing the log queues of nodes before they become candidates. With the increase of the number of nodes, the more complex the network structure of the system, the more serious the impact of outdated nodes. LTRaft can reduce this impact to a certain extent, allowing the system to operate stably.

4.3 Throughput

This section simulates the three algorithms of Raft, LTRaft, and VBBFT-Raft to send transactions in the system with different numbers of servers. This experiment has two variables, the number of nodes and the number of transactions sent by the client. Therefore, this experiment is divided into two small parts. In the first experiment, the number of nodes is varied from 4 to 20, but the number of transactions is fixed at 1000; in the second experiment, the number of nodes is fixed at 5, but the number of transactions is changed from 200 to 1200 to compare the throughput performance respectively. The results of the experiments are shown in Fig. 7(a) and Fig. 7(b).

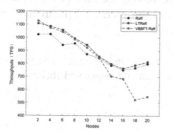
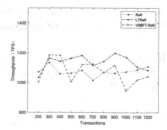

(a) when the number of nodes changes   (b) when the number of transactions changes

Fig. 7. TPS

In Fig. 7(a), when the number of transactions remains unchanged and the number of nodes is changed, the throughput of the three algorithms decreases as the number of nodes increases, while the waiting time increases accordingly. The reason is that as the number of nodes increases, the waiting time for submission and confirmation becomes longer. Compared with the VBBFT-Raft algorithm and the Raft algorithm, the LTRaft algorithm has a relatively stable throughput. When the number of nodes increases to 20, the TPS does not drop sharply, which indicates that the high scalability of LTRaft. Figure 7(b) shows the TPS performance of the three algorithms when the number of nodes is constant and the number of transactions varies. It is clear that when the number of nodes is the same, the performance of the three algorithms is relatively similar and the data is stable. However, the fluctuation of LTRaft is significantly smoother than other algorithms.

5 Conclusions

LTRaft algorithm is proposed in this paper. First, the algorithm has a pre-election state monitoring mechanism, which can prevent outdated nodes from participating in the leader election by comparing their log queues. Secondly, on the basis of the three roles in the Raft algorithm, the role of the alternative leader is introduced. In LTRaft, the appendEntry() protocol is modified to enable it to select the alternative leader node based on votes. When the leader node is normal, the alternative node is responsible for receiving the leader node's log for replication, just like any other node. But if the leader node triggers a timeout election, the system will first determine whether there is an alternative leader. If there is an alternative leader, the authority of the origin leader node will be transferred to the alternative leader first. Then the alternative leader will carry out the consensus until the next leader is elected, which will save the time of an election cycle. Under normal circumstances, the consensus time required by the LTRaft algorithm is similar to the consensus time required by the Raft algorithm. However, if the leader timeout occurs, the time overhead of LTRaft is shorter than that of the Raft. This can bring a significant performance boost in large distributed systems. But the LTRaft algorithm still has some problems. For instance, the alternative leader's log may be quite different from the log of the leader, which will prolong the time of log replication, and cause the broadcast data redundancy because of the increased parameters in the AppendEntry RPC, etc. These all require further study.

Acknowledgments. This work has been supported by the NSFC under Grant No.61961029, Key Research and Development Plan in Jiangxi Province Department of Science and Technology under Grant No.20171ACE50025.

References

1. Nakamoto, S.: Bitcoin: a peer-to-peer electronic cash system (2008). http://bitcoin.org/bitcoin.pdf
2. Yuan, Y., Wang, F.Y.: Blockchain: the state of the art and future trends. IEEE/CAA J. Automatica Sinica (JAS) **42**(04), 481–494 (2016)
3. Lamport, L.: The part-time parliament. ACM Trans. Comput. Syst. (TOCS) **16**(2), 133–169 (1998)
4. Ongaro, D., Ousterhout, J.: In search of an understandable consensus algorithm. In: Gibson, G., Zeldovich, N. (eds.) USENIX Annual Technical Conference 2014, USENIX ATC'14, pp. 305–319 (2014)
5. Lamport, L.: Fast Paxos. Distrib. Comput. **19**(2), 79–103 (2006). https://doi.org/10.1007/s00446-006-0005-x
6. Lamport, L., Massa, M.: Cheap paxos. In: International Conference on Dependable Systems and Networks, p. 307. IEEE Computer Society (2004)

7. Burrows, M.: The chubby lock service for loosely-coupled distributed systems. In: Symposium on Operating Systems Design and Implementation, pp. 335–350. USENIX Association (2006)
8. Chandra, T.D., Griesemer, R., et al.: Paxos made live: an engineering perspective. In: Twenty-Sixth ACM Symposium on Principles of Distributed Computing, PODC 2007, Portland, Oregon, USA, August. DBLP, pp. 398–407 (2007)
9. Corbett, J.C., Dean, J., Epstein, M., et al.: Spanner: google's globally-distributed database. In: USENIX Conference on Operating Systems Design and Implementation, pp. 251–264 (2012)
10. Wang, J., Zhang, M., Wu, Y.W., et al.: Paxos-like consensus algorithm: a review. J. Comput. Res. Dev. **56**(04), 692–707 (2019)
11. Liskov, B., Cowling, J.: Viewstamped Replication Revisited. MIT CSAIL, Cambridge (2012)
12. Medeiros, A.: ZooKeeper's atomic broadcast protocol: theory and practice. Aalto University School of Science 20 (2012)
13. Tan, D., Hu, J., Wang, J.: VBBFT-Raft: an understandable blockchain consensus protocol with high performance. In: 2019 IEEE 7th International Conference on Computer Science and Network Technology (ICCSNT), Dalian, China, pp. 111–115 (2019)
14. Wang, R., Zhang, L., Xu, Q., Zhou, H.: K-bucket based raft-like consensus algorithm for permissioned blockchain. In: 2019 IEEE 25th International Conference on Parallel and Distributed Systems (ICPADS), Tianjin, China, pp. 996–999 (2019)
15. Mao, Y., Junqueira, F.P., Marzullo, K.: Mencius: building efficient replicated state machine for WANs. In: 8th USENIX Symposium on Operating Systems Design and Implementation, OSDI 2008, San Diego, California, USA, Proceedings. DBLP (2008)
16. Moraru, I., Andersen, D.G., Kaminsky, M.: There is more consensus in egalitarian parliaments. In: Proceedings of the Twenty-Fourth ACM Symposium on Operating Systems Principles, pp. 358–372. ACM (2013)
17. Shi, R., Wang, Y.: Cheap and available state machine replication. In: Proceedings of the 2016 USENIX Annual Technical Conference (ACT'2016), pp. 265–279. USENIX Association, CA (2016)
18. Wilcox, J.R., Woos, D., Panchekha, P., et al.: Verdi: a framework for implementing and formally verifying distributed systems. In: Proceedings of the 36th ACM SIGPLAN Conference on Programming Language Design and Implementation, pp. 357–368 (2015)

Load Balancing in Heterogeneous Network with SDN: A Survey

Jingbo Li, Li Ma[✉], Yingxun Fu, Dongchao Ma, and Ailing Xiao

School of Information Science and Technology, North China University of Technology,
Beijing 100144, China
mali@ncut.edu.cn

Abstract. With the rapid development of the interconnection of things, a large number of different types of network protocols and network resources have emerged. There are traditional wired networks and wireless networks. Wireless networks include 4G/5G, NB-IoT, and industrial Internet of Things, world-ground integrated networks, satellite networks, ocean networks, and so on. Multiple networks enrich the scenarios and requirements, eliminate information islands. Building a consistent view of heterogeneous networks and load balancing of heterogeneous networks are realistic requirements for certain applications of future networks. The emergence of Software Defined Networking (SDN) has provided a brand new idea for this scenario and has become an important technology and hot research object in this direction. According to the research field of SDN in heterogeneous network load balancing strategy, this paper analyzes the research status and trends from two aspects: load balancing of data transmission and load balancing of resource allocation. Comprehensive research status and advantages show that the characteristics of centralized management, completely decoupled forwarding plane, and control plane provided by SDN can play an important role in the design of load balancing routing strategy. Using the SDN method can make the load balancing strategy more flexible, clear and controllable, which is of great significance for future development and has a far-reaching impact. Finally, it analyzes and predicts the development trend of SDN, and provides a reference for the construction of a new generation of network routing.

Keywords: Software defined networking · Routing strategy · Heterogeneous convergent network · Load balancing

1 Research Background

With the advent of the information age, technologies such as mobile communication networks, industrial Internet of Things, spatial information networks, and new types of Internet have developed rapidly, and various network forms have been varied. With the improvement of living standards and the increase in demand for new things, the integration of these different technologies is imperative, which forms a heterogeneous network environment. In this new type of network environment, traditional load balancing strategies can no longer meet the current dynamic requirements for information transmission,

© Springer Nature Singapore Pte Ltd. 2021
L. Cui and X. Xie (Eds.): CWSN 2021, CCIS 1509, pp. 250–261, 2021.
https://doi.org/10.1007/978-981-16-8174-5_19

acquisition, and forwarding. With the explosive growth of data scale, netizens' demand for network bandwidth has increased rapidly, and the continuous expansion of the number of users has caused various traditional routing technologies to have to change with the changes of the times. As traditional routing technology uses a distributed network architecture, functions such as data forwarding and control need to be installed on each router and switch, so much so that network devices become increasingly bloated with too many protocols installed inside them, unable to meet the needs of network management, control, addition, deletion and maintenance due to the growth in the size and traffic of the Internet. At present, the traditional load balancing routing strategy of such a network cannot effectively cope with this change. At this time, the heterogeneous network load balancing strategy to become more flexible and changeable.

In 2008, Professor Nick McKeown of Stanford University and others based on the research results of the Ethane project [1], a paper entitled OpenFlow: Enabling Innovation in Campus Networks [2] was published in ACM SIGCOMM, in which SDN was introduced in detail for the first time. In 2009, the research team further proposed the concept of SDN, which has attracted great attention from the entire industry. In 2011, Google, Facebook and other companies jointly established the Open Networking Foundation (ONF), and formally proposed the concept of software-defined network SDN. In essence, SDN is an idea of separating control and forwarding, a programmable network architecture, and a new network design concept. This kind of thought and concept can be directly introduced into a heterogeneous network system dominated by IP, and the introduction has the following benefits:

- The network control function can realize decoupling, which solves the bloated situation of the edge gateway due to too many protocols, and also releases the ability of hardware resource equipment to packet forward;
- It can effectively abstract and encapsulate the physical resources in network, without considering the heterogeneous characteristics of physical hardware, and can realize the overall deployment and sharing of the underlying physical resources;
- The visibility of upper-layer services can be realized. Due to the heterogeneity of different services, different services can be disassembled through the northbound interface after using SDN, thereby achieving business scalability.

After more than ten years of development, software-defined network technology has developed rapidly. The combination of SDN technology and heterogeneous converged network technology can integrate the advantages of both aspects and play the greatest role in the future communication network. The progress of globalization and social development is of great significance.

In the past research reviews on SDN, most of them combine deep learning and other technologies with SDN to summarize and summarize from the application point of view. This article summarizes the research from two aspects: load balancing of data transmission and load balancing of resource allocation. Section 1 of this article introduces in detail the research background and significance, as well as the advantages of introducing SDN into the load balancing strategy. Section 2 summarizes the load balancing strategy based on data transmission. After different networks are connected, how to enable different networks to effectively transmit data to achieve the overall network load balance is also the key content of many scholars' research. Section 3 summarizes the resource-based load balancing strategy. For heterogeneous networks, the types and efficiency of resources used by different networks are different. How to achieve a fair distribution of different resources is also a different study, one of the difficulties of constructing a network. Section 4 summarizes the existing problems of existing research centers, analyzes the research direction of SDN in the future heterogeneous networks, and looks forward to the direction and trend of future development. Figure 1 shows the technical architecture diagram of the SDN-based heterogeneous network load balancing strategy studied in this paper.

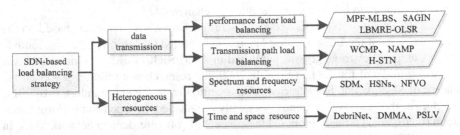

Fig. 1. SDN-based heterogeneous network load balancing technical architecture diagram.

2   Load Balancing in Data Transmission

As one of the common strategies to improve network performance, load balancing in data transmission has always been a hot issue and a difficult issue [3]. Load balancing can improve network performance because it provides a transparent, low-cost and effective method to expand the bandwidth of servers and network devices, enhance network data processing capabilities, and improve network availability and flexibility [4]. In the actual network use process, due to the characteristics of heterogeneous networks, the use of traditional load balancing routing strategies cannot effectively obtain real-time network link status, and thus cannot allocate and schedule network traffic transmission for load balancing in real time according to the actual situation. It is prone to problems such as excessive single-path transmission load, uneven resource allocation of the link, and poor data flow transmission efficiency, which is not enough to meet the development and needs of today's heterogeneous network environment. The maturity of SDN technical ideas provides new impetus for load balancing strategies. At present, common classifications in data transmission load balancing strategies include load balancing strategies based on performance factors and load balancing strategies based on paths. The characteristics of these different classification research programs are shown in Table 1.

Table 1. Comparison of data transmission load balancing strategies.

Literature	Load balancing		Put forward the model	Using technology	Advantage	Shortcoming
	Performance factors	Path				
5	√	–	√	SALB	Low energy consumption	High communication cost
6	√	–	MPF-MLBS	MPF	Low delay, high rate	A lot of data preprocessing
7	√	–	LBMRE-OLSR	SAGIN	Dynamic balance	Poor stability
8	√	–	√	QBA, QSR	Low delay, high speed	High communication consumption
10	–	√	–	WCMP	High bandwidth	Delay problem
11	–	√	NAMP	LPM	Low delay	Cutting complex
13	–	√	√	LTE/WLAN	Multicast communication	Poor scalability
14	–	√	√	MNO, H-STN	Spectrum sharing	Complex data preprocessing

2.1 Load Balancing Mechanism of Performance Factors

With the rapid increase of user groups and rapid growth of communication volume, the load and required energy of SDN equipment have increased significantly. Therefore, an SDN controller model that can load balance and reduce equipment energy consumption is needed. This demand document [5] proposed a new type of SDN controller energy-saving heterogeneous network load distribution framework, which is a combination of load balancing technology (SALB) and energy optimization framework. According to the communication requirements of different performance indicators, load balance is performed, and then efficient routing algorithms and selection procedures are combined to reduce energy consumption. In this way, combining the two technologies can interact with each other, so that the controller can reduce energy consumption while balancing network traffic to a large extent to achieve the purpose of load balancing. Literature [6] proposed an SDN multi-path load balancing strategy (MPF-MLBS) based on multiple performance factors (MPF). The strategy is divided into two stages: algorithm design and routing strategy implementation. In terms of algorithms, first, based on the characteristics of the SDN network architecture, combined with the advantages and disadvantages of the existing load balancing algorithm, considering the delay, bandwidth and link rate of the existing network links, a design based on multiple performance factors is designed Load balancing algorithm (MPF-CMP). In terms of strategy, first, build a multi-path network topology based on the SDN architecture, use the depth-first traversal algorithm to traverse the entire network topology to obtain various information about the link, and then combine the MPF-CMP algorithm and the OpenFlow group table technology to complete The network traffic of each available path is distributed proportionally, so as to realize the load balancing of the SDN network multi-path.

The transmission efficiency of traffic in the space-ground integrated satellite network is very important to the use of the satellite network. Due to the limitation of transmission distance and technology, if reasonable data flow load balance is not carried out, the space-ground integrated network will not be put into actual use. To solve this problem, literature [7] studied routing algorithms in a software-defined space-air-ground heterogeneous network (SAGIN) to optimize load balancing in a heterogeneous communication network. First, a new software-defined network was proposed (SDN) model to solve the network topology is the characteristics of real-time changes because this model can improve the flexibility of the network. Based on the above model, the author proposes a new dynamic routing load-balancing algorithm, namely the load balancing algorithm based on multi-dimensional resources and energy (LBMRE-OLSR), the routing algorithm considers the multi-dimensional consumption of resources and energy, experiments The results show that the algorithm in SAGIN's dynamic routing effectively reduces the end-to-end delay and packet loss rate when the load changes, realizes the convenient and intuitive unified deployment of the complex three-dimensional heterogeneous network framework and improves The fluency of the overall network operation and the efficiency of routing. Literature [8] proposed a software-defined network framework based on software-defined networking (SDN) and network function virtualization (NFV) for heterogeneous satellite communications. The purpose of this framework is to realize flexible satellite network traffic engineering and a fine-grained QoS guarantee. Based on this framework, a prototype implementation method based on delay-tolerant network (DTN) and OpenFlow is given, and a QoS-oriented satellite routing (QSR) algorithm and a QoS-oriented bandwidth allocation (QBA) algorithm are proposed to ensure QoS requirements for multiple users. Experimental results show that the framework is effective in terms of file transmission delay and transmission rate.

2.2 Load Balancing of Transmission Path

At present, some multi-path load balancing routing is optimized and improved on the traditional single-path routing strategy, without changing the routing strategy in essence. There is also some multi-path load balancing routing strategies that use multiple paths to evenly distribute network traffic. This strategy does not allocate link resources according to requirements, which will easily cause partial link congestion and low overall traffic transmission efficiency [9]. Using the traditional ECMP algorithm will result in lower overall bandwidth utilization, especially when the path difference is large, the effect is very unsatisfactory. Aiming at the shortcomings of ECMP, literature [10] uses Weighted Cost Multi-path (WCMP) to solve the load balancing problem under the resource constraints of the data plane. The purpose of WCMP design is mainly to solve the problem of data center traffic load balancing and to solve the problem of unequal handling of topological problems by ECMP. However, WCMP usually sets the weight according to the bandwidth attribute of the path and does not consider the delay change of each link during the service transmission process. There is still a lot of room for improvement. On this basis, literature [11] proposes and implements a NAMP, a multi-path scheme that considers network heterogeneity, effectively optimizes the transmission time of stream groups. Experimental results show that NAMP is 50% shorter than WCMP and 60% shorter than ECMP.

In the beyond 5G (B5G) era, the scale of wireless networks will grow very rapidly, which is believed to lead to scarcity of network capacity and degradation of service quality [12]. In a heterogeneous network, many cellular network users cannot enjoy high-quality multimedia services. To improve the service quality of these users, multicast uses an efficient spectrum method to transmit content. This method is considered to be a very effective method. Literature [13] proposed an SDN-based heterogeneous LTE/WLAN network architecture, which logically supports end-to-end (D2D) flexible multicast communication; because D2D communication can realize wireless peer-to-peer services, so in the vicinity directly establish a link between users for communication, which reduces the flow pressure of the backhaul. In addition, the introduction of SDN technology into heterogeneous networks can provide D2D users with reliable multicast content. Literature [14] established an SDN architecture that realizes spectrum sharing and traffic offloading in a heterogeneous satellite-terrestrial network (H-STN). This architecture supports efficient resource management and load balancing strategies and achieves large-capacity transmission and co-channel Interference control. In addition, this document also proposes an auction-based mechanism to facilitate the negotiation of traffic offloading between the mobile network operator (MNO) and the satellite. That is to say, the MNO announces its offloading rate threshold, and each beamed group of the satellite is based on its own Submit an unloading bid for the transmission rate of the MNO, and then calculates the best bidding rate for the beam group at different rates according to the different unloading rate thresholds announced by the MNO. This framework realizes the competition between the cellular network ground base station and the satellite-to-ground communication system multi-beam group and has achieved the purpose of traffic load balancing.

2.3   Brief Summary

In a heterogeneous network environment such as the Internet of Things, the number of various devices is huge, and the demand for transmission traffic is beyond imagination. How to distribute this traffic to a variety of devices in a balanced and reasonable manner requires extremely complex policy support. And the quality and effect of data transmission directly affect the experience of using heterogeneous networks. Although the use of performance factors considers many factors for load balancing, this method does not work well in the case of particularly large traffic. In the path-based load balancing strategy, the multi-path load balancing strategy has great advantages in robustness, fault tolerance and QoS compared with a single path. The use of a multi-path reduces the single link between different locations. Dependency risk, increase the transmission bandwidth and data transmission of the backup aging link without packet loss. However, multi-path routing will increase storage overhead. Data packets may require additional information, which increases the size of the data packets, and it also consumes additional processing power to propagate to other routers through multi-path.

3 Load Balancing of Heterogeneous Resources

Resource heterogeneity is a major feature in the context of the Internet of Things. According to the existing resources in the heterogeneous network, it is mainly divided into four aspects: frequency resources, space resources, time resources and power resources. With the development of the times, there are higher requirements for resource allocation load balancing strategies in heterogeneous converged networks. It is necessary to deploy resource load balancing with more flexibility, better scalability, and greater revenue costs for different types of services strategy. The main idea of SDN is to decouple the data plane from the control plane, and its controller can obtain a global view of the network, which facilitates the implementation of load balancing strategies. At present, resource load balancing strategies are classified according to different types of resources, including load balancing strategies based on frequency and spectrum resources, and load balancing strategies based on time and space resources. The characteristics of these different classification research programs are shown in Table 2.

Table 2. Comparison of load balancing strategies for heterogeneous resources

Literature	Resource allocation		Put forward the model	Using technology	Advantage	Shortcoming
	Frequency spectrum	Time space				
15	√	–	√	NFV, CCCP	Low power	Algorithm complex
17	√	–	√	A3C, EMC	High resource utilization	Low compatibility
18	√	–	HSNs	DRL	Intelligent manage	A lot of data preprocessing
19	–	√	DebriNet	PSLV	Low delay	Simple allocation strategy
20	–	√	√	PON	Delay monitoring	Poor scalability
21	–	√	DMMA	DHT	Strong scalability	High communication costs
22	–	√	√	K-means	Strong robustness	High deployment cost

3.1 Frequency and Spectrum Resource Balance

Load balancing strategies based on frequency and spectrum resources have certain similarities. For frequency resource allocation, on the one hand, according to Shannon's theorem, in a single user scenario, the efficiency of the system can be increased by increasing the bandwidth reasonably. On the other hand, according to Orthogonal Frequency Division Multiple Access (OFDMA) technology, in the scenario of multiple users, increasing the transmission bandwidth of one user will reduce the bandwidth of other users, so bandwidth allocation is very important; For the load balancing of spectrum resources, it is mainly through the reasonable allocation of spectrum to improve the utilization rate of spectrum resources. Due to the rapid development of diversified communication services in recent years, the data transmission rate and the frequency spectrum are limited in the case of limited spectrum resources. The contradiction still remains unresolved, and this problem can only be solved through a reasonable allocation of spectrum resources.

The load balancing strategy for resources is different in different environments. In a heterogeneous cellular network environment, literature [15] proposed a joint load balancing allocation algorithm based on SDN power and bandwidth resources, which considers the main purpose of the fragmentation technology of network function virtualization is to achieve maximum energy efficiency for the different QoS requirements of fragmentation. Because it is difficult to realize the resource allocation algorithm using virtualization technology, we choose to transform the problem into a DC structure problem, so that the problem is transformed into two sub-problems, and the interior point method and the CCCP algorithm are used to iteratively find the optimal solution. The simulation results show that compared with the bandwidth optimization algorithm and the power optimization algorithm, the energy efficiency of this algorithm is increased by 201.5% and 1.8% respectively. Aiming at the problem of load balance distribution of space-based information networks (SIN), literature [16] first established space-based information network control architecture based on SDN. To solve the problem of unified management of SIN network transmission, caching and computing resources, intelligent resource load balancing distribution method based on A3C algorithm in deep reinforcement learning. In this architecture, the transmission resources depend on the degree of satellite coverage and the state of the communication link. The cached resources are provided by the cache, and the computing resources are provided by the EMC server. The load balancing distribution scheme can effectively improve the resource utilization rate of the space-based information network. Literature [17] proposes a new generation of heterogeneous satellite network resource management frameworks (HSNs), which realize the cooperation and resource load balancing between different satellite systems, and supports the mutual communication between different satellite systems. This framework integrates and manages heterogeneous resources based on SDN, applies deep reinforcement learning (DRL) to the system, combines DRL with resource allocation, and realizes integrated management of resource load balance across satellite systems.

3.2 Time and Space Resource Balance

Load balancing of time and space resources in a heterogeneous converged network is very precious and essential. In terms of time resource load balance distribution, due to the heterogeneous network protocol's disparity and randomness, the data in the device is also changing at any time. To improve the efficiency of data transmission, real-time scheduling must be carried out according to the delay of different services. In terms of space resource load balance distribution, it is mainly because of the use of multi-point joint transmission that the placement of relay nodes is very important. Choosing a reasonable relay node can bring great space freedom to the system and improve transmission effectiveness.

In terms of time resource load balancing, literature [18] proposed a software-defined network platform concept: DebriNet, which uses the fourth stage of PSLV to establish a low-cost space-based communication network, which is a rocket fragment (called spent fuel level) low-cost software-defined network platform, which can be accessed by user equipment using ultra-low-cost terminals and extremely low latency. DebriNet uses an opportunistic packet handover mechanism that uses pre-calculated satellite positions on the orbit to optimize time resource allocation to ensure that packets are delivered to the destination as soon as possible, reduce network delays, and save time in the network Resources. Literature [19] proposes a real-time delay measurement based on SDN and it's the monitoring of 5G mobile converged passive optical network (PON). It is a real-time delay measurement scheme used to determine whether the network delay meets the requirements of the mobile network. The measurement scheme is based on the SDN idea. The implemented system can accurately measure the delay during network operation, and Monitor the real-time delay status, and judge whether the time resource load balance distribution is reasonable according to the delay status.

In terms of spatial resource arrangement, SDN requires a controller to manage the entire network, so how the controller is arranged in the space like relay nodes is particularly important for the load balancing of the entire network. This is also the focus of research in SDN. A reasonable controller distribution and optimal switching technology are essential for the load balancing of space resources. It can effectively reduce link delay and save a lot of time and space resources. Literature [20] proposes a seamless mobility management solution for users moving from one SDN controller coverage space to another SDN controller coverage space in a 5G heterogeneous network: DMMA, using key-value distributed hash tables (DHT) to capture user mobility in the distributed SDN controller. It solves the scalability and seamlessness of heterogeneous networks, that is, mobile devices can connect and leave between different associated SDN controllers. Literature [21] proposed an SDN-based air-space-ground integrated network framework, and designed an optimized K-means controller space configuration load balancing algorithm based on the characteristics of the dynamic topology of the UAV segment. Compared with the traditional K-means algorithm, this algorithm can effectively reduce the average delay and the maximum delay between the controller and the switch through a reasonable controller space configuration. This framework has the advantages of high throughput, wide coverage and strong robustness.

3.3 Brief Summary

In a heterogeneous network environment, resources are complex and scarce. Various resources are mixed together, and the load balance distribution of heterogeneous resources must be considered comprehensively. How to allocate these resources reasonably is extremely important to achieve load balancing in a heterogeneous network. Resource management in the existing resource management model is mainly for the management of a single resource within the network. Whether it is frequency, spectrum, virtual resources, forwarding resources, or time and space resources, it is an isolated management mode, without considering the available resources of other networks. In the future load balancing of heterogeneous network resources, it is necessary to coordinate the processing of resources between multiple networks, and allocate the best network resources in real-time according to the user's business characteristics and needs, so as to ensure the quality of service of the heterogeneous network and maximize the Make use of heterogeneous network resources.

4 Research Trends and Prospects

With the flexible features of software-defined networks and the in-depth application of various network technologies, the integration of SDN and heterogeneous networks has become an inevitable trend in research and network design. In such an extremely complex environment as heterogeneous networks, SDN has the advantages of centralized control enable more precise decision-making, flexible management and intelligent judgment of load balancing strategies in heterogeneous networks, making it possible to deploy in actual environments in the future. At present, there are many research results on load balancing strategies for heterogeneous networks at home and abroad, but there are still some drawbacks and shortcomings. For example, load balancing strategies cannot fully integrate the characteristics of different networks for distribution and integration; some load balancing strategies have poor scalability. It can only be used in a specific heterogeneous network; some load balancing strategies need to consume a lot of various resources, and the cost is too high; although SDN increases the flexibility and adaptability of the network, how to design and improve dynamic adaptation Sex requires in-depth research. This article believes that the field of heterogeneous network load balancing strategies should be deeply integrated and explored in the following aspects in the future:

- The ability to handle large-scale complex heterogeneous networks. The idea of separating the control plane from the data plane in SDN can be abstracted and simpler for solving complex heterogeneous network environments. The trend of future heterogeneous networks must be large-scale and complex networks, and the scale of data must also be larger. It puts forward higher requirements for the load balancing strategy of heterogeneous networks.
- The ability to adapt to the dynamic changes of heterogeneous networks. At present, the actual operating network has dynamic characteristics, and the nodes and connection status on the network and the transmission environment are changing all the time. Introducing the network protocol that has the ability to monitor the network status in real-time in SDN is of great help in solving the problem of dynamic load balancing, and there is still room for further optimization in future development.
- The ability to integrate with new network technologies. The integration of heterogeneous networks and new technologies is a trend. Combining the advantages of each technology will help the efficient operation and processing of load balancing strategies and bring out huge potential. The combination of new technologies has higher challenges and requirements for the stability and security of the load balancing strategy.

- Broaden scenarios and application areas. The future network form will be more complex and changeable. For example, the emergence of new complex heterogeneous network scenarios, such as the industrial Internet, integrated spatial information networks, and world ground integrated ocean networks, requires an in-depth analysis of load balancing strategies in different application fields. Look for entry points to introduce new ideas and technologies such as SDN, better integrate the technology with the scene, and expand to a wider range of applications.

5 Conclusion

This article elaborates and analyzes the load balancing strategy of SDN in heterogeneous networks. The solution of introducing SDN into heterogeneous networks is an effective and feasible choice, but the future heterogeneous networks must have huge mobile bandwidth requirements and ultra-low mobile bandwidth requirements. With delay requirements, high reliability and more access devices, in the face of these high-quality requirements, a heterogeneous network load balancing strategy must not only increase the transmission range, but also ensure the reliability of the network. In the face of such requirements, the research and application of load balancing strategies based on SDN in a heterogeneous network environment are not very mature, and it is still in an exploratory stage in practical applications, and there are still many deficiencies that have not been discovered and resolved. In future research, a large amount of scientific research personnel will be required to invest. It is necessary to conduct an in-depth analysis of load balancing strategies in different application fields in a heterogeneous network environment combined with SDN research to find an entry point and apply SDN to a wider field of heterogeneous networks, Make a good theoretical foundation for practical application.

Acknowledgment. This work was supported by the National Key R&D Program of China (2018YFB1800302), Natural Science Foundation of China (62001007), Beijing Natural Science Foundation (KZ201810009011, 4202020, 19L2021).

References

1. Casado McFreedman, M.J., Pettit, J., et al.: Ethane: taking control of the enterprise. ACM SIGCOMM Comput. Commun. Rev. **37**(4), 1–12 (2007)
2. McKeown, N., Anderson, T., Balakrishnan, H., et al.: OpenFlow: enabling innovation in campus networks. ACM SIGCOMM Comput. Commun. Rev. **38**(2), 69–74 (2008)
3. Liu, Y., et al.: A novel load balancing and low response delay framework for edge-cloud network based on SDN. IEEE Internet Things J. **7**(7), 5922–5933 (2020)
4. AlKhatib, A.A.A., Sawalha, AlZu'bi, S.: Load balancing techniques in software-defined cloud computing: an overview. In: 2020 Seventh International Conference on Software Defined Systems, pp. 240–244. IEEE, Piscataway (2020)
5. Priyadarsini, M., Kumar, S., Bera, P., Rahman, M.A.: An energy-efficient load distribution framework for SDN controllers. Computing **102**(9), 2073–2098 (2019). https://doi.org/10.1007/s00607-019-00751-2

6. Li, D., Liu, H., Jin, Y.: MPF-MLBS: a multi-path load balancing strategy for sdn networks based on multiple performance factors. Math. Comput. Sci. **5**(3), 64–71 (2020)

7. Qu, H., Luo, Y., Zhao, J., Luan, Z.: An LBMRE-OLSR routing algorithm under the emergency scenarios in the space-air-ground integrated networks. In: 2020 Information Communication Technologies Conference, pp. 103–107. IEEE, Piscataway (2020)

8. Li, T., Zhou, H., Luo, H., Yu, S.: SERvICE: a software defined framework for integrated space-terrestrial satellite communication. IEEE Trans. Mob. Comput. **17**(3), 703–716 (2018)

9. Lu, L.: Multi-path allocation scheduling optimization algorithm for network data traffic based on SDN architecture. IMA J. Math. Control Inf. **37**(4), 1237–1247 (2020)

10. Wang, H., et al.: PrePass: load balancing with data plane resource constraints using commodity SDN switches. Comput. Netw. **178**, 107339 (2020)

11. Cheng, Y., Jia, X.: NAMP: network-aware multipathing in software-defined data center networks. IEEE/ACM Trans. Netw. **28**(2), 846–859 (2020)

12. Nawaz, S.J., Sharma, S.K., Wyne, S., Patwary, M.N., Asaduzzaman, M.: Quantum machine learning for 6G communication networks: state-of-the-art and vision for the future. IEEE Access **7**, 46317–46350 (2019)

13. Bukhari, J., Yoon, W.: Simulated view of SDN based multicasting over D2D enabled heterogeneous cellular networks. In: 16th International Bhurban Conference on Applied Sciences and Technology, pp. 926–929. IEEE, Piscataway (2019)

14. Du, J., Jiang, C., Zhang, H., Ren, Y., Guizani, M.: Auction design and analysis for SDN-based traffic offloading in hybrid satellite-terrestrial networks. IEEE J. Sel. Areas Commun. **36**(10), 2202–2217 (2018)

15. Ma, J., Pan, C., Yin, C., Li, X.: Slice-aware resource management in SDN enabled heterogeneous cellular networks. In: 2019 IEEE/CIC International Conference on Communications in China, pp. 869–874. IEEE, Piscataway (2019)

16. Meng, X., Wu, L., Jiao, J., Gong, X.: Research on resource allocation method of the SIN based on SDN. In: 2019 IEEE International Geoscience and Remote Sensing Symposium, pp. 10071–10074. IEEE, Piscataway (2019)

17. Deng, B., Jiang, C., Yao, H., Guo, S., Zhao, S.: The next generation heterogeneous satellite communication networks: integration of resource management and deep reinforcement learning. IEEE Wirel. Commun. **27**(2), 105–111 (2020)

18. Suraj, R., Babu, S., Dalai, D., Manoj, B.S.: DebriNet: an opportunistic software defined networking framework over PSLV debris. In: 2019 IEEE International Conference on Advanced Networks and Telecommunications Systems, pp. 1–6. IEEE, Piscataway (2019)

19. Oh, J., Ryoo, Y., Kim, K., Doo, K., Lee, H., Chung, H.: SDN based real-time latency measurement and its monitoring for 5G mobile convergence passive optical networks. In: 2019 Asia Communications and Photonics Conference, pp.1–3. IEEE, Piscataway (2019)

20. Alfoudi, A.S.D., Newaz, S.H.S., Ramlie, R., Lee, G.M., Baker, T.: Seamless mobility management in heterogeneous 5G networks: a coordination approach among distributed SDN controllers. In: 2019 IEEE 89th Vehicular Technology Conference, pp.1–6. IEEE, Piscataway (2019)

21. Qu, H., Xu, X., Zhao, J., Yue, P.: An SDN-based space-air-ground integrated network architecture and controller deployment strategy. In: 2020 IEEE 3rd International Conference on Computer and Communication Engineering Technology, pp.138–142. IEEE, Piscataway (2020)

Author Index

264   Author Index

Printed in the United States
by Baker & Taylor Publisher Services